# LARRY MILLER TIME

*THE STORY OF THE LOST LEGEND
WHO SPARKED THE TAR HEEL DYNASTY*

Neal:
Enjoy the book
AN Best Wishes

Larry Miller

# LARRY MILLER TIME

*THE STORY OF THE LOST LEGEND*
*WHO SPARKED THE TAR HEEL DYNASTY*

## Stephen Demorest

### with LARRY MILLER

TAMARIND PUBLISHING

Published by Tamarind Publishing, 106 East Union Street, Hillsborough, North Carolina 27278

larrymillerunc@gmail.com

ISBN: 978-1-09830-462-1

eISBN: 978-1-09830-463-8

Photos courtesy of University of North Carolina Athletics, Larry Miller Collection, Nancy Demorest Collection, *Sports Illustrated, Durham Herald Sun, Charlotte Observer, Greensboro Daily News,* Getty Images.

Cover design by Jaimey Easler

Edited by Nancy Lee Cunningham

*For Nancy, a dream come true.*

—Stephen Demorest

*Achieving and enjoying my personal private paradise, little did I know a random encounter with a lost child from my past would result in a myriad of exciting experiences. Aside from the obvious, incredible new friendships, a revival and expansion of past relationships, a fifty-year reunion with my old Carolina teammates, a visit to the Basketball Hall of Fame, acting in an ambitious movie, continued fantastic visits to UNC with hometown friends (called the Carolina Experience), and now a terrific book that promises to explain it all. Enjoy the journey!*

—Larry Miller

*People need to understand, Larry was the winner who made Coach Smith a winner. Like Bill Russell started the Boston Celtics tradition, Larry Miller is the tradition that Carolina talks about. Everything starts with him.*

Charles Scott

*So hello, Bobby Lewis, and hello, Larry Miller. I salute you from the secret place to which lost nights go. I tell you how splendid the two of you were that night and the next night and all through that long season. I have never forgotten the dark fire of Larry Miller or the breathtaking swiftness of Bobby Lewis and I did not deserve to be in the same building with them.*

Pat Conroy, *My Losing Season*

*I believe that the one thing that's largely gone out is what made sport such fertile literary territory—the characters, the tales, the humor, the pain, what Hollywood calls "the arc." That is: stories. We have, all by ourselves, ceded that one neat thing about sport that we owned.*

Frank Deford, 2008

# TABLE OF CONTENTS

# FOREWORD

*by Nancy Curlee Demorest*

When I was growing up in North Carolina in the sixties, the name Catasauqua was lodged in my lexicon at least as deep as Hiawatha or Timbuktu. So recently, when my husband and I wound up in a hotel just outside Allentown, Pennsylvania on Catasauqua Road, the first thing that came to mind was Larry Miller, "the Big Cat from Catasauqua," a legend of almost mythic proportions, the hard-driving, sure-shooting, movie star handsome captain and undisputed leader of the 1968 Tar Heels, my all-time favorite Carolina team.

I had a scrapbook stuffed with newspaper clippings and programs from games in Chapel Hill that my parents brought back—those I had to hide to keep my big brother from confiscating. On the playground at school, you could hear the older boys "playing" Carolina versus Duke or State, and every one of those kids diving and elbowing and scrapping for the basketball wanted to be Larry. When my friends and I played Barbies, we wound up stealing my little brother's GI Joe to play Barbie's boyfriend, who was now Larry Miller. (Ken was Dick Grubar.) My affection for #44 was so great and widely known that a local family I didn't even know very well invited me to go see him at an ACC All-Star game in May of 1968. I was ten years old and so excited to be going to Newton-Conover to watch him play, you'd have thought I was off to the Oscars. I couldn't sleep the night before. I will never forget how thrilled I was at last to be standing before him, thrusting my crumpled index card forward for an autograph. By then nervous exhaustion must have caught up with me because I blurted something which I've never been able to fully recall—probably that I knew Ursula Andress was his favorite female star—but whatever it was made him laugh and say, "You're so cute" and put his hands on either side of my cheeks before he took my card to sign. I *never* forgot that.

I grew up and became a television writer in New York before eventually moving back to North Carolina with my family. Larry Miller went on to have a whole big life of his own after that little encounter, in the limelight and out of it, but in recent years he had become something of a mystery. He had stopped coming back to Chapel Hill for games and reunions since Coach Smith's retirement. After Coach's death, no one seemed to hear from him much at all. The rumor was that he was reclusive, really not much interested in Carolina anymore.

As a former professional writer and a constitutionally curious person, I couldn't get this close to Catasauqua without checking him out. So I persuaded my very reluctant husband, Stephen Demorest, to drive by the address I had found. I would stop in with a coffee and see if Larry was willing to chat with me for a few minutes on his porch. Yes, it was intrusive, but I would leave immediately if he was at all annoyed.

Fifteen minutes later we found ourselves parked in front of a freshly painted colonial house with knockout roses climbing its white porch railings and fence. I balanced my phone and tray of coffees and pen and pad and headed for the door. Stephen would take the dogs for a run in a nearby park and then swing by to pick me up once I sent him a text. I knocked and waited . . . knocked and waited. The coffee was cooling.

I went to a door alongside the driveway that might've been the kitchen, knocked and waited . . . No answer. Stephen was beckoning me back to the car at this point. But the garden in back looked intriguing. From where I was standing, I could see a potting table, with rows of neatly labeled clay pots with fresh sprouts, and beyond it, thick grapevines twining over an arbor, a spreading Japanese maple . . . I stepped in farther. There were neat garden beds planted with rows of tomatoes and peppers. Arborvitae lining the other side of the yard, explosions of flowers and vines, and an open cellar door against the house. I went toward it, ready to call down, when I realized at the other end of the yard down toward the garage was a faded green chair, and in it, a big craggy white head facing the other way.

"Larry Miller?"

He unfolded from the chair like a long wooden yardstick. There appeared to be a lot of him. He was blinking and bewildered as I rapid-fired my prepared speech and offered to vacate the premises immediately. But as soon as he recovered from his surprise and had ascertained that (a) I was sane and (b) had transportation and would be leaving soon, he offered me a chair and we fell into a remarkably warm and relaxed conversation.

It turned out I wasn't the first intrepid fan to find her way to Larry's door. In fact, it was a fairly regular occurrence. His legacy still loomed large in the memory of the Tar Heel faithful, not to mention Lehigh Valley fans and ABA cult followers.

We talked about our shared history as a childhood fan and college player back in the late sixties, and about certain thrilling games and Coach Smith. But other things as well: about what it's like to come back to the place where you grew up after nearly a lifetime away. About how the air there feels just right on your skin. About that Dorothy in Oz moment of "There's no place like home." We talked about the mail he had received over the years from fans, particularly the kids who wrote while he was at Carolina and how he had loved those letters. And the stories he'd collected while playing with the Heels and later in the ABA. We talked about storytelling in general. I told him he should think about telling his.

As he walked me out to the car, I remarked on how beautiful his garden was. He told me it had been nothing but hardscrabble when he bought the house eight years before. I said he must have a gift for gardening. "Nah," he looked around, satisfied nonetheless. "Just good soil."

Larry Miller had nothing but happy memories of his time at Carolina, and fond feelings for the people who'd been so generous to him during his time there. But I couldn't help thinking how fortunate he was to have come back to this town, to these familiar sidewalks, to the friends he'd played Knee-Hi baseball with. The place that made him, where he grew up and was nurtured. His good soil. He seemed to be a happy man, at peace with his past and in love with his present. But I still wanted him to think about telling those stories . . .

*Nancy Curlee, Larry Miller, and Carole Kivett after an ABA East-West all-star game at Charlotte Coliseum on May 16, 1969. Miller was leading scorer for the West team coached by Bill Sharman.*

# PREFACE

I'm idling in my SUV with two dogs in the back, double-parked in front of a beautifully kept house on a quiet side street in a forgotten town in the Lehigh Valley of Pennsylvania, waiting for my wife to be arrested for trespassing.

I somewhat deserve this for marrying a North Carolina girl with such a love of UNC basketball that she can still recite the entire 1968 Tar Heel roster she memorized as a ten-year-old. She is sentimental about Coach Dean Smith and the voice of announcer Woody Durham, but I long ago realized that the only name that really matters is "Larry Miller." This was the first true legend of Carolina basketball, whose protean feats are still related with awe by those lucky and old enough to have seen him dominate in the era before videotape, before he veered off into memory uncaptured by ESPN. For decades now he has seldom been seen or even reported, his legend surviving on rumor and myth—and today she hopes she has found him.

I met a lot of legends in my time as a journalist in New York—rock stars and actors and even a Ringling Bros. tiger-trainer—but never an athlete so hungry to make himself great that he weight trained as a child by practicing in a vest loaded with buckshot. Never a prodigy who matched up with full-grown Eastern League pros in his summer after eighth grade—and led that team in scoring. Never a phenom who broke Wilt Chamberlain's high school scoring record, becoming the top recruit in the nation, so beloved by his town that caravans of buses drove seven hours to watch his JV games in college.

When the legendary Coach Smith was still a struggling thirty-three-year-old fledgling, hung in effigy by a frustrated student body, Larry Miller was the recruiting prize whose take-no-prisoners confidence became the rock on which Smith founded his Tar Heel dynasty. Twice the ACC Player of the Year, twice an All-American (and a member of the greatest All-America team ever), Miller put Carolina on his back and willed them to the National

Championship game, arguably saving Smith's career and all the glory that was to come.

(I have also been schooled that he was a major heartthrob, blending the dark good looks of "Route 66" star George Maharis with the unsettling power of Robert Mitchum . . . and he was admired for giving his all in that arena, too.)

His "44 MILLER" jersey hangs in the rafters of the Smith Center now, camouflaged in the back row by those who followed after him, a holy relic of tales told by aging men and sports writers, who sometimes refer to him as a man of mystery, still pursued half a century later on the outskirts of fame. And right now by my wife, as I await a sharp rap on the glass at any moment from protective neighbors strongly suggesting that I move along.

Before I'm rousted, though, she comes waving out of the driveway, followed by the man himself. Larry looks great—lean and tanned from hours in his garden, a full shock of steel white hair shading his eyes—and he's cautiously amiable and gracious about this home invasion. He's even engaging with the dogs, who dance about like excited coeds. I decide that I like meeting him now, as a regular guy around my own age, happy to talk about dogs and his roses and not the old accolades. I like that my wife and I can look at his kaleidoscopic life from opposite ends.

Moments later we have left the man in peace. Steering back to the interstate, talking through long hours down the Shenandoah Valley, I become ever more curious about the whole arc of Larry Miller's star turn through the changing mores and expectations of late twentieth century America:

- How did the blue-collar hunger of a post–World War II steel town shape Larry's character for stardom?
- How did a kid growing up using an outhouse feel when Kennedys and corporate CEOs courted him to attend their alma maters?
- How did his family cope in the besieged home of the most hunted high school player in the nation?
- Why did Larry choose UNC, and how did he become Dean Smith's most beloved—and vexing—prodigal son?

- What was Miller's pivotal role in convincing Charles Scott to break the color barrier at UNC?
- Why did Miller sign with the upstart ABA, and never play in the NBA?
- How did he navigate life as "the Joe Namath of the ABA," winning "The Dating Game," belly dancing with Little Egypt, and barely missing a visit from the Manson Gang when flower power LA turned crazy?
- Why was he let go by the Carolina Cougars the same year he set the ABA scoring record (which he holds forever now), averaging more rebounds per minute than All-Star guards Jerry West, Kobe Bryant, or Michael Jordan?
- What happens when someone's character is at odds with changes in his sport's industry?
- What can Larry teach today's heroes about how to survive American stardom after your dreams come true?

By the time we reach home in North Carolina it's clear that the full story of how and why someone this beloved simply disappeared has yet to be told. But is the reclusive All-American likely to address such personal questions after all this time?

A few days later, my wife is surprised to receive a package from Larry in the mail. Inside is a friendly note saying he enjoyed their visit and a headshot from his foray into acting at Universal in the 1970s. But the real stunner comes next. It's a faded letter in a child's round lettering. A fan letter she had written and dropped into a Statesville mailbox in 1968, stored by Larry's mom with others in a trunk for fifty years, and now returned like a message in a bottle, along with Larry's phone number—proof of the enduring bond of devotion between superstar and fan.

She stares at it for a long time . . . looks at me a moment . . . then picks up the phone and dials.

"Larry? I think I know someone who can help you with those stories."

I don't know whether my wife has hooked Larry Miller or he's hooked her, but I do know we've sighted the great white whale of Carolina sports, and she—still feeling the absence of Carolina's first basketball god as surely as Ahab yearns for his missing leg—wants to chase the rest of his story. And I, well . . . Call me Ishmael.

# CHAPTER 1

# FORGING IRON

The day the boy's life changed began like any other in that golden summer during the Eisenhower years. Banging out of the house, he barely heard something Mom said about a picnic, so eager was he to round up his buddies and escape to the water. But this would be no wholesome trip to the sun-dappled pool in the park. The boy and his cronies were slipping away to an abandoned canal down the hill for a clandestine rite of passage. He was ten years old, a smart aleck, and a thief . . . doling out cigarettes stolen from his father.

The play was simple: You took a deep drag, sank underwater, and then blasted a lungful of bubbles that broke the surface with little pops of smoke to the cheers of your pals. Taking turns, he was just another guppy blowing smoke and spouting nonsense . . . until the laughter died and the boy looked up to see his old man glaring down at him.

"Up here," the man ordered.

Instantly the boy knew a whipping was coming and, sure enough, his father kicked him mercilessly up the hill, all hundred yards to the car—not sparing the rod, not spoiling the child. By the time they caught up to the family picnic he was too bruised to swim any more.

Eight years later Larry Miller would be on the cover of *Parade*, the most widely read magazine in America. In those days—back when the nation had just won the world and was bigger, stronger, and younger than anyone around, just like him—he and the country tried to do it right: building your strength, helping your teammates, playing fair, and deserving what you won because you worked harder than anyone else. His generation was told that you could become anything—even All-American—if you worked your heart out for it. Larry Miller is one of those who did. And if you wanted to forge a working class hero for all America, there was no better place for it than right here on this bend of the Lehigh River.

*

Today "Catasauqua" is just another long Indian name signifying nothing to most people, but it wasn't always that way. Catasauqua was simply a great little town so long ago that, by the time Larry Miller put it back on the map, the rest of the country had forgotten how this area transformed the nation. This is where the Crane Iron Works fired up the first furnace on the new continent for mass producing iron in 1840, arguably making Catasauqua the birthplace of the Industrial Revolution in America.

The little settlement that grew in the mud streets around the coal furnace was primitive, most of the workers living in tents at first, and fear of fires discouraged indoor cooking. Instead, everyone heated water and did their cooking over fires in the community burn-pit on Front Street next to the mill. It was a hard life, but in forging what became the hard skeleton of industrial America, Catasauqua soon became known as "The Iron Borough."

They made iron rails for horse-drawn carts before locomotives were invented to ride them. Six hundred men worked twenty-four-hour shifts producing horseshoes for the British and Russian armies in World War I.

And they devised massive cast iron tube segments for the tunnels of New York City. Today, anyone riding Amtrak lines under the Hudson and Harlem Rivers into Manhattan . . . anyone driving in from New Jersey through the Lincoln or Holland tunnels . . . or arriving by taxi from JFK and LaGuardia airports through the Midtown or Brooklyn-Battery tunnels, is protected by Catasauqua iron.

As the town made iron, the iron made Catasauqua rich. The Crane replaced its grubby tent city with solid row houses for its employees. Meanwhile, town patriarchs stepped up to organize and fund public works, including the town's first electric light plant, designed and constructed by a nearby Jersey guy named Thomas Alva Edison. By 1900—scarcely fifty years after the iron mill's founding—little Catasauqua had the highest percentage of self-made millionaires of any town in America.

And then, as iron was supplanted by steel, Catasauqua's preeminence was swallowed by surrounding Allentown and Bethlehem until, today, most residents of the Lehigh Valley are likely unaware that this little borough was the seed from which the entire region sprang. In the aftermath of World War II, though, this area was still ground-zero for toughness. And 300 feet up the hill from the old iron works and its paved-over burn pit, in the row house at 116 Wood Street—so original that some claim it was once the Crane company store—lived the family of Julius Miller.

*

Julius Miller was the son of German immigrants, a veteran, a union man on the assembly line at Mack Truck, and, at 6'3", a fine enough athlete to make a few extra bucks playing semi-pro basketball for a local sporting goods team. His wife, Mary Magdalene—but everyone knew her as Peggy—had herself played fast-pitch softball in an era when the sport drew thousands of paying spectators to games in Allentown. With a young family to raise at the tail end of the Depression, though, the Millers had to quit playing, dropped out of high school, and Peggy came to like being a homemaker. By all accounts the Millers were nice people, although Peggy—a small lady at 5'4"—was fully capable of throwing her imposing husband out of the house when he missed supper one night and came home drunk. (It only happened once.) The couple's oldest child, Lorraine, was a good girl called by some "the darling of the nuns." And then there was the kid, Larry . . . the troublemaker.

It was foreordained that the Miller children would attend St. Lawrence, the neighborhood Catholic school, but as much as young Larry respected his mother and father, his high spirits rattled the strictures of Catholic education, and he always considered his enrollment a mistake. Though he would wind up an honor student, his marks were very poor in the early grades, barely above passing. He never felt comfortable with the priests. He was never an altar boy. And he hated communion and confession so much that he and his pal John McCarty would sit in the back until they could sneak out. When forced to participate, Larry entertained himself by making up bogus sins until, one day, he finally admitted the truth—that all of his previous confessions were lies. That was the last time Larry Miller confessed . . . to a priest, anyway.

His irreverence guaranteed that Larry was always in trouble. (It didn't help that Lorraine specialized in tattling on him.) Larry would later boast in an autobiographical sketch assigned in high school, "I had evidently chosen the wrong people for my cohort. I acquired a nice, shiny police record and began smoking. At that stage in my life, many people were disappointed in my character. I was not really concerned since I was having a great time."

We're talking about a third grader, here.

The mature Miller concedes that, while some of these kids had records, he was only pulled down to the station a couple times for questioning. The nuns, however, were quick to see what hardwood opponents would one day discover—that energetic Larry could be a handful. So when Lorraine aged out of St. Lawrence and headed to public school, the Sisters firmly suggested it was time her little brother moved along as well.

"They didn't want me around without her to rat me out," surmises Larry, who was more than glad to go. "They weren't being mean, they were just being *nuns*. It wasn't fun."

*The Cigarette Thief, 1954–55.*

\*

When an older Larry recalls a happy 1950s childhood, he's remembering summers of running wild and free with his pals. The families knew where their boys were—"out"—and they'd roam all day through the neighborhood, all doors open to them, going miles in any direction. They had bikes, but mainly they explored on foot. They had the Lehigh River to swim in at the dam. They had Jordan Creek out in the woods if they wanted to fish. And then they'd head for Catasauqua's spectacular, seventeen-acre town park, a legacy of the early town fathers and the WPA.

You could spend the whole day at the park's two playgrounds, swimming in a huge twelve-foot-deep municipal pool with three diving boards, playing a little touch football, a little basketball, watching the girls on the tennis courts, and then cooling down with swimming again while waiting for concerts on the lawn. Perhaps best of all, there were no cell phones, so you didn't have to check in. This was an age of unscheduled days for adventure, pretending, pranking, and soaking up sunshine that would never end.

"With a river, two streams, and all the other kids you didn't want for much," Larry says. "When summertime came, you didn't see me from dawn to dusk."

. . . Unless he was careless enough to forget a family picnic and his dad came looking for him. Julius quickly put an end to the little tough's walk on the wild side because Larry's pilfering had gone on for so long that his unsuspecting father, thinking he was smoking too many Pall Malls, had tried to cut back by eating sweets . . . only to develop cavities instead.

"And all the while it was me," says Larry, now chagrinned. "That's probably why he kicked the crap out of me, for what I was doing to *him*. He was a big person and I was still pint-sized, and he beat my ass so hard that day I couldn't take my shirt off at the picnic. It took me two weeks to heal. But I didn't think too much of it because I deserved it."

Scott Beeten, who scrimmaged with Larry in summers as a teen (and went on to coach at Temple, Penn, and George Washington), testifies that Larry's dad was not a guy to be messed with. "Sitting around the kitchen he used to tell me that he hadn't been happy with the guys Larry was hanging out with back then. It was nothing serious compared to today—no drugs, no gun violence—and it wasn't unusual for any of us to be like kids, when smoking and being a tough guy was cool. But Mr. Miller would tell me stories of the things he'd do to straighten Larry out."

However Mr. Miller chose to get his feelings across, Larry got the message just days after his dad caught him down at the canal: "He said, 'If you keep on this way, you're going to get in trouble.' So he gave me a basketball—I wasn't particularly interested in basketball before he did that—and he said, 'Do this or you're gone.' " From that moment, as Larry bounced through the rest of his years in Catasauqua, everywhere that Larry went the ball was sure to go.

\*

After Labor Day, Larry entered fourth grade—this time in public school—which he later considered one of the most significant steps placing him on the straight and narrow path. He made new friends, he began to get good marks and, perhaps most important, he learned to have good times without getting in trouble. The key to this turnaround was new friends interesting him in organized athletics, where success could be savored by keeping score. Once his exuberant playground moves, rehearsed in pickup games in the park, were channeled through the rules of a game, Larry discovered he had a gift which, for young boys, is more valuable than money—he was a "natural."

He played Knee-Hi baseball and is easy to find in team photos from this era—just look to the back row for the kid standing a head taller. But it wasn't only his dad's physique that stood out. Even in adolescence, he was alert for the winning play. In the Downtown Youth Center championship game, Larry came to bat in the bottom of the last inning with the bases loaded and two out. The tie score guaranteed he'd either be a hero or a bum, and soon he was down two strikes. As the pitcher wound up, Larry knew that one more strike would kill his team's hopes . . . and in the blink of a fastball whizzing toward the plate, the boy suddenly saw his chance. It was a wild pitch—and with the savvy, nerve, and reflexes to pull this off, all firing in a split-second, Larry swung and whiffed by a mile as the ball went careening behind the umpire, intentionally striking himself out to end the game. But wait—*except* for one of the most arcane rules from the early days of baseball: that a dropped third-strike is still a live ball.

Larry streaked for first base, knowing without looking that the desperate catcher was scrambling after the escaping ball, that the runner on third base was simultaneously charging home, and the panicking pitcher was racing to cover him at the plate as the sideline screams of agony and joy flipped sides of the field in an instant. By the time the catcher dug the ball out of the backstop, the batter was safe, the runner had scored, the game was over, the championship was theirs, and Larry had accomplished the near-impossible: He'd "batted in" the winning run by striking out. It was bedlam, one of the sleepy summer game's rarest plays.

It was a heady play, too, but one that boyhood brains are made for, and in the years to follow Larry's knack for finding the winning play at the end of a game was never again a surprise.

Larry found he liked being a team man, and has kept some of these friendships for life. He will proudly point out several pals in a Knee-Hi photo who are still married to their high school sweethearts past retirement age. In his high school autobiography, he even credited athletics as "the deciding factor in my life so far."

*

At a time before ESPN or even color TV, the citizens of Catasauqua had three religions: their church, their company, and local sports—not always in that order. This was a region where a man's net worth was measured by the stories he could tell, and among those who remember every kid who played on local playgrounds and school courts across half a century is Don Canzano, an Allentown native who played with and against Larry as a teen a lifetime ago.

"To let you know how big it was with basketball around here, we're almost equidistant from New York City and Philadelphia, where high school basketball was great. When I was in third grade they were all fanatics in the neighborhood—the barbershops, the little mom-and-pop shops—they talked basketball and football all year 'round. Every Tuesday and Friday night, religiously, everybody went to the games. High school football and basketball, they were our aspirin, an escape from our miserable daily lives."

Don saw Wilt Chamberlain play as a high school junior when Philadelphia Overbrook came up to play against Allentown. He remembers that local high school legend Bill Mlkvy led the nation in scoring at Temple in 1951 and had the best nickname ever—"The Owl Without a Vowel"—and that his younger brother Bob shattered Bill's record six years later. He remembers Bob Heffner of Allentown, who became Pennsylvania's first *Parade Magazine* All-American. "We had at least three or four superstars before Larry came along. But Larry James Miller was the apex of the empire of the Lehigh Valley."

*

The only thing standing between the old iron works and the Miller house was the Boys Club on the corner, which soon became Larry's second home. Mr. Miller took his son out on the playground there and schooled him hard. Still in his mid-thirties, he didn't hesitate to bang against Larry with the fervor of a man accustomed to playing for money—banging on the boy until he had to bang back, shaping the boy's energy into skills like a blacksmith hammering iron into shape—and for the first year or two the matchups were no contest.

Julius knew how much strength his son would need, and soon devised a homemade form of weight training. Remembers Scott Beeten, "In those days, they wouldn't let us lift weights. They thought it would make us too stiff and bulky, not agile enough. But Larry's dad was a smart guy. He got him an old hunting vest and filled the pockets with buckshot, and had him run and jump with the precursor of a weight vest."

Larry stepped up to the challenge, and when Julius was working at the plant Larry lived at the Boys Club. The building had a pool table and ping-pong, but Larry's domain was the compact gym on the third floor where the ceiling was so low that he had to arc his practice shots through the rafters. "Out of bounds" were the walls padded with mats, and on hot days, playing with the fire escape door open, chasing the ball could mean a three-story fall. It was there that the kid grooved his shooting stroke—and stayed out of trouble—by becoming a gym rat. As soon as he got home from school he'd dump his books, grab a sandwich, and dribble over to the gym next door until dinner called.

"I didn't know much about discipline back then until I started working out and realized I had it—a *lot* of it. My parents never got involved. They knew I was working hard." He became so devoted to these lone, but not lonely, hours with the ball—learning the weight, the arc, and spin of it—that, even on biting cold winter mornings before the Club opened, he could be seen shoveling snow off the outdoor court so he could practice for an hour before walking to school, literally clearing a path to stardom.

"You know, Larry's dad was a child of the Depression," notes Don Canzano. "He never even finished high school, but at Mack Truck he became an inspector at Changeover. It's a place where they make all the corrections on all the trucks before they're finally sold to the customer. There can't be any mess ups. And the only way you can get in there, you have to know everything and you have to have your own monstrous toolbox. So this was a blue-collar guy with a reputation around here for grit and determination, and he passed that on to Larry. It's hunger . . . It's blue-collar hunger."

Soon Larry began playing rec league contests with kids his own age, picking up the team game. The youngest kids would have to earn their fun, learning fundamentals and being put through drills by ex-high school players priming the next generation, before they could run in a full-court game. By seventh and eighth grades, as the talent stood out, the best of the boys began playing other Boys Clubs in the area.

Playground rules were different, of course, following the law of the jungle: If you lost, you couldn't play again. You had to move on to another playground and get in line. But it wasn't long before all the kids realized if you had Larry, you had nothing to worry about.

Julius had the know-how, the bulk, and still half-a-foot of height to train his son, but he hadn't played in years, and the changing of the guard came fast in the Miller household. By the time Larry was twelve, the "old man" realized he couldn't keep up with his energetic boy. It was time to call in reinforcements. He needed a younger man, but a big enough man . . . one with semi-pro basketball experience, but still rooted in the community . . . He needed someone like Bobby Nemeth.

*

Bob Nemeth became a pivotal figure in Larry Miller's surge to stardom. A fine athlete who'd signed with the St. Louis Cardinals at age seventeen, Nemeth played three years of minor league baseball before an injury sent him home to work at Mack Truck and play for the company basketball team. He played well enough that the Eastern League's Allentown Jets tracked him down while he was having a beer after a game and asked him to suit up for them that night. At that time the semi-pro Eastern League was strong, stocked with veterans from the New York Knicks and the Harlem Globetrotters who, it was said, were one injury away from being in the NBA. Still in his early-twenties, Nemeth was good enough to stick with the Jets for another three years and earn the respect of coworker Julius Miller.

Recalls Nemeth, "I had a phone call from Julius—who I'd never met—saying, 'I have a son I'd like you to work with,' so I said, 'Where does he play?' And Julius said, 'He doesn't—he's in middle school. He's a diamond in the rough.' I said, 'Are you kidding me?' I thought it was a prank. But I believe in giving a guy a chance and . . . now I'll never forget that call."

This was a step beyond father-and-son good fellowship and character building. What Mr. Miller had given the boy was a discipline that had long since transcended punishment, and now he could see Larry embracing it as a path to mastery. Having once earned walking-around cash playing roundball himself, Julius was now arranging a serious apprenticeship for his son.

Nemeth remembers sizing up middle school Larry as about 5'10" and skinny, but noticing he had tremendously big hands. Clearly there was a growth spurt still coming, so Nemeth gave the kid a shot. He started working Larry on the playground, playing him one-on-one, and was first impressed by the kid's work ethic and tenacity. "Any time I was on the court that summer, he was there, going against me in the hot sun. After his dad put that basketball in his hand, you couldn't take it out anymore."

Nemeth soon recognized that the boy hadn't been game tested, and gave him two critical lessons. "I used to say you couldn't go anywhere if you didn't play defense. Larry had quick feet to begin with, and great balance, so he really improved there." Down the road, Larry would be known as a scorer, but his ability to turn a game around playing defense, making steals at the defining moment, became an underappreciated hallmark of his game—and that began here.

Bobby also recognized the weakness in Larry's offensive game: "When we started playing one-on-one, he was always jump shot . . . jump shot . . ."

Of course, that was what Larry could practice alone in the Boys Club gym, and was the easiest way to score against his looming dad. Bobby Nemeth, at 6'4" and in top condition, was an even bigger challenge. "I said, 'Larry, you've got to go to the basket once in a while.' So we got him to do that. I used to bump him, he bumped me, and he got tougher." Larry was only 160 pounds at this point, but one day his ferocious charge to the hoop would become the weapon that rattled the Atlantic Coast Conference and made Nemeth's apprentice an All-American.

Nemeth knew, however, from his three-year odyssey through minor league baseball up to Triple-A, that once you reached the next levels of college and professional sports, there was so much talent waiting on you that mere excellence might not be enough. "The way Larry built his body up to make it stronger—that really helped him the most. It's almost like he was born to play basketball, but he had a heck of a work ethic. I remember him telling me one day, 'I can't dunk the ball.' And I had to laugh, 'Just wait until you get a little older.' Then he kept on growing and putting on weight, and all that time he was lifting weights. He'd put the bar across his shoulder, and the bar would *bend*. He used to pump those weights, and that's how he got that spring in his legs to get up there. He made that happen. A lot of guys are good, and he could have not worked out and still been a good player. But he *made* himself a great player."

Larry won't disagree, saying he always knew he had to work. "I had more self-discipline than anybody I ever knew. I still have it."

The payoff was obvious when the Miller boy led his junior high Boys Club team to a Lehigh Valley divisional championship, scoring 69 points in just two games while making 17 of 18 free throws. Clearly, on the hardwood against kids his own age, Larry was dominant from the jump. In later years, when fame cozied up to him like a lonely girl who'd found her man, it only felt natural to Larry. "We'd won since middle school," he'd shrug. "It wasn't a dream."

Before long, Bobby Nemeth was having trouble handling Larry, too. As the primary witness of Larry's growth spurt on the basketball court, Nemeth realized that the kid was not just a man among boys, but was unafraid of grown men as well. So by the time Larry was finishing eighth grade, he was a tough enough customer that Nemeth agreed to give him a shot with the big boys and allowed him to join a summer league team loaded with Allentown Jets.

*

In an era with few television channels and scant coverage of sports, the Eastern League pros were a tremendous draw in winter, playing in front of 3,500 fans at Central Catholic's Rockne Hall every Saturday night. (With admission only thirty-five cents, twenty-five regulars came from Don Canzano's neighborhood alone.) The summer league, though, was playground basketball at its purest—an amalgam of Industrial and Eastern League semi-pros (not being paid here) joined by ambitious college and high school players testing themselves for the love of the game. The outdoor courts in Catasauqua Park were the summer league's mecca, with admission open to all who brought beach chairs which ringed the court four and five rows deep, some in the back rows standing on theirs. The weaker teams played at 4:00 PM, followed by the main attractions starting at 6:00 PM, stoking the crowd for boisterous summer evenings.

The Miller kid was no stranger to the Jets, who already knew him as Bobby Nemeth's project. For a couple of years, Nemeth had taken Larry to their games so he felt at home with these older guys. Larry was excited to be practicing with experienced men, a whole team of Bobby Nemeths, knowing his skills would grow by leaps and bounds over the summer, testing him at a whole different level.

Then the plan hit a snag. Before the first game, Bob Mushrush—the supervisor of playgrounds who was also Catasauqua's high school coach—hurried over to insist the kid couldn't play on a team with pros or he'd lose his high school eligibility. Mushrush had earned considerable respect in the region by just winning the Lehigh Valley League championship with a very small school, and having seen Larry play at the Boys Club he wanted this incoming freshman for his JV team in the 4:00 PM early games. Larry was stricken, realizing that playing JV—not even with the varsity!—meant he'd be playing with children again, instead of learning from the best.

As Larry balked, his eyes welling up with tears, the grownups wrangled over this injustice until someone thought to ask Mushrush a simple question: Why should Larry have to follow high school rules when he hadn't even enrolled yet? Eventually Mushrush caved to the inescapable logic: The kid was simply too good too soon for the rules to apply to him.

Initially Nemeth told his teammates to take care of his pupil on the court, but as Larry held his own with the big guys, he wound up playing the entire summer. Before long, word filtered through the league that the Jets team had a new hotshot. If you wanted to beat these guys, you had to stop the kid. Whitehall tried that.

"They thought they could intimidate me because they were older, and they played a big guy named Eddie Folk," Larry recalls. "He whacked the hell out of me. Suddenly my dad was rushing out of the stands and on to the court—and now I wasn't pissed at Eddie Folk, but at my dad. I was just a skinny kid, maybe 170 pounds, but I pulled him aside and said, 'Don't you ever do that again. I appreciate your help, but I can take care of this.' And I did, and we won the game."

They won often enough that, as summer drew to a close, Nemeth's team found itself in the championship game. Larry had started all summer long, and was leading the team in scoring, but the men worried he might not handle big game pressure and they wouldn't start him this time. (Some have speculated they were embarrassed to be led by a kid.) Even after halftime they wouldn't start him—and they were losing. Don Canzano was there that day and witnessed it all . . .

"All of a sudden, this kid comes off the bench. I didn't even know who he was; I just remember he was really, really thin then—about 6'1". And down by the gazebo end of the court, they down-screened for him, and he came from the lower box, flashed out to the foul line extended, and hit a 17-foot jump shot. Then a minute later, same play, he does it again in the heat of the game. And I said to this person, 'Who's *that?*' He goes, 'Well, his name is Larry Miller and he's only going into ninth grade.' I said, *'What??'*"

Larry scored in a hurry and soon had 8 or 10 points to catch his team up. But now there were just a few seconds remaining as the team huddled on the sideline, setting up their last shot for the kid with the hot hand.

Let's call a time-out to digest this: When a team of veteran pros designs the last shot in their championship game for a fourteen-year-old kid, that kid is now officially a phenom.

In the moment, the play didn't work and they lost a game they might have won easily if they'd played Larry sooner. "So that was my first lesson that you're not always in control of your own destiny." It was also the first public display of what would become a hallmark of the Larry Miller legend: that when it was winning time, you wanted the ball in his hands.

Bobby Nemeth put it most succinctly: "Everybody knew who he was after that."

# CHAPTER 2

# THE BIG CAT

As a youth, Larry Miller's goals were pretty limited. "Sure, I had ambition: I wanted to live in a house with an inside toilet—so I didn't have to go to an outhouse at 11:30 at night in winter."

Still, in an era when good blue-collar jobs were creating the middle class, the older Millers were doing pretty well for a couple without high school diplomas. They owned the house on Wood Street, they had a '56 Dodge station wagon that was one of the first cars on the block, and one of the first televisions in the neighborhood. "I never wanted for anything," Larry remembers. "And they taught me how to work if you wanted something else."

What they couldn't afford, Julius Miller often made for himself. Coming home from work, he'd go straight to the basement where he had a huge workbench with all kinds of tools. In Larry's early memory there'd been an apricot tree in the yard and a large garden supplying the family with fruit and vegetables, some of which they canned. But then Julius began taking his son up to the Mack Truck dump to harvest discarded wooden crates that parts had arrived in. They'd pull the nails out and load the station wagon with lumber which Julius used to build a garage where the garden had been.

Later on, the Miller men used reclaimed lumber to build a cabin up in the Poconos. "We built the walls at home and then carried them up there. I helped him put up the walls and anything else he asked me to do. He's the one who really taught me about recycling and making things out of old or discarded stuff. He didn't talk about work, he just did it. That's how he taught me—by example."

Mr. & Mrs. Miller trusted their tight-knit community so much that, by the time the kids were in their teens, the parents would often head off for their getaway cabin, leaving the kids unsupervised. On balmy nights, young Larry would grab his sleeping bag and sleep on the front porch.

*

Catasauqua was small and safe enough that everyone walked everywhere in those days, including to high school. (Girls had to wear skirts, even in winter, and often arrived with their legs stung red by the cold.) With bridges over the river connecting the neighborhoods, everyone either knew or recognized everyone else, and even visitors from nearby schools were familiar from summer playgrounds and sports programs.

Nancy (Konye) Cunningham, a classmate and neighbor of Larry's on Wood Street, remembers a small town America right out of the movies. "There was ethnic diversity, but not racial diversity. It was common for us to visit each other's churches on Sundays, and nobody locked their doors. And John Kennedy was elected President when we were freshmen, so that was inspiring to everybody.

"I think our graduating class was about 106, so we knew each other well. And being in a small school you could really participate in just about anything you wanted to. It was a charmed upbringing. It was separated from other parts of the country that were not experiencing that idyllic kind of upbringing, so I've always felt very lucky to have grown up in Catasauqua."

When Larry Miller entered high school that fall, his court prowess was not the talk of the hallways. After all, it was football season and, for all his athleticism and the barefoot games of touch he'd played in the park, he had never suited up to play organized tackle football before. Trying out for the varsity everything was new to him, yet he earned a starting safety spot and lettered as a freshman.

Basketball season was a different story: Many people have said that little Catty could have won multiple state titles if they'd played to their size in Class B or Class C, but they always played up against bigger schools in the toughest Class A division. And the Rough Rider team from the small Iron Borough was already too tough not to be respected, having just won the most recent Lehigh Valley championship.

This year, however, Coach Mushrush's district champions had a problem: They'd lost their top seven players to graduation, and were strictly a team of rookies. Mushrush was known on the playgrounds as a great organizer, and knew how to build the other guys as best he could around Larry. But essentially the entire team was tipping off for the first time, and as the season began the results were predictably dire.

Larry didn't even start the first game of the season, and up in the bleachers Bob Nemeth surely had déjà vu watching his protégé suffer the same summer coaching slight of sitting out the entire first half. Once Mushrush bowed to common sense, though, the kid came in and scored 18 points in the second half. After that Larry started every game, often leading the team in scoring.

As the team lost game after game—eight games in a row with press clippings more like obituaries—the playground hotshot had to learn about losing before he could win. By the middle of the season, though, Mushrush had found Larry a running-buddy in a junior walk-on from the football team named Jimmy Murtaugh. Catty went 13-4 the rest of the season, surprising everyone by winning the Lehigh Valley League's second-half championship, and were dubbed the Cinderella team at the season-ending tourney thanks to

the unexpected strength of their youngsters. And now the papers were starting to run photos of Larry in action, too.

In a playoff, Catty then crushed the first-half champ, Palmerton—so
a team that began its season in a death-spiral had developed so rapidly that
they won the overall league crown, and Miller was the difference. He had the
league's fourth highest scoring total and was voted to the Lehigh Valley All-
Star team—the first freshman so honored in league history. The next time a
Larry Miller team would lose eight games in a row was never.

The accolades were still local at this point, but choice. From the
Allentown *Evening Chronicle*: "A fourteen-year-old basketball player who has
made [his] team a weapon of unexpected power . . . Miller is the flywheel
of the Catasauqua team . . . If a lot of other coaches feel envy for Coach
Mushrush, they cannot be blamed. Possessing the talent of such a boy for
three more years is like owning a hundred acres of oil-bearing land."

Wrote another paper, "One of the yearlings is 6'2" Larry Miller, who
gives promise of developing into Catasauqua's all-time great basketball
player . . . He can do almost anything with a basketball except eat it."

In the years that followed, Bob Nemeth would occasionally scrimmage
with Larry in summers or in the off-season until the kid headed off to college. But the perfect mentor, found by Julius at just the right time, knew that
his work was done. "I could see how he was improving. He was just head
and shoulders above everybody. He was a joy to watch, it was like poetry in
motion. In high school he was unstoppable."

*

As a homegrown talent, Larry's path from the Boys Club to local playgrounds
to high school seemed clear. But unlike others, this fourteen-year-old—
already touted to "conceivably become one of the greatest to be developed in
this region"—soon got a hint that he was more than a star. He was going to
be a commodity.

Rumors swirling through the *Evening Chronicle* that spring stirred alarm
in the borough that the Miller family might be moving to nearby Bethlehem

Township, where Catty's boy wonder would be poached by District champion Liberty High. The paper even passed along gossip that the Bethlehem coach was already talking to Larry's father, before dutifully adding the coach's adamant denial: "There's nothing to it, absolutely nothing. I don't know how some of these things start."

Clearly, Larry's talent was chum for the imaginations of others, and although that lone rumor's dorsal fin was harmless as a porpoise this time, it was an augury of the feeding frenzy to come.

*

Larry Miller's stature as a superb schoolboy athlete was confirmed that May when the Pop Warner organization chose him for the Little Scholars All-American "A" Team, winning a three-week tour of the Holy Lands that summer. Being chosen one of twenty-four winners out of 660,000 national participants in Pop Warner games was astonishing—the odds of winning were .00003636, or more than twice as rare as anyone's odds of winning an Oscar—but it wasn't astonishing to Larry.

"I had a premonition the day the letter came. I knew it would be in the mailbox, and I knew I was going to win. And I didn't want to win, either, because it meant being away from home and your pals for the summer, which you look forward to as a kid. But after it was over, I was so glad it happened."

This was the first national recognition of Larry's athletic ability and, perhaps most remarkable, it came for a sport that he'd barely played at all—football. Because Larry had always been over the weight limit for his age group in the younger leagues, he never did play Pop Warner Football. Nevertheless, he qualified because the town did have a Pop Warner team, he was eligible at the cutoff date (still fourteen), and he'd played very well in school as a freshman. Naturally the local papers gushed with pride over the young "goodwill ambassador" putting their town on the national map. When the *Chronicle* noted that $1,200 would have to be found to pay for the trip, someone in town sponsored Larry anonymously—no one ever told the Miller family who.

*Julius and Peggy Miller admire their fifteen-year-old son's*
*Pop Warner award.*

None of the boys who flew out of Idlewild that summer of 1961 had ever been on an airplane before—nor had most of their parents—and they kissed the ground when they landed at Lod Airport in Israel. What the boys found was a different world, where more people still rode camels and mules than rode in cars, and where songs sung with local kids on a kibbutz were accompanied by the sound of tanks clanking by in the night to defend a nation that was two years younger than the boys were.

This trip to the Holy Land was tailor-made for a Catholic kid, even one as lapsed as Larry, who swam in the Jordan River from which he drew a bottle of water to bring home to his mom. They also visited the actual Room of the Last Supper, right on the border between Israel and Palestine. "We had to get permission to go there, and there were soldiers everywhere with guns. It was kind of a rude awakening to what the world is really like over there. And it had no windows—so that painting by Da Vinci is wrong."

Then it was on to Italy, markedly different with big cities like Rome, where they had an audience with Pope John XXIII in Vatican City. What Larry had the good sense to leave out of his well-bred school report that fall was his own individual heroism one night in Rome when the entire trip could have ended in disaster.

Photos of the group show Larry already a head taller than his teammates, and he was also the oldest. The previous summer he'd been the kid playing with grown men, but among this group there was no question of who the big dog was. Fortunately, he was ready to take a leadership role from the court to the streets when things got strange one night at a street festival. Some of the kids went missing and Larry went to check on them. What he found was a group of locals hectoring his teammates who were out of their depth. Then he saw something he *really* didn't like—and suddenly the locals were facing an iron pumping enforcer from Allentown.

"My Pop Warner contact had warned me that they'll try to cut the wallet out of a kid's pocket, and I saw someone trying to do that to my guys. So I had to challenge them and we almost fought . . . And then we all just ran and scattered. I got lost, and it was like being in any big city at night—you walk in the middle of the street, saying 'Ou est Coliseum?' Once we found that, we just walked around it until we found the right street. We got back around 12:30 in the morning. The other guys had seen people chasing us and they thought we were dead."

Instead, the boys cruised home on the Italian liner Leonardo Da Vinci, and some became pen pals for years. "Before that, I hadn't spent many nights away from home, so that was pretty good for a little high school kid. Some people don't get to do that their whole lives. That was a quick summer."

\*

*A head taller (with hair in a classic 60s flattop), Larry returns from
the Holy Land on the liner Leonardo da Vinci.*

Back in Catasauqua, it was too late to rejoin the adult league season,
and Larry never did play with Nemeth's team again. Instead, he worked his
first job setting up bowling pins by hand at the American Legion alley behind
his house, earning spending money when he wasn't keeping in shape. He did
play at basketball camps in the mountains, though, and after one of these
games he met a man who nearly shaped the course of his life.

Duke University coach Vic Bubas, allegedly vacationing with his wife
in the Poconos, dropped by to watch Larry play and became the first college
coach the boy met and really liked. "When you're a kid who's been around a
little bit, you can tell when they're trying to b.s. you, but he was a really nice
man—down to earth, a family guy—the type you like to hang around with."
Over the next three years they would form a close bond. In fact, Bubas had
been tipped off by a Duke alumnus that this Lehigh Valley kid was special
and in seasons to come the coincidence of coaches "just passing through"
Larry's orbit would become ever less surprising.

*

By the start of his sophomore basketball season, Larry had grown to 6'3" and 187 pounds, muscled up by quarter-squats using the weights at a nearby boxing club. Still wearing weighted spats in practice, he worked on dunking with a medicine ball—"My goal was to hit both elbows on the rim"—and he was now able to dunk a basketball with ease, just as Bob Nemeth promised he would. And this year, Coach Mushrush gave Larry the green light to play all over the court—sometimes in the corner, sometimes the pivot—so he could go wherever the action was.

After wobbling to a 1-3 start in close games, the Rough Riders ripped through 22 wins in their next twenty-four games, winning Catty's third straight Lehigh Valley League title. No one cared more about the team's success than Larry, who told Paul Reinhard of *The Morning Call* years later, "I was so dedicated that I couldn't sleep the night before a game. I could hardly eat and my stomach would be churning. Bill Russell said he used to throw up every game. Well, I was a nervous wreck until I got on the court. I was home then, and when I got going I didn't see anything else."

Let us not imply that Larry's life was all work and no play, though, because after the games he enjoyed the rewards of a job well done as much as anyone—especially after the night games. In the 1960s, the high school offered three programs—Business, College, or General Studies—and students gravitated to three after-school hangouts. The General kids went to Fuzzy's on Front Street for sodas and pinball. Up the street was the Varsity, favored by the Business kids. But Larry would hang with the College preps— the athletes and cheerleaders—who went to Mooney's on Howertown Road for their burgers and soda. There they would celebrate the thrill of victory and cruise around in their awesome cars.

Like most boys in the car-crazy '60s, Larry had gotten his hands on a steering wheel before he got around to girls, when an older boy named Hoagy Carmichael (no relation to the famous songwriter) taught him to drive at fourteen. (Hoagy's claim to fame was that when a teacher once asked him who Pontius Pilate was, he'd bluffed the guy was a navigator for TWA airline—proving that in towns as small as Catasauqua everyone gets famous for something.) For now, though, fifteen-year-old Larry could only dream of having his own wheels, so he got his hands on the next best thing.

"Sometimes after a game I was too keyed up to sleep. And my neighbor was a cheerleader, a couple years older, but of course we'd be getting home from games at the same time. So we'd go to her place, just making out and . . . exploring in a confined space. Then I'd get out of there about 3:00 or 4:00 AM and just walk across the street—and my sister would rat me out! I mean, what's my sister doing looking out her window at 3:00 in the morning??" [Note: Here and hereafter names may be omitted to protect the not-so-innocent.]

The more serious courtship of Larry Miller began in earnest this spring of '62 with a trickle of letters from colleges making eyes at the boy to gauge his interest. Virginia and St. John's sent letters inviting him to visit, and Davidson's coach Lefty Driesel initiated a three-year full-court press of mail from Lehigh Valley undergrads and well-wishing alumni. But while the schools could barely contain their dreams of golden nights and settling down to raise NCAA championship banners together, Larry's guardians would spend the next two years keeping the sweet-talkers at bay.

Coach Mushrush knew what was coming, and warned the Millers that they'd be hounded all the time now, but with Lorraine applying for scholarships that would make her the first Miller to go to college the family tried to accommodate all comers and would talk to anyone. Mushrush, by contrast, put up what guardrails he could by decreeing that no one could interrupt the boy in school, no matter how far a coach had driven to get there (including one who drove from New York in a blizzard only to find the school was closed). They could leave messages for Larry at the Guidance office and, of course, watch games from the bleachers like anyone else.

What they saw was a team that went 23-5 for the league title, and this time the District 11 championship, too, with a revenge win over Bethlehem. Some observers consider this squad on which Larry was the only sophomore the best of his high school era, going on to win their Class A Eastern Regional semifinal in front of 9,000 fans at Harrisburg, before losing in the finals to a much bigger school.

Larry's individual progress was even more dramatic. He bumped his scoring average from 17 to 24.7 points per game, finishing as the top scorer in the league. Remarkably, by season's end the fifteen-year-old had already scored more points in two years than any other Catty player before him had done in four. When he won Second Team All-State Honors, the local papers didn't hold back, crowing that "Larry has been one of those spectaculars who come along once in a lifetime."

*District 11 Champions. And one of the last times Larry celebrated a championship with a soft drink.*

The "spectacular" was still a very down-to-earth boy, though, and if you traveled the Pennsylvania Turnpike that summer of '62, he might have made you a soda. When Larry turned sixteen, his dad bought him a black '54 Studebaker for $150—making it clear the insurance, maintenance, and gas were on his son from now on—so Larry could take a job twenty miles out of town at a Howard Johnson on the Turnpike. "I was a soda jerk, a busboy, I was everything. Sometimes I worked double shifts, 7–11 and 11–7. On a Sunday they'd put me on the front fountain, and you can't believe how crowded a HoJo's on the Turnpike would get on a Sunday back before the fast-food chains came along. They'd be standing ten deep. You should only put one scoop on a cone, but I couldn't do that to people, so I'd pop on a bigger scoop and put a little extra on it. I never had any trouble. They were happy to have me because I'd take on all the work. I kept that job the whole summer."

The old Studebaker had cloth seats, a 6-cylinder engine, and an awkward post in the middle between front and back seats, but Larry was the first among his friends to have a car, and on days off he'd load it with teammates and friends and head for the Poconos. But if the boys were ready to range far and wide, the car wasn't quite ready for them. "There'd be five of us, and everybody weighed close to 200 pounds, so we'd have to get out and push the car to get it up the hills. It wasn't the car's fault. But it was more fun going down."

*

Entering his junior year, Larry was now on the radar of *The Basketball Yearbook* which tabbed him as a Third Team preseason High School All-American— the only junior on the first three teams—still preeminent among his peers, and now on a national level.

He was on the opposition's radar, too. In the third game of the season, against Central Catholic, Larry had 21 points—in the first half. When the game resumed, the desperate opposing coach resorted to a unique strategy. Don Canzano reporting: "They said, 'To heck with this!' So they put a 6'4" guy in front of Larry, they put another 6'4" guy in back of him, and every time the ball got near him they had another guy go right at him. They *triple-teamed* him for the whole second half, and they were bulky, too. He had no room to move and he only got 6 more points because his team couldn't get him the ball. And he didn't have the supporting cast, so they lost the game."

Sure enough, sportswriter Dave DeLong's coverage of the game concluded: "Miller cannot carry the load alone. Coach Mushrush will need to rustle up another man to supplement Larry like Murtaugh did last season."

Before long, the answer emerged in senior Dennis Fehnel, who had upped his scoring every year. In this campaign he became a reliable double-figure scorer averaging 14 points (and several times hitting for more than 20), ably making opponents pay for obsessing too much on the star. As Fehnel and the team got rolling, Catty clobbered most opponents by 20 points, losing only two more games the rest of the season.

That January of 1963, Larry set a new league scoring record by hitting 19 of 26 shots, 15 of 16 free throws, and grabbing 24 rebounds, pouring in 53 points (more than the entire opposing team) to bury Lehighton 90–51. (Oh, and Coach Mushrush sat him down for the last 3:30 of the game.) The numbers in the box score tell us how he did it: Of the 18 free throws taken by Catasauqua, Larry shot 16 of them, clearly battling on the boards while the rest of his team got out of the way.

That Larry would break Bob Mlkvy's single-game record had long seemed inevitable, and the press was ready for him. DeLong called him "one of the most phenomenal youngsters to have crossed this region's basketball stage in decades." The Allentown *Evening Chronicle* said he was "currently establishing a career record that promises to stand untouched for generations." Another writer noted, "He's a fundamentalist—put the ball through the hoop. He may run over a few opponents to get there, and if they persist in hanging on he may put them through the hoop along with the ball."

*

Not all of the attention was pleasant, though. Larry already had a full day practicing before and after school, working a part-time job, and studying enough to maintain a 90 average, but now last year's trickle of college suitors was turning into a flood. Despite Mushrush's guidelines, coaches began haunting the playgrounds, dropping by Larry's job saying they were "just in the area," and showing up at school at all hours, annoying the principal and teachers.

They called the house, too, and after a while Larry pleaded to his mother that he didn't have time to talk to all those people. "God bless her, she would answer the phone because my dad was working and I wasn't around. And she was a talker—she enjoyed it." But practical Mrs. Miller also extracted a price for managing her popular son's dance card. "My parents said let's set up a time we'll go out to dinner one night a week with one of these guys who had an expense account—might be Davidson one week, someone else the next—so she could reap the rewards of working the phones. That was the deal: I had to sit and listen to somebody's line over dinner for two hours at Walp's Restaurant in Allentown, so my parents could get a nice meal."

There were all kinds of suitors—big name universities, small private schools, handwritten notes from local schools, and off the wall places you've never heard of—all of them hoping Larry would pick up their glass slipper. Parsons College of Iowa had written early that November, followed by Grove City College . . . East Stroudsburg State . . . Carroll College of Montana . . . Gannon College . . . Stout State of Wisconsin . . . Even nearby Millersville University, which facetiously offered to name the school after him.

Well, they had to try.

The Ivy League—with Bill Bradley lighting up nearby Princeton—took their shots, too. Dartmouth sent a formal letter from the Director of Admissions while Larry was still a junior. Princeton, Cornell, and the others followed suit, with a stranger who played his high school ball in nearby Easton, PA writing a personal letter to extol the virtues of Yale, where "you will meet the people who will be the leaders in all walks of life in twenty years."

Perhaps most intriguing was the Harvard educated go-between who dangled, "You have not only earned the attention of basketball coaches across the country, but also of one U.S. Senator, Kennedy by name . . . Harvard's problem is that Ivy League rules prohibit coaches and College from contacting you; however, there is no rule against your contacting us." That was powerful stuff with JFK and Jackie reigning over Camelot.

Meanwhile, Vic Bubas stayed in the hunt by sending Duke's All-ACC forward, Jeff Mullins, up to shoot around with the young prospect in Catasauqua High's Lincoln Gym. By now many people were assuming that Larry was going to Duke—"And I might have thought the same thing."

*

All across America, coaches recognized that Larry Miller could be a job saver, and few of them needed saving more than the young coach sitting up in the Lincoln Gym bleachers one afternoon as Larry shot around at practice. "Our manager, Louis Hilt, came up to me and said, 'Who's that bum up in the stands?' And I said, 'That's no bum—that's the coach at the University of North Carolina.' And Louis laughed, 'What did he do, walk all the way up here? He's got a big hole in the bottom of his shoe!' So that was the day I met Dean Smith."

The future dean of college coaching was only in his second year as a head coach, struggling for respectability after a major recruiting scandal had forced the resignation of former coach Frank McGuire. The Tar Heels had finished 1961 ranked #5 in the country and Smith's first squad still included Larry Brown and Donnie Walsh, but they'd finished a dismal 1962 probation season with a record of 8-9.

Thanks to McGuire's last recruit, Billy Cunningham, moving up from the freshman team, the current year was going somewhat better. And Smith was about to get lucky, with Vic Bubas passing on a sharpshooter from Washington, D.C. named Bobby Lewis. So if the rookie coach could land the Big Cat from Catasauqua *next* year . . . well, he just might survive.

Even if Coach Smith hadn't walked all the way from Chapel Hill, though, he had to feel dispirited watching the powerful Miller in practice . . . who, by coincidence, was wearing a Duke sweatshirt that day. Realizing he'd picked the wrong time to wear it, the youngster apologized, "I don't have a UNC sweatshirt, Coach." Smith replied, "You know, we're not allowed to give those out." So Larry told him, "Oh . . . well, I got this one from a friend."

*

Following Larry's record-setting game against Lehighton, the wins kept coming—ten more in a row, as the Rough Riders wrapped up their fourth consecutive Lehigh Valley League title. Perhaps unsurprisingly, though, not everyone loved playing in the phenom's shadow.

Coach Mushrush later conceded to sportswriter Bob Rubin, "There were a few boys that were envious of Larry. My problem was keeping unity, so I called the team together to talk about it when Larry wasn't there. I told them it should be an honor to play with a boy of his ability."

Larry remembers a day he got sick at practice and had to go home, and figures that's when Mushrush talked to the team. "That's all I knew—I never felt anything from them. They probably got sick and tired of everybody asking stuff about me, and I can understand that. But I never saw any resentment."

In fact, Larry was uneasy with the accolades, himself. Sportswriters could revel in the ecstasy of their words and move on, but the down-to-earth boy had to live with them, when actually he preferred a team game because that's how the game was meant to be played. He routinely complimented other players, and once even gave an opponent a congratulatory pat for stealing a pass from him, simply because the guy made a good play.

In later years, Don Canzano played with Larry on the Allentown Summer Basketball League All-Stars and remembers, "He was such an unselfish player it was a pleasure playing with him. On rebounds Larry would pitch the ball out to me on the wing, I'd dribble to the middle on a fast break, and would dish it off to a cutter or go all the way myself. But I always knew I had a safety valve, because coming down behind me was Larry Miller, and you weren't going to stop him. So I could throw him a flick or a behind-the-backer for two points.

"Connie Hawkins, the first mid-air acrobat basketball player, made a statement which applies to Larry Miller. He said, 'If you don't like a guy's game, if he's a selfish guy on the court, you're not going to like him off the court either.' And that's why people liked Larry so much—because he was *not* selfish. He was a great team man, and he gave it up to lesser players when he didn't have to—but he did."

Mushrush generally approved of Larry getting his teammates involved in the first half, and then coming on strong, himself, at crunch time for the win. But now, aware of his teammates' unrest, Larry tried to solve the beef the only way he knew how—and Mushy had to step in. "He began passing the ball off even when he had a good shot. I had to tell him he was our big scorer and rebounder, and I wanted him to use what he had."

*

Catasauqua won the rest of their league games by a merciless average of 25 points, with Larry (and Fehnel) hitting on all cylinders. Larry won the scoring crown for the second year in a row, and broke another of Bob Mlkvy's records, for total points in a season, while averaging 30 points per league game and better than 24 rebounds, hitting 60% from the floor. But it's not the statistics fans remember, it's the proportion and the poetry they inspire. Thirty points per game is a lot—but others have done that. Twice as many season points as the next kid in the league is dominant. And his playing style inspired such rhapsody in observers you'd think they were watching Secretariat run away from the field in the Derby.

Bob Mlkvy's former coach said, "I feel Miller is better . . . He's like lightning. You never know when or where he'll strike next."

The Harrisburg paper wrote, "As an individual, Miller is a pat-on-the-back man. He's never too tired to help a fallen opponent to his feet. But he goes about the job of scoring points and collecting rebounds with the powerful efficiency of a bulldozer." The same paper was so impressed it dubbed him "Hoop Houdini . . . Basketball's Wizard of Wows."

And it's not the names of the rivals Catty beat that echo even now, it's the pride of a small town gaining a reputation for slaying surrounding Goliaths. For even as his name got bigger, Larry Miller still belonged to his town. One neighbor whose home overlooked the playground testified to watching him practice every day, winter and summer—the year 'round business of plain hard work that led to the headlines.

His neighbor Nancy (Konye) Cunningham was class Secretary to Larry's President. (Well, of course—his classmates honored him three straight years.) She tells of coming home early one day to find herself locked out . . . until Larry came along. "I explained my plight, and the next thing I knew he had effortlessly climbed up on the porch's roof, climbed in a window, and walked downstairs to let me in. All in a day's work for my favorite knight. What a sweet, sweet guy." (Larry later wryly noted, "Normally I have to crawl *out* of those things.")

The basketball team's student manager, Doug Miller, also knew the more famous Miller from German class where they were known as "Herr D" and "Herr L." He proudly remembers teaming up for a skit, in German, about a wise elder and his complaining son (Larry was the son)—and getting an A together.

Judy Fletcher's favorite memory of Larry was simply walking home one day from high school, on Second Street near the American Legion. "I was about half a block behind him, and I heard him singing "Swing Low, Sweet Chariot" very quietly to himself. He was totally unaware that I was listening. That day he became very human to me, not some unreachable basketball star."

*

"Catasauqua" is a Lenni-Lenape Indian word meaning "earth is thirsty," and the hard-working citizens of the borough addressed this with thirty-two neighborhood bars—one on almost every corner—to match their thirty churches—one on almost every block. No matter where you lived, you had the devil or angels on opposite shoulders to indulge or repent with. Larry's local (though he never drank there underage) was McCarty's Farmer's Hotel—named for the family which has owned it since 1867—and in his generation the heir apparent was his childhood sidekick in ducking confessions at St. Lawrence.

*Class President Miller, Class Treasurer Loretta Hauser, Class VP and basketball team manager Louis Hilt, and Class Secretary Nancy (Konye) Cunningham at the Freedom Shrine. The Rough Riders always wore brown blazers with a CHS emblem to away games.*

During playoff season—as Catty's league champions traveled for District, Regional, and State tournaments—these bars would charter buses for their regular customers and send long, boisterous caravans off to Hershey and Harrisburg and Philadelphia. Others, who couldn't get a ticket, would drive over anyway and listen on their car radios in the parking lot, just to be there. Witnesses have testified that on weary, late winter playoff nights in these years, so many followed the team that the borough itself was a ghost town.

This year, little Catty won their first two playoff games against other league champions by 27 and 23 points to grab the District 11 title. Then it was on to the Penn Palestra in Philadelphia—the mecca of Big 5 college teams—for the Pennsylvania high schools state tournament in front of a raucous crowd of 9,000. As usual, they were matched against a larger school, this time Plymouth-Whitemarsh.

It was a seesaw battle—Larry knocking in 28 point with 20 rebounds—and Catty was up by two with less than 2 minutes to play. And then came a play that will haunt Catasauquans as long as they live. Someone stole the ball for Catty and fast-breaking Larry got it mid-court, looked up, and saw a teammate way ahead of him, wide open. Instinctively making the unselfish play, he flicked a pass for what should have been an easy layup and a four-point lead with the clock ticking down. But the kid bobbled it. He bobbled it out of bounds, and Rough Rider fans moaned in the stands, moaned in their cars, in their bars and their bedrooms, as the win slipped through Catty's fingers.

The bitter irony of literally throwing away a shot at the state title by making the sportsman-like play wasn't lost on Larry, years later telling writer Paul Reinhard of *The Morning Call,* "In retrospect, I should have taken it in. I think we would have won the state championship that year." Instead, Plymouth-Whitemarsh inbounded, tied the game, and then won the chance to advance on a shot in the last 7 seconds. Instead, they went on to win the state title.

Afterward, the press was very kind, showering Larry with the lesser balm of compliments. Writer Ed Gebhart said he looked like a schoolboy edition of Princeton's heralded Bill Bradley, calling him "unstoppable once he gets the ball in the pivot" and "downright mean off the boards." And Bobby Nemeth can take credit for coaching up this line of praise: "It's on the drive-ins that Miller really shines. He has the God-given knack for being able to weave his way through five defenders between the foul line and the basket. Bradley can do it. Oscar Robinson can do it. Not many schoolboys can. Miller does it beautifully."

*The Morning Call* wrote, "His all-around greatness becomes most apparent in the face of a serious challenge. In three playoff games—the 'must' games—he scored 38, 36, and 28 points. Even in the loss to Plymouth-Whitemarsh he was outstanding in the second-half comeback that nearly won the game."

The praise was nice, and splendid awards were on the way, but still . . . the season had ended two games too soon.

As expected, Larry again made Pennsylvania's All-State team, this time with more votes than anyone else. Gushed *The Morning Call*, "Miller did everything but sweep the floor for the District 11 champs . . . in a league peopled by small schools gaining a rep as one of the most rugged in the state." (Larry also felt gratified that his "feeder," Dennis Fehnel, made the All-State Fourth team.)

Nationally, he was chosen a Second Team High School All-American, a terrific honor for a junior and one of only three underclassmen in the thirty-five-man group picked by scholastic magazines. An even bigger honor was being tabbed one of the nation's top six High School All-Stars by *Basketball News*. The only other underclassman chosen for that group was a kid from New York City named Lew Alcindor.

*

The end of the 1963 basketball season only turned up the pitch of the recruiting season, with Larry's awards goosing the telephone to ring ever more insistently. The coach of Wichita State was so eager for Larry's game that he called the Miller house one Saturday morning, pressing the boy that time was running short and they needed his decision *now*. Startled, Larry politely replied, "Coach, I'm not a senior. I've still got another year of high school to go."

A few years after this, Peggy Miller saw a newspaper article about the recruitment of a New Jersey high school football star and offered the boy's mother advice in a seven-page handwritten letter: "I must say for one year before Larry made his decision it was quite hectic around here. Every day our phone rang between four and a dozen times an evening, starting right when we would sit down for dinner. I would have to put our phone on busy signal so we could get through our meal without being disturbed. Sometimes our doorbell and telephone rang at the same time.

"Larry tried to keep a lot of the coaches away from *us*. His coach tried to keep a lot of coaches away from *him*. I tried to keep a lot of coaches away from *Larry*. You see, in the end Julius and I got to see the ones Larry had an interest in . . . In Larry's last year, there were coaches that wanted to see us after every game. Sometimes three coaches would walk over at the same time. I'm proud to say I didn't lose my temper during all this time, but there were times I almost did."

*

Since being ousted at North Carolina, Frank McGuire had flicked the scandal off his shoulders and spent a year coaching the NBA's Philadelphia Warriors. Now, restless after two years of PR work in New York, McGuire was back in the college game that spring, pulling into the Miller driveway in a big Cadillac one afternoon with assistants Buck Freeman and Donnie Walsh. Larry was just heading off for practice, but McGuire said he wanted to speak with Larry's mom anyway because at that time, especially in a Catholic household, the parents made the decisions.

"They thought she was the way to get to me. They didn't understand my parents weren't going to make the decision, that it was totally up to me. But here's the amazing part: They came up to sell their wares—and they didn't have a college! They might be at St. John's . . . or they might be at South Carolina . . . here or there . . . He actually tried to recruit me without a college!"

Finally, at the end of Larry's junior year, Mr. Miller had had enough. Julius told his son to cap his list at fifty schools, which they would then whittle down to twenty-five . . . then to ten, and so on. This allowed Mrs. Miller to thank any straggling suitors for their interest, politely saying, "I'm sorry, you're not on Larry's list, but if anything changes we'll let you know . . ."

\*

That summer of '63, Larry checked his glory in his locker and did what every working class schoolboy did—he went to work. "I always had my own money. I worked all the time." The seventeen-year-old initially got a job at the local Holiday Inn, where he was a bellhop and a maintenance guy. But then he found a job that was dearer to his heart, working for a family friend—Buff Schwenk—who hired him at the local Esso station. Because this son of a Mack Truck worker loved cars—oh, did he love cars—almost as much as he loved basketball, and maybe a little more than girls.

"I did everything—pumping gas and mechanical work—I think I was making almost $100 a week. Some of the engines were so big I could stand in them. I worked there three summers, and I built up his business. At the time Buff didn't know a lot of people, but all the guys in Catty were car people and I brought the guys from school there, and we'd work on their cars and soup 'em up."

One customer named Tommy Mueller used to bring in his burgundy '58 Corvette convertible to be tuned up on Friday nights, and Larry would jack up the points for him. "One night he said, 'Let's take a ride,' so I hopped in and we took off. Gunned out of the gas station headed out to the country roads around Bath. We must have been going 120 mph—the telephone poles were flicking by like a picket fence—and I thought about jumping out, but that wasn't an option. Finally I just laughed my ass off—we were smokin'!—and when we got back to Buff's he said, 'You guys are tuning this thing *right!*' That's when I realized I liked to go fast."

Larry had already traded in the old Studebaker for a black '57 Ford, but he didn't have that car for long. It was parked on Front Street one night, where he could see it from his bedroom window, when someone totaled it. Unfortunately, the impact also popped the trunk where he'd stashed two gallon jugs of wine. The jugs were smashed and the trunk reeked, but the police appeared not to notice. So Larry replaced that car with a beautiful, azure blue '55 Chevy with new bucket seats, a really nice engine, and three-on-the-floor that he got for 500 bucks. In that, he and his friends would drive east and west across town all night, windows down, music cranked up, hollering back and forth.

Some Friday nights in summer they'd go drag racing the big 4-barrel Chevys and Fords on a strip by the airport that ran parallel to the runway. It was dark there between Catty and Allentown—with no local jurisdiction so the police didn't patrol out that way—and the action usually kicked off around midnight. Then they'd move on to the City Vu Diner around 3:00 AM before heading home. Nobody ever got hurt.

"I was pretty wild," Larry concedes. "But I was good at being wild. I didn't get caught, so my parents trusted me."

*

Whenever he wasn't risking his neck, or working at Buff's, Larry blew off steam by honing his basketball moves in another adult summer league, where they'd put up lights in Trout Creek Park. He played for a team sponsored by a neighborhood blue-collar bar, Sportsman's Café, facing off against thirteen other teams. Once again, Larry was the youngest guy on the team, but now he was an All-State and High School All-American talent and, paired up with Allentown high schooler Bob Riedy, already set to start college at Duke that fall, they went undefeated.

Playing for Franklin A.C., Don Canzano was on the wrong side of the court: "We could have had a chance against Riedy, but once Sportsman's picked up Larry Miller, that changed the whole complexion of the league. We had no prayer. Once he got to the square and the basket, it was like getting run over by an 18-wheeler. He was so strong, a tremendous player and a tough guy, too—but nothing ever dirty. He'd elbow you and bang you, just a hard-nosed player, because I don't think his dad would have tolerated anything less. And you had to like him because he was so darn good. I never heard anybody who said a bad word about him."

Toward the end of the summer the league picked an all-star group that barnstormed all over eastern Pennsylvania, playing other regional all-stars. At Jewish resorts they played under assumed names (because some of the players may have been paid), and Larry still recalls a contest in Quakertown against a team of Latvians who spoke their own language so no one knew what they were talking about. This is when Don got to play *with* Larry, and one Sunday night that August they went up to Jim Thorpe, PA to play under the lights along with Riedy. "Of course, Larry was the attraction, but we had a good team and beat them pretty bad," Don recalls. "And in the crowd along the sideline was Vic Bubas watching Riedy, but still hot on the trail of Larry James Miller. He came up to us after the game and said, 'I like your fast-break attack'—because he was from Indiana, which was a running state. So everybody still thought Larry was going to Duke."

*

Entering his senior year, already a High School All-American, class President, and honor student with a 90 average, Larry Miller found himself in the choice position of having more college offers than he could count. The Millers therefore decided it was time to go window-shopping before basketball season began.

Naturally Larry's first official visit that November of 1963 was to Duke, where his pal Riedy—now on the Blue Devil freshman squad—showed him around the Durham, NC campus. On Saturday afternoon, Coach Bubas got him a seat in the football stadium to watch Heisman Trophy winner Roger Staubach's #2 Navy team hand Duke a respectable 38–25 loss. There was only one problem with the visit: Larry couldn't fall in love.

"Duke was Gothic, it was gray stone and felt cold to me. And we didn't party, or go to clubs and sororities—they didn't do that over there."

Underwhelmed, Larry didn't head across the state to look at scrappy Davidson, either, despite the school's freshman coach pitching its connection with graduates Woodrow Wilson and Dean Rusk, the 1931 basketball captain and current Secretary of State. (Now, there's a fun couple of guys.)

Instead, Larry returned home looking forward to the following weekend's official visit to the academically esteemed University of Michigan, where he could join a stellar team with three-time All-American Cazzie Russell. Larry was still in school that Friday afternoon, crossing the hallway bridge over the driveway, ready to head home to pack, when he, along with the rest of the world, was blindsided by the news that America's first Catholic president had just been gunned down in Dallas. With the entire country in a daze over President Kennedy's assassination, Larry flew to Ann Arbor the next day and went through the motions of seeing the vast football stadium and meeting Cazzie Russell. But nobody felt like doing anything. "That was the most miserable weekend of my life. As much as I liked Michigan, it was a horrible time to go there to visit." Through no fault of its own, Michigan's chances never recovered.

*

The best thing for Larry's spirits at that point was a new basketball season, beginning just in time. As the world turned cold, his classmates, the townspeople, and civic leaders turned desperately to the homegrown superstar to be their aspirin now, helping little Catty lift its chin and feel they once again counted, not for iron, but for this one kid. The 900-seat Lincoln Gym that had sold 25 season tickets in Larry's freshman year had 800 season ticket holders now. Fans without them would line up three hours before game time, hoping to join the packed stands even before the early JV game started, smelling the surge of adrenaline to come. (Anyone they didn't recognize was bound to be a college scout.) Those who came too late stuck close by anyway, listening on their car radios in the parking lot, eager to join near-guaranteed celebrations flooding out of the gym.

Larry's senior basketball campaign was expected to be a victory march into the pantheon of Lehigh Valley legends, and the All-American did not disappoint. He attacked the season with trademark ferocity, notching scores in his first five games of 38 . . . 38 . . . 25 . . . 32 . . . 41 . . . Clearly, here was a young man whose skills had outgrown local competition.

The only bump in the road came in the Johnstown Invitational tournament over Christmas break, when the Rough Riders ran into national power DeMatha of Washington, D.C. which, just the week before, had knocked off Lew Alcindor's Power Memorial team. DeMatha overpowered little Catty 87–58, and some Lehigh Valley rivals exulted that someone had finally stopped Miller. But considering that Larry scored 40 points in that game— and none of his teammates scored more than 4 (count 'em: four)—it wasn't Miller they stopped. With no Murtaugh or Fehnel chipping in points, Larry's senior squad had simply run out of options.

Returning to league play, though, Larry was more than enough, and rounding the turn into 1964, Catasauqua rolled through opposing teams like they were duckpins.

*

Meanwhile, even the Miller family's best intentions for whittling Larry's college list couldn't stop the blizzard of letters pouring into their mailbox that winter. These solicitations, often from adult businessmen trying to cloak their awkward pleas with forced bonhomie, were variously coy . . . respectful . . . inveigling—the whole spectrum of human desire—not dissimilar to the approaches from coeds and stewardesses that would greet the boy in years to come. Some letters were brief, others were lengthy confessionals, and many offered advice or reminisced about halcyon college days. All of them wanted to be the talented teen's new, unknown best friend.

Mr. Lester Mendelsohn of the Paris Handkerchief Company touted the advantage of playing for NYU at Madison Square Garden "under the eyes of every sportswriter of note and very many coaches of the NBA."

A stock broker in Winston-Salem paid lip service to Davidson's strong academic rating before really laying the goods on the table: "There are (it seems) a million girls' colleges within easy range of Davidson. The dance weekends have a good mixture of Northern and Southern girls, so one really has a choice."

Gary North of Philadelphia's Westminster Seminary typed four sin-gle-spaced thoughtful pages addressing the "nightmare" of having 200 col-leges breathing down Larry's neck. His recommendation was John Wooden's UCLA—"the land of milk and honey (quite a few honeys)—if you want to work for a coach who is, in every respect, a Christian gentleman who never swears or makes crude comments about his boys"—but North's "little secret" was that Larry should first go to Junior College.

Realizing that all of these well-wishers were simply overflowing with earnest alumni and community pride, and still appreciative of Pop Warner's adult boosters who had cared for his Little All-American pals so well, Larry responded as often and as respectfully as he could . . . as long as it didn't cut into basketball practice. Not all of those approaching him were pure of heart, though . . .

*

As the 120 . . . or 150 . . . or 200 colleges—the Miller team eventually lost count—jockeyed for advantage, the more desperate and ethically challenged schools began approaching Larry with outright bribes.

"I never seriously considered under-the-table offers, but I liked to hear them just to learn my value. In those days, the colleges used go-betweens—like, a guy from Mama Leone's restaurant in New York offered me a Corvette from a school in Florida. A Big Ten school offered a summer job, a car, and a clothing account. A local Big 5 college offered me a summer job at Mack Truck where my father worked—where I'd be making more money than him! That was unacceptable even to think about. I never would have accepted any of that. And, besides, there'd be no enforceable contract between you and the coach. You go somewhere, and the coach gets fired or moves on, and there goes the deal. And if the NCAA finds out, everything is tarnished and you're screwed. Besides, I knew how to work. I'd been making my own money since I was fifteen. Even in college, I worked summer jobs.

"I was offered all kinds of crap, and if it embarrasses anyone for me to talk about it, then maybe they shouldn't have offered me. But, fortunately, the big guys were pretty aboveboard." This was an era when the only "one-and-done" players were guys who flunked out as freshmen. As Larry told *The Morning Call* in 1999, "Our morals and expectations were different then. I played for pride, for my town, for the school, for my team. Now it's all about money. It's a sad thing."

*

Larry kept the pressure in perspective by following the motto he always shared with friends and future teammates he recruited: " 'We work hard and we play hard.' If you get stuck on working all the time you lose your focus. You've got to enjoy what you do in the moment." His Dad was pragmatic about this and, not wanting his well-known son going into places illegally looking for beer, he started buying cans that they'd keep in the basement. "But then they'd be gone in two days, supplying the neighborhood, and my dad said, 'That's it—I'm not doing it anymore.' "

Larry was more circumspect about a relationship he had with a local businessman's daughter. "She was older, it was very clandestine, and I never told anybody about it before. She'd pick me up on various street corners and sneak me in the back of the place, and then we'd hurry up to her bedroom on the third floor and fool around out of sight—nothing serious. Later, she married a really nice guy and had a great life."

*

By mid-season, Larry was scoring 30 points in his games more often than not. Bob Nemeth recalls, "I've asked a lot of college coaches what they're looking for in recruiting, and they told me, 'We look for the kid who can dominate a game.' One play that sticks in my mind, senior year Larry came down on a fast break and got tied up in the air . . . so he threw the ball against the backboard, followed the ball, got his own rebound, and stuffed it in with two hands. I looked around and everyone had their mouths open. They couldn't believe it. You didn't see that in a high school player."

Catty rolled into perennial nemesis Bethlehem's home court still undefeated (except for DeMatha), and all of their games had been sellouts. This was a tight contest, too . . . until the game was suddenly halted at 1:30 of the first period for a public announcement: Larry Miller's latest basket had just broken Wilt Chamberlain's career high school scoring mark of 2,231 points. The crowd of 4,100 erupted for a standing ovation—this was the enemy's house, remember—and the first man out to congratulate Larry was the Bethlehem coach.

Decades later, Don Canzano would say Bethlehem was the top team in the Eastern Penn League of that era. "But Bethlehem had one problem: Miller. That was everybody's big problem. He ruined a lot of high school hoop dreams."

The Bethlehem win earned Larry an honor that was a dream come true for any kid in America: He was featured in *Sports Illustrated*'s "FACES IN THE CROWD" section—his first (but not last) appearance in the country's premier sports magazine.

Nearing the end of the season with a 19-1 record, the Rough Riders seemingly could do whatever they wanted on a basketball court. That spring Larry played his farewell home game in front of 1,100 in the Lincoln Gym (capacity: 900, but the Fire Marshall was busy tying his shoes), and his teammates—any whiff of jealousy long forgotten—thanked Larry for the memories as only another player can: They fed him the ball. They fed him, and fed him, and Larry feasted all night long against poor Stroudsburg, sinking 24 of 40 shots, 15 of 18 free throws, and obliterating his own single-game league scoring record that he'd set as a junior by racking up 65 points—again outscoring the entire opposing team in a 93–60 victory. Knowing the town would never see his like again, Mushrush allowed the points to pile up, no one in the stands wanting the Miller era to end . . . until, with 32 seconds left, the coach pulled Larry out of the game to a roaring standing ovation.

*

Entering the playoffs at 21-1 that March, the little giant-killers with the All-American were a marked team. It didn't help that one of the Catty starters strayed down that fork in the road Larry had avoided, getting caught with a gang stealing TVs and tossed off the team. ("I guess he wanted to be someone else," Larry remarked.) But two games later they were District 11 champs and moving on to the States.

What happened next was a performance for the ages, in what one writer called "arguably the greatest basketball career, and greatest career of any local high school athlete, playing in some of the most memorable games in local basketball history." (But how do you really feel?)

Steelton was considered a tough, hard-nosed, blue-collar town right on the edge of Harrisburg, so the PIAA quarter-final in nearby Hershey Park Arena made this contest practically a home game for the Steamrollers. They had tremendous pride in their school, and during warm-ups they were showing off, dunking and staring down the Catty star while their fans punctuated each dunk with taunts . . . "Mil-ler *Who?* . . . Mil-ler *Who??*"

Larry purposefully didn't dunk while running through his own team's layup drill until the buzzer ended warm-ups. Then he wheeled suddenly, drove to the basket, soared and double-clutched—holding the ball over the rim, then pulling it back, underneath, and up the back side of the basket to jam it in behind his head—before finally coming down. In the sudden dead silence, he ran back to his team past the Steelton bench, pointing to himself and announcing: "Miller Who." Don Canzano remembers, "They had this 6'6" guy, a defensive end on their football team who was taunting Larry—bad move—and he paid for it. When Larry 'went off' there wasn't a thing you could do about it. He was like a quiet assassin."

The next day one paper headlined its story "Mr. Everything!," saying Larry carried the Rough Riders into the Eastern Class A State Championship practically single-handedly. Tom Taylor reported, "Larry Miller had the greatest game I have ever personally seen a high school player have with 46 points (19-29, 8-10) and 20 rebounds." When John Kunda, the sports editor of the Allentown paper, retired thirty-four years later, he called this easily the best basketball he had ever seen—noting that Larry's 46 points most critically included his team's last 11 points in the tight 65–62 victory.

"I don't think anyone realizes the pressure that is on him," Coach Mushrush told *The Morning Call,* highlighting Larry's shrewd ability to save himself from fouls until the final quarter. "In four years he has never had a bad game. He relaxes when he can in the first half, and then comes on strong. He has started 103 games for me and he's never fouled out."

This was no surprise to Catty's next opponent, defending state champion Plymouth-Whitemarsh. As their worried coach noted before their semi-final showdown, "He plays for an average team, and it's unbelievable how far he might take them. I respect him as the finest opponent we've faced. He doesn't commit the foolish foul. He's always there to kill you at the end."

∗

That spring, the Associated Press wrote, "His name is Larry Miller, and he's got the college basketball world in an uproar. Coaches from every major basketball power in the country are beating a daily path to Miller's door in an effort to woo the seventeen-year-old sensation . . ."

Among those sitting in the stands for the state semi-final against Plymouth-Whitemarsh were the coaches of Pitt, Syracuse, and Illinois. What spectators saw that night was one of the most versatile games of Larry Miller's young career. He started the game at center, out-jumping the 6'6" All-State center across from him, and stifled him with 10 blocked shots while snatching 19 rebounds. He also showed his defensive quickness with at least 5 steals. Unfortunately, scoring nearly half of Catty's points wasn't enough this time. Plymouth-Whitemarsh played a box-and-one defense (four men each covering a quarter of the court, with the fifth dedicated to hounding Larry), holding him to 26 points in a 75–57 loss.

The final stats for Larry's senior season averages were staggering, though: 35 points per game . . . 30 rebounds per game . . . 8 assists per game. Any one of those would make him a superstar wing . . . or a star power forward . . . or a star point guard. This kid was three studs in one. With 2,722 total points, he had led Catty to 68 wins in seventy-two league games, the last forty-four in a row. And, pointed out Mushrush whose "oil-bearing land" had indeed been a gusher, "He could have scored a lot more points, except there were times we had to take him out early because the score was too high."

Five decades after his last game, Larry Miller is still the all-time leading scorer in District 11 boys' basketball history.

Within a week of his last game, the awards started pouring in. UPI announced that not only was Larry selected All-State for the third time, but he'd received more votes than the other four members of the First Team combined. The AP followed suit with a record vote of more first-place votes than anyone in state history. National honors came from *Parade Magazine's* 8th Annual High School All-American team, confirming Larry's leap from regional hero to being widely considered the most coveted college recruit in America. The one ding on the honor: For the first time, *Parade's* high school stars were not invited to appear on the Ed Sullivan Show so Larry missed sharing the stage where, just two months earlier, The Beatles had first performed in America.

More touching were expressions of local pride. A commendation was extended by the Mack Truck bulletin—not to Larry, but to his dad for not getting a swelled head. "Enough has been said about Larry Miller and his exploits, but now let's talk about his overjoyed father. Julius Miller works at Plant 5C, "F" Model Jungle and his co-workers are very proud of the way he has conducted himself in the wake of his son's publicity . . . Julius was quite an excellent player himself in the old days. In those days they never received scholarships like they do today. If they ever gave them out, Julius would have received many such honors."

Another admirer wrote to Larry: "After the way you played Wednesday, holding PW's Ed Szczesny scoreless in the entire first half, big Ed was 0 for 15 from the field. Not only did you play a good offensive game, but a heck of a defensive one. Everyone who was in ear range of my radio Wednesday said you were the best they ever heard. Even the bosses at the Camden Post Office where I work stopped to listen. So I thought I would write you a let-

ter and express the sentiments of the employees of the Camden Post Office who wish you the best, especially Andy Kovalchuck, whose mother lives four blocks away from you. Again, all the success in the world in college . . . Larry O'Brien, Clerk."

Fifty years later, Larry Miller auctioned off most of his awards and memorabilia to benefit the Catasauqua Public Library. But he still has the letter from the guy at the post office.

CHAPTER 3

# FULL-COURT PRESS

That spring, Larry was the big name invited to the annual B'nai B'rith Schoolboy Classic, in which the best players from eastern Pennsylvania, New York, Philadelphia, and Washington, D.C. played each other in Allentown. Larry had watched this tourney as a kid, studying talents like future Hall of Famer Dave Bing. Just the previous year he'd watched *Parade* All-American Bobby Lewis from Washington, D.C. become the tournament MVP (before moving on to star for North Carolina's freshman team), leaving Larry thinking, "Man, I could really play with *this* guy." The Lehigh Valley had never done well in this tournament, so the hometown star was looking forward to going against the best of the rest.

As chance would have it, though, for the first time the Pennsylvania officials decreed a preliminary game right across town at Dieruff High to assess the talent pool—and it cost them their best man. Larry was destroying the opposition with something like 20 points in the first quarter, and was going up for a dunk when another player undercut him and he fell hard, dislocating his shoulder.

Come tournament time a week later, the player headlined as "The Hottest Schoolboy in the Land" was sidelined in a sports jacket and tie, his court time limited to accepting a halftime standing ovation while collecting a jeroboam-sized silver trophy honoring him as the greatest basketball player to come out of the entire area in twenty-five years. (This invites the question: Why did a consensus All-American with an inscribed silver trophy waiting for him have to play in a qualifying game in the first place?) The silver cup was a beauty, and Larry appreciated it . . . but he'd rather have played in the game.

*

By now, the recruiting world's Big Cat had cut his list of preferred colleges down to ten, and it's revealing to note what he didn't want. He didn't want a school so small that he would have to be the Lone Ranger again. He didn't respond to the Ivy League, which gave no athletic scholarships and so was seen as a haven for rich kids (although he could have qualified there academically). And he couldn't love the nearby Big 5 schools, despite his respect for their strong teams, mostly because three of them—Villanova, St. Joseph's, and LaSalle—were Catholic. (He also ignored a dangle from New York Catholic power St. John's.) They were big schools, and fine schools, with good programs . . . but they all had *nuns*. "Even my priest—they threw me out of Catholic school in third grade—and my priest, of all people, tried to recruit me for Notre Dame!"

Larry's injury didn't discourage the colleges one bit. Even schools that he chose not to visit found a way to make their pitches in person. When Larry went to Philadelphia's Penn Medical Center for treatment on his shoulder, to no one's surprise the Penn basketball coach, Jack McCloskey, made sure to "just happen by" as the boy was checking in. Moments later, as the coach offered his concern, a couple of McCloskey's players also showed up. "So I was being recruited there, too. It wasn't official, but it was a visit."

Some continued to tout Villanova as a late dark horse, rumoring it to be Mr. Julius Miller's favorite . . . or was the local press just trying to tease its readership? (Only many years later was Villanova coach Jack Kraft informed by a man from Duke that the Blue Devils had employed a woman who lived down Wood Street as a spy. Her mission was to record the make and license numbers of visitors' cars in the Miller driveway and report back to Durham— and to prove it, the man cited the exact date Kraft had come calling, himself.)

Even far-off UCLA, beginning its long championship run under John Wooden that year by beating Duke to win its first national championship, had reached out with letters and partisan callers. But Larry was more impressed that Duke's Coach Bubas had telephoned him from the arena in Kansas City right before the championship tip-off to share the excitement live and in person. "That was pretty impressive."

Meanwhile, UNC had stayed in the hunt with freshman coach Ken Rosemond making repeated trips to Wood Street, drinking Pabst with Mr. Miller on the front porch. (Only later did he confess to *Sports Illustrated's* Frank DeFord that he actually hated beer.) In DeFord's telling, Rosemond remarked to Larry one day that spring, "The saddest thing is that, if you went from here down to Duke, then you'd be going all that way and you'd still be 5 minutes from heaven."

That caught the boy's attention.

*

Finally, that April, it came down to three big universities: Duke, with the attentive Vic Bubas, always in the lead . . . Michigan State which had become very persistent . . . and late closing North Carolina, with an asset Duke would find hard to match.

No, it wasn't Dean Smith. It was Billy Cunningham.

"Frank McGuire dressed sharp and had that Irish personality," recalls Cunningham, the final recruit of the disgraced coach. "When he walked into a room, it lit up. Whereas Dean Smith just melted into the woodwork." (This from a gifted player who loved the man.) But Smith was smart enough to turn the Lehigh Valley visitor over to Cunningham, another playground kid from the industrial north (Brooklyn), asking Billy and teammate Mike Cooke to show the kid around a campus bursting with spring flowers and sap rising a month ahead of chilly Pennsylvania.

Strong in Billy's memory is that everyone on the team was more than willing to take a recruit out, because then you could go for a big steak dinner at The Ranch House, where Chapel Hill lore claims they used to cook steaks on bedsprings back in the 1950s. "We didn't have the talent because the scandal in 1961 had limited Dean to recruiting in-state. And at that time there was segregation, so you only had white players from the state of North Carolina, which did not have an abundant amount of talent. I always say the worst stretch of time for Dean Smith as a coach . . . I guess that's my legacy. My teams weren't very good, but they knew how to enjoy themselves. So here came Bobby Lewis . . . but the big one was Larry Miller. Everybody wanted him."

Larry remembers Coach Smith telling his lettermen to show him around. "But I'm sure he didn't mean the kind of good time that we had. Billy told me they had a reception with a bunch of students wanting to greet me at Woollen Gym. We could go there or have some beers at The Shack. [Motto: "Come down before it falls down," where legal age was then eighteen.] And I said, 'What are you, crazy? Let's go drinking!' And that's what we did. I fit in right away with those guys."

Mike Cooke, a senior guard about to graduate, recalls the contest was coming down to Duke and UNC, and confirms the newly-minted head coach was not a great recruiter in those days. "Dean pretty much just gave Larry to us and said, 'Do something with him.' Well, okay, we had this *really* good looking girl at Carolina, and we fixed him up with her. The bunch of us ran around together, and hung out at fraternity parties having a huge time. It was spring and there were a lot of parties going on in Chapel Hill. And Duke is not Carolina. Duke is pretty staid; they're not much fun over there." It wasn't lost on Larry that all the guys from Duke would come over to Carolina on weekends.

As Cooke remembers it, the recruit was supposed to visit UCLA the following weekend—swimming pools, movie stars—so they figured that was the last they'd see of Larry Miller. "And we really liked Larry, he's a loveable guy. But the next Tuesday in practice, the manager comes running down calling, 'Coach! You've got a long-distance collect call from Larry Miller!' So Coach took the call, and after practice he says, 'Mike! Billy! Come here! Larry wants to come back this weekend—he's cancelled his UCLA trip—do whatever you want to entertain him."

Larry remembers this differently: "Carolina thought I was slipping away and asked me to come down again, and because I hadn't visited a lot of schools, and my parents had the opportunity to go down and see why I liked it, I decided to do it again. We flew down and that was their first-ever plane ride."

When Larry returned to the land of early springs, Coach Smith and his wife kept his parents occupied with a reassuring get-together where the Millers were welcomed by other young couples in town. Meanwhile, Mike and Billy were waiting on Larry with Bobby Lewis and his roommate, Pennsylvanian Tom Gauntlett. They hosted a feast at The Pines restaurant, which set aside a private room for them with appropriate provisions so the whole team and their dates could indulge to their hearts' content.

The Catasauqua kid from Buff's garage also burned up the backroads after meeting a recent Carolina grad named Reggie Fountain, destined to make a name for himself in offshore powerboat racing. "I told him we were into drag racing up in Catty where I had a hot, amped-up '55 Chevy, but when Reggie offered me a spin in his Corvette, that was almost a big mistake. Reggie was a teetotaler, and didn't understand he was handing his keys over to someone who was . . . not. I'd had a few, it was nighttime, and I took UNC forward Charlie Shaffer's wife out driving that Corvette 60 or 70 mph through the dark on some dirt back roads like I knew what I was doing—and I didn't. It scares me today to think about, because I could have rolled that car over and hurt somebody. I still have nightmares about it."

\*

Peggy Miller described the impact of these visits in her letter to the recruit's mom in New Jersey: "After Larry made his first visit to UNC, I think Julius and I felt Larry was terribly impressed, but we wanted him to be sure and asked him to visit a few more colleges, but Larry went back to UNC a second time and after the second visit to UNC Larry didn't want to visit any more colleges."

That's when the boy cut his list to three (including Michigan State), which should have simplified his decision. But the success of these visits also put Larry in a pickle: He'd long had a coaching family he had grown to love and admire, at a school that left him cold. And now he had a school and teammates he felt at home with, but a coach he barely knew who had just managed a 12-12 season. If Bubas had been at Carolina, it would have been a no-brainer . . . but how could he mix and match those feelings?

Of course, the Duke coaches eight miles down the road got wind of Larry's return visit to their rival and, sensing Larry might be leaning UNC now, Bubas made a beeline to Allentown for a meeting at the same Holiday Inn where Larry had recently worked a summer job. "It was really emotional," Larry recalls. "I was so close to them, and they were telling me they really wanted me and what they could do, and saying 'We know you don't want to be offered money' . . . and I appreciated that. I was almost in tears, because I just didn't know at that point where I was going." Finally Larry went home from the meeting with a Letter of Intent committing him to Duke in his pocket—still unsigned—and Bubas returned to Durham still one promise short of the finish line.

With his head and his heart in a muddle—torn between wanting to please those he respected and hoping to please himself in ways he could only guess at, someplace five hundred miles from home—Larry bought himself time by making the three remaining schools on his list an identical promise: He would announce his final decision by inviting the head coach of his chosen college to his high school graduation in early June.

*

Meanwhile, Catasauqua High School was organizing a May athletic banquet, replete with awards ranging from Most Improved Benchwarmer to, this year, the High School All-American presentation to the #1 schoolboy in the land. First, Catty took a shot at inviting the great Boston Celtic guard, Bob Cousy, to be their guest speaker. And Cousy was willing, on two conditions: He wanted a $500 speaking fee . . . Oh, and he wanted a guarantee that Larry Miller would commit to Boston College, where Cousy was now coaching. Of course, the high school was in no position to pledge Larry's services, so Coach Mushrush redirected his invitation to the coach of the recent national championship runner-ups—Vic Bubas—who quickly accepted, hoping this was the break he needed.

It should have been a triumphal spring for Larry, the payoff for years of hard work. But if the boy thought stalling his college decision another month would relieve the pressure gnawing at his gut, he soon discovered that— unlike the anxiety he felt before games, when he could play away the tension that night—being the darling of the country's top recruiting war brought a never-ending queasiness that was even worse.

Two days before the banquet, and determined not to be forgotten, Michigan State's coach kept the pressure on by dangling a team trip in Hawaii.

He also included a chart of his proposed freshman team, boasting "This is an NCAA Championship club! We have the animals for the circus—all we need is the Ringleader!"

*

The May 2nd gala testimonial banquet at the Lincoln Gym, home of its League and District basketball champions—and especially the All-American who brought them national attention—promised to be Catasauqua's biggest night of the year. Coach Mushrush was there playing the host, justly proud of his program's strong legacy. All the Rough Riders were there, too, surrounded by proud parents, all of them (including parents) stealing looks at the stalwart Duke coach who was hoping this would be the night that his intended would say, "Yes." And of course all eyes flew to the Millers as Julius and Peggy entered, accepting congratulations from friends as they found their seats. But Mushrush, casting his eyes across the expectant crowd, must have stalled a bit, his puzzled look mirrored by others in the room, flitting glances from table to table because . . . Where was *Larry??*

The Millers had to admit they didn't know where the boy-of-the-hour was, either. For the first time in his very public career, the local hero was a no-show. Eventually the festivities proceeded without him (somewhat less festive for the underlying bewilderment). Awards were given, speaker Bubas gamely gave them his best, and the evening built to Peggy Miller's and Coach Mushrush's anticlimactic acceptance of Larry's All-American First Team citation on behalf of the missing star. Speaking to reporters afterward, Mushrush sympathetically described the severe strain on Larry of deciding his future plans, the pressure of a hundred recruiters literally lining up in the office all year, of the Miller's home phone ringing incessantly since the playing season ended, overwhelming the youth until his nerves must have finally snapped.

The following day, Sunday, the AP sounded the alarm that the missing star had been under severe strain, giving rise to all sorts of worried speculation. Local newspapers played up the mystery, reporting that Larry's friends had told Mrs. Miller that he hadn't been himself for a couple of weeks. Some even surmised that the prospect of being loaded with awards might have weighed on his natural modesty. As word got around the small borough, friends and police began knocking on doors, and Bobby Nemeth stopped by Wood Street to ask Julius and Peggy if there was anything he could do.

Reporters calling the Miller house were told the truth: The parents had no idea where Larry was. These articles quoted Mrs. Miller saying "Larry's head was spinning. The boy has never missed a basketball game . . . Now, because he missed the banquet Saturday, some people want to crucify him. All of this has simply been too much for an eighteen-year-old to carry on his shoulders."

By Monday afternoon, with Larry missing two days, what local papers called a "major mystery" had the entire Lehigh Valley buzzing: Had he run away from home? Was he lying injured somewhere? Had he even hurt himself?

In fact, Larry was contentedly holed up right there in Catasauqua, just a few blocks from home. Having decided to skip the banquet, and knowing he couldn't lie low at a teammate's house with the gala looming, he'd gone to spend the night with a buddy on the wrestling team, Harry Mauger. Next day, the cops who were all over town looking for Larry stopped by the Mauger house three or four times, but Harry's parents never gave him up. "I stayed right there, and we had a good old time, day and night—I even have pictures."

Initially, Larry figured he could handle skipping the gala and it would soon blow over. Once he realized the "Basketball Star Missing" story was rocketing around the country, though, the situation became serious and he had to put it to rest. "I called a couple of guys Monday evening—I think Riedy was one if he was home—and we met at the Irving Street playground in east Allentown and just started playing. It didn't take long before somebody recognized me, and then the cop cars started coming around, and people were on their porches gawking. But there was no warrant because I hadn't done anything wrong, so a couple of days later it was all over."

And yet the mystery persisted. Three years later, a local paper claimed to have finally scooped the secret of Larry's disappearing act: "It is reliably reported that Larry's dad's insistence about Villanova is the real reason behind the Larry Miller Episode. Larry was heading out of the house for the banquet when his dad told him it was an excellent time to announce the Villanova offer."

Well . . . No.

＊

The true story behind the disappearance of the All-American could have happened to Any-American family in 1964. The afternoon of the banquet, Larry's mother was doing laundry and going through her son's pockets when she found what she thought was candy. When Larry came by moments later, she confessed that she'd sampled a few—she thought they were something like PEZ—and they were good. Larry went ballistic.

What Mrs. Miller couldn't know was that, the night before, someone at Mooney's—the hangout favored by jocks and cheerleaders—had given the lozenges to Larry, telling him they were "Spanish Fly," the mythological aphrodisiac advertised in comic books, along with X-ray glasses and Sea Monkeys, which teen boys fantasized would make the girls go wild.

"I just took it, put it in my pocket, and forgot about it," Larry recalls. "I was never going to use it, because you couldn't know what it really was. We were from beer country up here. We had three or four breweries in town, one right around the corner from my house. That was our culture. But strange pills were something new back then . . . unpredictable. I was really worried about her, and then my dad picked up on it and got furious at me, and we almost got into a fight. Finally I just said, 'Screw it!' and stormed out."

That night, Larry's parents went to the team banquet, not knowing if their son would show up . . . or what strange trip Peggy Miller's brain might be on as the night unspooled with unknown chemicals dissolving inside her. "They had the burden of handling the press that night—God bless them. They accepted all the awards I got, and Mom was fine so maybe it was just candy after all. But to this day, I don't know what those things were.

"In retrospect, I think there was something deeper going on there. I wasn't avoiding Coach Bubas—I really felt close to his family—I hated that he was subject to me not showing up. But I'm thinking I just didn't want to go that night with all the awards. They even had a bust made of me for the Youth Hall of Fame. It would have felt like a eulogy."

*

Larry Miller, the champion of Pennsylvania, had played his last high school game. He had set new records that would last for generations and won all the awards that his town, his state, and his nation had to give to a schoolboy. But the torment of unlimited potential was still far from over.

"The last couple of weeks were really tough on me. I kept an open mind the whole time—I really did—but at that point Duke was the most persistent, and Carolina was close behind. And, I'm telling you, I was sitting on the fence on that one."

Another coach, far away and fading down the stretch, made his last offer on May 27 by sending Larry a snapshot of a girl in her prom dress, wearing what appear to be devil horns and an inviting smile. "I hope your prom date looks as nice as the enclosed picture," the desperate coach wrote. "Incidentally, this is my daughter Barbara . . ."

Unfortunately for that school, this was not an area in which Larry Miller needed coaching.

*

The day before his graduation, Larry awoke to find himself still on the fence. "I asked my mother and father, 'Okay, you've been close to this, you've met all the coaches. What do you think?' They said, 'We like Coach Bubas and we like Coach Smith and we like their assistants. But it's your decision. You're the one who's going to spend his time there.' I could not get them to say a bad word about either one of them—they wouldn't commit—and that was so wise in the end.

"I'll respect them forever for doing that, because I've heard these horror stories where parents act like a kid is their property, and they dictate the terms. My parents were totally the opposite way. They just said, 'Whatever you do, we're with you all the way.'"

Down on Tobacco Road, graduation day started early in the offices of the *Durham Sun*, serving both the Duke and Carolina fan bases. Sportswriter Elton Casey chronicled his hunt for the scoop that day, which began with a 7:55 AM phone call bearing a tip from the Raleigh-Durham Airport: An Eastern Airlines flight was leaving at 9:35 for Washington D.C. . . . and one of the passengers was going to be Dean Smith, the head basketball coach of North Carolina.

Casey quickly called the airport to confirm the 9:35 flight to Washington, but was unable to wheedle the flight's passenger list. Was there a connecting flight to Allentown, PA that day? Yes, there was.

A call was then placed to the Smith home, where Mrs. Dean Smith said her husband was at his summer basketball clinic.

A long distance call to the Miller home reached a lady (presumably Peggy Miller) who said Larry was at school already.

Stymied, *The Sun* took another tack by checking whether Duke coach Vic Bubas was present at his clinic in Durham. He was. Conceding that he had not been invited to that evening's graduation ceremony in Pennsylvania, Bubas said that was all he knew. (But knowing that was everything.)

A call to Dean Smith's office at UNC was answered by a secretary who finally confirmed the coach was out of town. But this was her first day on the job, and she didn't know where he was. Only that he was due back the next morning.

A call to Carolina sports publicist Bob Quincy yielded only that he didn't know where Coach Smith was, but he would check.

By now the *Sun* sports desk had its scoop of the year—Casey *knew*—but he couldn't publish without attribution . . . and the deadline for the afternoon edition slipped by.

Finally Casey left the office, took an afternoon nap at home, and then rallied to join an anniversary dinner party for friends who had been married twenty-three years. Also at the party was Bob Quincy, the sports PR guy, who drew Casey aside and made it official: At that very moment, Coach Smith was in Pennsylvania at Larry Miller's graduation.

Dean Smith had walked into the Miller house late that afternoon to find his prized recruit and dad in the kitchen having a whiskey together to celebrate. At that point, just hours from graduation, the boy was thinking, "I work hard and play hard, and you'd better get used to this." If the coach was nonplussed, he nevertheless got the minor's signature on the Letter of Intent typed up the previous evening in the Tar Heel state and Mrs. Miller's signature as well.

The key to Coach Smith's win at the buzzer, in Peggy Miller's opinion, was later revealed in her letter to Mrs. Jilleba in New Jersey: "I think these two coaches, Mr. Ken Rosemond and Dean Smith, handled Larry just perfectly. Of course they listened to me, his mother. I told them not to be pushy and they respected my word, which so many didn't do. Some of the coaches were too persistent. Larry is the kind of boy who likes to make up his own mind . . . We felt he worked very hard for this right.

"In all our conversations with Mr. Ken Rosemond and Dean Smith, Julius and I never heard them say a word against another college or another coach. And believe me, Mrs. Jilleba, that is rare in this recruiting business."

*

Down in North Carolina, news of the Miller signing electrified the state. One local restaurant owner was so "happy out of his mind" at the Tar Heels landing the basketball whiz that he served T-bone steaks all day for only ninety-eight cents.

"Solid gold walks on two feet," gushed Charlotte writer Max Muhleman. "At 6'3", 210 pounds he reminds you of a bigger, younger Mickey Mantle. He is far more muscled than the average basketball player, but suffers no loss of agility, smoothness, or speed for it."

The *Charlotte News* equated Carolina's signing of Miller with the Louisiana Purchase, adding "In Allentown they speak as prideful of his character as of his ability." Sure enough, the sports editor of the *Evening Chronicle* told Elton Casey that Larry "has a certain degree of humility. He likes to shy away from publicity."

The classiest reaction came from rejected suitor Vic Bubas, who told the Durham *Morning Herald*, "Larry Miller is a fine student, a gentleman, and an exceptional basketball player. We would have been very pleased if he had chosen Duke . . . He's a fine kid. He'll do a good job on and off the court."

This was third-year coach Smith's first big win over his crosstown rival, all the more startling with Duke coming off the second of three Final Four runs in four years. Sometime later Smith acknowledged, "Vic taught us all how to recruit. We had been starting on prospects in the fall of their senior years, while Vic was working on them their junior year. For a while, all of us were trying to catch up with him."

Ultimately, the blue-collar kid from the Iron Borough simply made a gut call in choosing the big public school in Chapel Hill that impressed him as warm and friendly. As he told Paul Reinhard of *The Morning Call* decades later, "I felt more comfortable as soon as I got there. I didn't feel good at Duke; it was just not the same atmosphere. Duke seemed to have the rich kids; Carolina was the state school. Then I met Billy, and he made me feel good."

To this day, Billy Cunningham says. "As good as Bobby Lewis was, I think Larry brought something to the program that really turned it around. It took off from there, and others guys came in after him—but he was the one who stirred the drink."

Mike Cooke is more blunt: "To be honest with you, Coach Smith was on the hot seat. I've always said, if he didn't get Miller, he probably would have lost his job."

*

Even now, Larry can't tell us how Dean Smith reacted to the biggest win of his fledgling career, because Larry doesn't remember calling him that Sunday evening before graduation. His mom had all the phone numbers, and he guesses she gave Smith the good news. He couldn't make himself give the bad news to Vic Bubas, either, so the Miller team sent wires to officials at Duke and Michigan State instead. And the guilt Larry felt at turning down a man he'd so admired for years tied another knot in his gut a few days later, when a letter from Bubas arrived in the Miller mailbox. This time, after years of tearing open multiple letters a day and tossing them aside, the boy was unable to face the Duke coach's last words. He kept the letter safe, but it would be another four years before he could bring himself to open it.

But all of this was still to come as a shiny Lincoln Town Car flew through that cool, dark 5:00 AM morning after graduation. The King of Catasauqua had borrowed the big beauty to drive the other kids around town all night, partying like the jubilation would never end. Now, with sunlight spilling over the Appalachians, the lanky youngster with sleepy blue eyes pulled into a parking spot at the Holiday Inn—relieved, fulfilled, and knowing his whole life was about to change.

What he couldn't know is how many other lives were about to be changed by him.

# CHAPTER 4

# TAR BABIES

Three months later, the Pride of Pennsylvania was coasting down Interstate 95, being chauffeured into "the southern part of heaven." Carolina freshmen were not allowed to have their own cars, so Larry's cohort now was Catty teammate Jim Van Horn—who he'd helped get a scholarship at nearby Elon with an assist from Coach Smith—Jim's older brother doing the driving, and a team manager to share the long drive home.

Larry still had the wind in his hair, having been chosen by Royal Crown Cola for an All-American tour of the New York World's Fair, ushered to the front of the line at every exhibit. He'd also worked on cars at Buff's garage, and—what would become an annual summer indulgence—done what it takes to balloon up to 223 pounds, before playing himself back into condition in games around Allentown and the mountains. Now he was in fighting shape, and with Billy Cunningham, joined on Carolina's varsity by Bob Lewis, Tom Gauntlett, and a Florida sharpshooter named Ian Morrison who'd been 1963's national high school player of the year, Larry foresaw years of winning respect from a wider world, and ultimately a college degree that would open doors he couldn't imagine yet. And if leaving the northeast behind meant his world would be warmer, more independent, and brimming with warm girls, too . . . Game on!

What Larry was not counting on were the riches of pro basketball, because at that time there weren't many. There were only nine NBA teams that were rarely seen on TV—maybe one game a week and always the Celtics—so with revenue dependent on game attendance, only the very best pros like Jerry West might be paid as handsomely as $65,000 per year. (Bobby Lewis would later guesstimate that Coach Smith was likely making around $9,000 a year, which was pretty decent for a teacher. Note that one can multiply times seven to convert 1960s dollars to values at this writing.)

Veering off the interstate, the Catty car wound its way along a rural road past old cotton fields for half an hour before it pulled up to every northerner's dream of a South that wasn't yet gone with the wind—a big antebellum house with pillars out front. No, this wasn't Chapel Hill. It was the family manse of Larry's new muscle car buddy, Reggie Fountain, who had invited Larry's crew to stop over in Tarboro on their way to the Spartan rigors of school. There they enjoyed a weekend of rare hospitality, with formal dinners, hot and cold running servants, and a bell in the floor of the dining room when you wanted their attention. For the blue-collar kids from Catty it was a gracious welcome.

Then it was on to the college town that Larry's mom had fallen hard for. "I can readily understand why Larry chose that college," Peggy wrote some months later. "It is strictly a college town. There are no industrial plants anywhere. It is a very clean town. The whole town has such a relaxed atmosphere you just have to see this to believe it. The people there are just out of this world they are so friendly and down to earth. I could really make myself at home in Chapel Hill."

When Larry was dropped at Avery Residence Hall in the heart of the UNC campus—a big dorm where regular students far outnumbered athletes—he found no luxuries, no servants, and no familiar faces waiting for him. The varsity players he'd met wouldn't return until after freshman orientation, so recruits arrived not knowing anybody, or even who else was recruited. You were just told what time to be at the gym.

There were only four scholarship freshmen that year, paired up in a three-room suite, along with two seniors in the third room. (Fellow freshman Jim Frye remains convinced to this day that Coach Smith had the seniors in there to keep an eye on the youngsters and steer them away from trouble.) Frye, from Illinois, and his roommate Greg Campbell, from New Jersey, soon found southern customs disorienting. "I remember the first day Greg and I went to Franklin Street early in the morning, and two older, heavyset black ladies were carrying buckets of flowers to sell. When they approached, he and I moved aside to let them pass—but they stepped off the curb to let *us* pass. And he and I looked at each other like, 'What's going on here?' I was used to playing with black players all the time, and here there were still white and black drinking fountains. That blew us away."

Larry was a new look for the nice boys, too, with his black leather jacket and the flattop haircut with combed back sides called a "ducktail" favored by tough guys up north. "I did get accused of having a lot of grease in my hair," concedes Larry, who appreciates a good ribbing. "The Duke cheering section used to say my hair needed an oil change." He had a ready parry, though, whenever a southerner asked him where the heck Catasauqua was: "I'd just rattle off, 'It's across the river from Hokendauqua, east of Punxsutawney, and north of Conshohocken.' That usually shut 'em up."

Right off the bat, Miller crowned Frye with a nickname. At that time the players ate meals at Ehringhaus dorm behind Avery, and their first time heading over there none of the four knew where they were going. Frye and Campbell were following a path down a flight of steps, followed by Miller and suite mate Jimmy Shackelford, when Larry called, "Hey, Frye, you look like one of those Slinky toys going down there." To this day the name has stuck, says Frye. "That's all Coach Smith ever called me—'Slink.' As sophomores on the varsity, whenever our bus would roll up to an away coliseum, I would say [Ed McMahon voice] 'Heeeeere come the Tar Heels!' It got so whenever we pulled in somewhere, Coach would call out, 'Slink!' wanting me to say that every time."

Like his fellow rookies, Larry did not party hearty—at first. "We were a little apprehensive. 'What have we gotten into, here? This is going to be me for the next four years; what are we going to do with it?' You don't want to screw it up right away."

Larry was here for basketball, telling Don Shea of the *Durham Herald,* "In the last three or four months I think I've felt every emotion that anybody can feel . . . There were times of frustration, anxiety and confusion; then elation, satisfaction and happiness. And now what I feel is just eagerness— eagerness to be playing basketball with North Carolina . . . Basically, I love the game."

In the 1960s, when players wore canvas high-top sneakers like Converse All-Stars decades before TV exposure made a player's name on a shoe worth millions to him, freshman athletes were not marketable—they weren't even allowed to play on the varsity. At Carolina, the early birds settling in for orientation found most of the campus wasn't even open yet, including the Woollen Gym. Instead, their first basketball was played at the Tin Can (offi- cially the Indoor Athletic Center), home of the program in the 1920s and '30s. This rudimentary steel shell was so primitive that it couldn't be heated in its early years, so cold that ice often formed inside and teams couldn't dress there. After Woollen was built, the Tin Can served as a dorm for returning World War II vets and later as storage for medical equipment. But in 1964, with the old basketball court still in the middle of a wooden track oval, it was apparently good enough for freshmen.

Early pickup games at the Tin Can were competitive, the newcomers scrapping for status in the pecking order, and everyone got along well . . . most of the time. But those early-century Carolina teams—known as the White Phantoms—would have had an awkward time with Larry's teammate Willie Cooper. "He was actually the first black basketball player at Carolina," Larry relates, "but he doesn't get the credit for it because he never played on the varsity. I think he was from eastern North Carolina—a nice guy and very athletic—but he was slower and couldn't guard me. He tried to, though, and he banged my knees. It wasn't intentional but he knocked the crap out of me. I worried some people might take it that I was against a black person, because I'd get frustrated and mad when basically he was hurting me. But I thought he was a nice guy. So he was the first, a couple years before Charlie Scott made history."

*

One day, biding his time on the empty campus by working out alone in the old Tin Can, Larry noticed a man in street clothes watching him shoot. When Larry took a break, the man introduced himself as Tommy Lloyd—an avid fan who had just stopped by to check out the source of all those headlines. In his mid-twenties, recently married with a small baby and a second one on the way, Lloyd had just started an insurance business, and once again Larry made an older friend. "Every weekend I'd get together with them, and sometimes he'd lend me his car which was great. You had to have a nice car because those frat boys had nice cars, and this was a nice car—a Buick Skylark convertible. How about that, I was hifalutin'!"

*

Once the varsity arrived and Woollen Gym opened, the freshmen followed the leaders, chiefly senior Cunningham. (Billy got away with driving an old '54 Oldsmobile, fondly called "Car 54" after the TV cop comedy, because he was already a First Team All-American and Carolina legend, destined to be 1965's ACC Player of the Year.) But the freshmen worked on a different schedule and remained pretty isolated from the varsity, not getting much mentoring from the seniors. Instead, Larry set about going to classes, and with his own money from working at Buff's—supplemented by mailing his wash home to mom and pocketing the $15 laundry stipend—it didn't take long for his social life to become operational.

UNC didn't have many women back in the day; most often they started at women's colleges before transferring in as juniors. Fraternities remedied this by casting a wide net of invitations, and Friday evenings down at the bus station saw bus after bus rolling in with girls piling off. Coach Smith, however—wanting to make sure his recruits established the right study habits—wouldn't allow his players to join a frat until second semester of their sophomore year. Larry's talents were not confined to campus, though. He was able to forage out to Greensboro and up to Hollins, exploring all over Virginia, making any off-season weekend a new adventure. "There was enough for me. I always had a girlfriend or two here and there."

As Jim Frye remembers it, the freshmen didn't do a lot of socializing together. "Larry was pretty independent. He was never for want of a young lady's attention, so he was out and about quite a bit, always with this young lady or that one. Certainly the rest of us were not on his level."

*

Woollen Gym was a step up from the Tin Can, but after twenty-six years its 6,000-seat capacity was no longer keeping up with the student body. Once the season began, the University had to ration tickets, limiting seats to undergrads whose last names ranged from A to L for one game, and then alternating to names beginning from M to Z for the next one. Everyone wanted to size up the Big Cat snared by Coach Smith, so the early freshman games were sometimes more packed than the following varsity contests. Larry, however, known since high school for being matter-of-fact, credits another player for the attention: "A lot of people came to those games to see Willie Cooper, thinking, 'Wow, if we've got a black player he's got to be good!' But it didn't work out."

The freshman team, innocently dubbed the Tar Babies, mirrored much of the Tar Heels' ACC schedule, leading off against opponents' junior varsities at home or around the state. And if the Tar Heels were playing out of conference in Charlotte or Greensboro, the frosh might play a nearby smaller school like Wingate. But if the varsity ventured out of state to Alabama, Indiana or Tulane, the rookies would be left behind to play someone more local, like Edwards Military Institute. Lehigh Valley fans chartered fourteen buses and rode 460 miles to watch Larry score 40 points in that one . . . and the Catty buses came back again and again.

For Larry, this year on the hardwood felt comfortable right away. Accustomed to stepping up with grownups since he was fourteen and setting high school records as a sophomore, he found playing against opponents only his own age was a piece of cake, even in the ACC. His collegiate debut against Clemson's JV before a packed house in Woollen netted 25 points and 23 rebounds in a convincing win, leaving one dismayed ACC scout to report, "Miller was just as good as we expected." That was followed by 39 points in crushing little Wingate in Charlotte (before the varsity played Kentucky) . . . and he did that despite coming into the game on a sprained ankle and spraining the other one in the first half.

By the time the team reached its holiday break after games against Davidson and NC State (in which he scored 19 consecutive points), Larry was averaging 32 points and 16 rebounds per game—in other words, business as usual. He wasn't overly impressed with himself, aware that future running buddy Bobby Lewis had averaged about the same in *his* freshman year. What mattered most was that he felt right at home: "I mean, this was what I do."

Jim Frye, the team's second leading scorer, says what Miller could do was obvious from the first day of practice. "He would kind of play angry— and I don't mean that in a negative way—he would just refuse to let something bad happen. He was so aggressive he could pretty much do anything he wanted. And you couldn't draw a charge because he was too quick, could see things in advance and do things in the air like Jordan did later to avoid going into people. He could stop on a dime and go right up with such a great vertical jump. I high jumped for the track team at Carolina, and I told Larry he could have jumped out of the stadium."

True to Bob Nemeth's advice that, one day, talent alone would not be enough, Larry's years of pumping weights as a teen were now paying off.

\*

*Novice coach Dean Smith, prize freshman Miller, and Smith's first*
*Assistant Coach Ken Rosemond. A member of UNC's first national*
*championship squad in 1956–57, Rosemond recruited and coached*
*freshman Miller before being named head coach at Georgia.*

Dean Smith took his mission to mold men of good character seriously, and held periodic meetings with each of his young charges. As a committed Christian, one of his tenets was that all players should attend church every week—and bring him the program to prove it. (Assistant Coach John Lotz's brother, Danny—a member of Carolina's 1957 national championship team—was married to Billy Graham's daughter, Anne, and had helped found the Fellowship of Christian Athletes in the state.) For the first several months, Larry skipped church and had fellow Catholic Billy Cunningham pick up extra programs for him to turn in at these meetings. That all changed, however, when Larry had gotten so comfortable in his new surroundings that he walked into the coach's office one morning in cutoff jeans and a sweatshirt, unshaven and totally wiped after drinking Purple Jesus all night long—clearly over-performing on the "play hard" part of his commitment. Smith took one hard look at his disheveled man-child and ordered him out of the office.

At their next interview, Larry arrived without a program and made his first religious confession since St. Lawrence. "I just said, 'Look, I ain't going to church, I'm sorry. And I'm not going to give you that program anymore and try to dupe you. I'm not that person and I'm not going to lie. That's more religious than the other way around.' Dean said, 'If you were home, wouldn't your parents make you go to church?' And I said, 'No, my parents would *not* make me go to church.' And that was it. End of conversation. I think afterward he understood and respected that I spoke up and said that. He accepted the fact that I was different." And that's how Larry Miller became the first known player of the Smith era to be excused from attending church.

It may have helped that Smith was aware of Larry's problems at St. Lawrence. "As a kid you get put into religion, and you're supposed to grow into it. But you have to embrace it, not deface it by lying. That was the first time I was starting to realize I was not a religious man, but a spiritual one. To this day I believe in a lot of things, but I don't believe in . . . well, you see what religion does. God wouldn't have created 17,000 different religions—man did that."

Curiously, a prominent feature of Larry's take-no-prisoners playing style at Carolina would be the St. Christopher's medal forever flying around his neck on a chain. But this was no prayer to a Higher Power. "It was a gift from my mother, so I wore it. I didn't believe in the Faith . . . but I believed in my mother."

*

Returning to action after the Christmas break, the Tar Babies kept on winning, burying Wake Forest's JV team in Winston-Salem, 104–74, as Larry scored 38 and "showed Wake Forest's freshmen every shot in the book and some that aren't," according to one writer. The varsity, however, had hit the skids. Creamed by Wake in the marquee game 107–85 for their fourth loss in a row, the Tar Heels were wallowing toward mediocrity again with a 6-6 record as the team bus rolled into campus and one of the most infamous incidents of the early Dean Smith era: Waiting for them was a mock-up dummy of the embattled coach, hung in effigy from a tree . . . by his own student body. As discouraged players stared in dismay, an infuriated Billy Cunningham bolted from the bus and cut the offending figure down. "That's how tenuous it was at that point," Larry recalls. "It was tough." Smith's response was already in hand, though: Larry Miller was waiting in the wings, in the back of that bus.

∗

Nearing the end of the season, Miller was leading the freshman team in scoring—with 30 or more points in seven of their twelve games—and also in rebounds, and assists. That near-impossible trifecta had one former pro coach working in the ACC saying, "Miller is the greatest freshman basketball player since Bob Cousy."

Dean Smith could hardly disagree: "Boys often falter when they meet college competition but Larry has actually exceeded my expectations . . . He has more polished moves at this stage of his career than any other I've been associated with. My only regret is that Larry is not eligible right now."

Miller agrees that he was good enough to play varsity from the jump, and probably would have started and averaged in the mid-teens. His own regret in these years was that he never did get to play with Billy Cunningham. "Quite frankly, with Billy in the center and Bobby and me on the wings, we could have won the whole thing. Because we were very good smaller athletes, and that's how UCLA won it that year."

Instead, Larry won where he could, leading the Tar Babies to the Big Four freshman crown over Duke, NC State, and Wake Forest with a 12-4 record. "Miller Explodes" headlined an article in *The Daily Tar Heel* by classmate Pete Gammons (later the revered "Peter" Gammons of *The Boston Globe, Sports Illustrated, and ESPN*) describing Larry pouring in a season-high 44 points for an emphatic beatdown of Virginia's previously undefeated frosh. A few days later, Larry racked up 23 points in the first half alone against Duke's Blue Imps before fouling out both Duke centers on his way to 38 points. (Explained Rosemond, "He has moves other players just aren't able to defend without resorting to a foul.") Fifty years later, Gammons would still remember Miller as "a character, and a great money-player with a propensity to come up with huge plays at the end of games."

Meanwhile, the varsity had finished strong, winning their last seven games in a row before losing in the ACC Tournament for a 15-9 record, with Bobby Lewis averaging 21 points in his first varsity campaign. But Billy the legend was leaving, and the season had exposed Morrison, the deadeye shooter from Florida, as a washout, his 20-point freshman average slumping to a lackluster 6.8 ppg against the big boys. "It turns out he wasn't really an All-American," Larry says now. "He just played for a high school where he had a lot of points, but he didn't know how to get them—great shooter, but he couldn't get open. He didn't turn out to be what was called for."

As for reinforcements from the freshman team, Coach Rosemond had said, "Whatever shortcoming we may have, Miller goes a long way toward camouflaging them." That was a swell compliment to Larry, but faint praise for his teammates, and he was becoming uneasy. "Coming down, I never thought we wouldn't be competitive."

Back in September, Larry had shared with the *Durham Herald* a personal motive for risking his future on the friendly school with the mediocre record instead of Vic Bubas' Final Four program: "I just couldn't see myself alternating on a team with eight starters. I like to play all the time, or a good portion of the time. Starters get the feel of each other, learning each other's moves and consequently can work together better as a unit." But if Duke was stockpiled with too much talent, Larry was beginning to wonder . . . did Carolina really have enough?

\*

With basketball season over, the toughest challenges for freshman Miller now awaited him off the court—including one that almost got him kicked out of school. Always a dedicated student, Larry carried a B average into that spring of '65, verging on the Dean's List. Everything was suddenly at risk, though, when the professor of his Geology class—known at even the nation's finest colleges as "Rocks for Jocks"—summoned him and accused him of cheating. Holding up two important labs with identical work as proof that Larry had copied from an upperclassman, the man demanded to know why he should not be expelled. Larry was trapped . . . but he knew exactly why not.

The prof had it backward: It was actually an older friend who had asked Larry for a look at *his* answers after the test was handed out. And Larry had no problem with that, but warned he wasn't going to ace this—it was going to be a B or C type deal—so the other fellow had better not copy him exactly. If their mistakes were identical, it was bound to be noticed. The senior was careless, though, and did it anyway . . . and sure enough the prof caught on and assumed it was the freshman who had cheated off the older student. Larry, knowing his pal was set to graduate in less than a month, just couldn't rat him out. It was an ethical stalemate. In desperation, Larry swallowed his pride for a buddy's sake and played the only card he had, promising this would never happen again. And of course it never did.

*

Larry was now allowed to meet high school seniors making campus visits and, from his own experience with Mike Cooke and Billy, realized that off-season recruiting was an essential part of the team game. Also, looking toward his future on the varsity, he was fully aware that the future needed help. Fortunately, Dean Smith had made a good head start on recruiting the Class of '69 with local basketball camps that he ran during summers.

A guard from western North Carolina named Joe Brown, who would become an Honorable Mention High School All-American, was good enough after his sophomore year to have come to Chapel Hill in the summer of '63. There, he met the captain of Smith's first team, Jim Hudock, along with Cooke and Cunningham. "Coach noticed me right then and essentially offered me a scholarship before I left camp. So even though I was later being recruited by Davidson, Duke, Wake Forest and others, Coach Smith was always at the top of my list. That made it easy my senior year when he said, 'It's time.' "

Even more critical for the Tar Heel lineup, Smith at last found some real height in 6'8" Bill Bunting and especially 6'11" All-State center Rusty Clark, almost certain to come to UNC after winning the state's most prestigious academic scholarship, the Morehead. He had been Brown's roommate at Smith's camp the previous summer.

That left the pipeline needing only a point guard, the critical floor general, and Smith had his sights on a dandy up in Schenectady, NY. A big guard so highly recruited he could go almost anywhere, Dick Grubar in high school had seen Billy Cunningham dominate NYU in a tight game at Madison Square Garden before fouling out midway through the second half. "I'll never forget that game—it was unbelievable—and it always stayed with me. That's why I paid attention to UNC."

Still, Grubar was probably slotted for Kentucky because Schenectady's Pat Riley was now a star there. Then Kentucky's legendary coach, Adolph Rupp, made a fatal mistake: "He came up to see me with an entourage of fourteen people. And I was a lower-middle-class kid—our family couldn't fit more than six people in our living room. He embarrassed my parents. And then he never spoke about a single player; it was all about *his* accomplishments. I thought to myself, 'I sure don't want to go there.' "

Meanwhile, Ken Rosemond had accepted the head coaching job at Georgia, and Dean Smith had just hired Larry Brown—Carolina's 1961–63 point guard, with an Olympic gold medal that would put his jersey in the rafters—to come take over the freshman squad. "He came up to see me, and he was pretty impressive," recalls Grubar. "A lot of people saw me as a small forward, but I wanted to be a point guard and that's how he wanted to use me, so that was exciting to hear."

The rest of Grubar's recruitment was a carbon copy of Miller's, only this time Larry was the northerner closing the deal. "I and my parents flew down—when we left it was snowing—and we arrived on a perfect April weekend in Chapel Hill with everything blooming. Then Larry and Bobby showed me around and . . . c'mon, Larry's a fun guy." What neither player realized at the time was how much their movie star looks would mean to the Carolina magic to come.

Says Miller, "I told all the recruits, 'You work hard and you play hard—and we're in a great place to do both here. We can win and we can have fun.' And that's exactly what I did the whole time. It was a total experience."

Not everyone approved of the "play hard" part of the program, though, as Miller, Gauntlett and crew discovered while auditioning a skilled, 6'9" player named Chris Thomforde. "We invited him to come along to a party and he took offense to it," Gauntlett recalls. "He said, 'No, I don't do that'—and wrote us off right away." Larry remembers, "He wanted to go to a Christian seminar, and I thought, 'Here we go again—this is against *my* religion.' " (Instead, Bill Bradley lured the center to a pretty decent place called Princeton.)

To this day, Larry feels that recruiting the Class of '69 was far more important than anything he did on the court for North Carolina that first year. "We needed some athletes. That was the big deal, to get those other guys—they were the important class—because if those guys didn't come in after me, we would have been up the creek. And Dean would have been done."

*

Jim Heavner was twenty-one years old and fresh out of UNC when he replaced broadcast legend Ty Boyd at Chapel Hill's radio station WCHL after working there as a student. He and rookie coach Dean Smith both got their new jobs in the summer of 1961, and as Program Director and all-purpose broadcaster Heavner began doing a live daily radio show with the basketball coach every weekday from the October start of practice to the last game of the season.

Heavner was also a neighbor of Coach Smith, who would sometimes give him a lift to games in his old car with a bum defroster, and together they'd scrape the ice off Dean's windshield. It was during these rides that Heavner, who went on to own WCHL and build a media empire, learned how to run his businesses by paying attention to the coach who was only nine years older.

"Dean was so structured in his view. He would say, 'From the first day of practice October 15 until we play our last game, everything is for the team. I am the commander, whatever I say goes, it's all for the team and the individual is not important. From the day of the *last* game until the beginning of the next season, I am the servant of every player on the team, and the goal of the individual is most important, and my goal is to do all I can to help you be successful.' "

That philosophy went into action when classes let out and exams were over that spring, because Larry didn't head home right away. Coach Smith had a paying job waiting for him right there in Chapel Hill, working as a counselor at his summer basketball camp. It was a sweet and legal deal for teaching what Larry did best.

First, though, a growing boy had to celebrate freedom by doing what Larry also did best—have fun the hard way. Lacking wheels, he got a lift to Myrtle Beach where he was hired for the stage crew of a Martha and the Vandellas show at a beach club. "They gave me $5 and all the beer I could drink—I only had to throw one guy off the stage—so I was a professional bouncer after that."

The next day didn't go so well. Larry missed his ride back to Chapel Hill, had to hitch over 200 miles, checked in too late to welcome Smith's arriving campers, and got reprimanded. "Who would do that?" he muses. "Well, apparently me."

*

Meanwhile, back in Pennsylvania that spring, Larry's mother had wrapped up encouraging advice to another mother whose son was about to leave home.

"Larry adjusted very well," she wrote. "I don't think he was very homesick either. He's doing well in his studies, too. Most of all, the people in Chapel Hill are treating Larry as good as they said they would. I think the most important thing is Larry is happy and what more can a mother ask than that.

"Well, Mrs. Jilleba . . . I hope your household doesn't get too hectic in the next few months. You may laugh at this, but sometimes my house is so quiet I wish the phone would ring."

*A North Carolina team issued photo, 1965.*

CHAPTER 5

# REINFORCEMENTS

Larry cruised into his sophomore year in his azure blue Chevy, now souped-up with a hot engine that he'd bought from Reggie Fountain and installed while working at Buff's garage over the summer. He'd found time for basketball, too, playing pickup games at the old playgrounds against Bob Riedy, home from Duke, with both men fully aware they were rehearsing for an ACC season in which they'd likely be guarding each other. So Larry was souped-up, too, now with 225 pounds of muscle and ready to be the big new engine of the Tar Heels. As eager as he was to jump into the varsity lineup in October, though, he knew all his hopes for this new squad would rest on his chemistry with top gun Bobby Lewis.

Lewis, from Washington, D.C., was a *Parade* High School All-American the year before Larry, and vividly remembers appearing on The Ed Sullivan Show. "I was standing next to Lew Alcindor [later Kareem Abdul-Jabbar] who was only a sophomore, and he was seven feet tall even then!"

Proclaimed by Dean Smith, himself, as his first star recruit, Bobby Lewis was a key player in the powerful relay of 1960s All-Americans at North Carolina—overlapping from Cunningham to Lewis, to Miller, to Charles Scott, and endlessly on into the future. In 1963, though, with no star in Smith's first recruiting class to take the baton from Billy, Carolina was on the brink of becoming just another forgotten also-ran, its lonely 1957 National Champion banner fading into memory, year after year. There's a fair argument that if Lewis hadn't risked joining the sanction-crippled program with its unproven rookie coach, there likely would have been no Miller, and thus no Scott, and no more championships for a long time to come . . . if ever.

And Lewis was badly wanted elsewhere. "I visited a lot of schools," he recalls. "I was recruited very heavily by Kentucky. Adolph Rupp came up a couple times to take me and my girl out to dinner. That was impressive to a kid like me. I wanted to go south, and I would have gone to Maryland—I told Coach Smith this—if the DeMatha High School coach, Morgan Wooten, who I knew from working his camp when I was sixteen, had taken that job. No questions, no visits anywhere else. But he stayed at DeMatha and never left. So we went down, and Coach Smith wasn't the greatest coach in the world back then—he was just starting—but he was very, very good with the parents. And I was recruited by Billy."

Like Miller, Lewis had responded to the confident Cunningham and his surroundings. "Back then, Carolina was a fraction of the size it is today. So the school sold itself as beautiful, not a big factory." It was also relevant to Bobby's interests that Lexington, KY was a nine-hour drive from Washington, while Chapel Hill could be reached in little more than four hours—close enough for his mom to drive down every weekend with his girl. (In the words of one teammate "a real sweetheart," who would still be Bobby's girl past their 50th wedding anniversary in the next century.)

Now a certified star, Lewis had lived up to last year's high hopes that he would join Cunningham in a formidable tandem—but the Florida washout had already transferred back home. And despite Miller's reassuring arrival from the JV to replace Billy (now having an All-Rookie Team year in the

NBA), the team still lacked effective size with 6'8" center Bob Bennett tagged "an enigma" and Willie Cooper quitting athletics to focus on his studies. The 1965–66 UNC press guide even acknowledged, "A successful season rests on what sort of muscle the Tar Heels can apply on the boards . . . Is there a replacement around for Billy?" Bobby was lauded as "the fastest gun in the South" and much was expected of Larry, but the rest of the write-up pressed to find one nice adjective for each of the other veterans, while passing over Larry's fellow sophomores, noting "Other than Miller the newcomers will have to make their way."

Meanwhile, Assistant Coach Larry Brown was hard at work drilling the new talent fresh out of high school. "Thank God he was there," says Joe Brown. "Many of our class will tell you he worked us so hard, but that taught us what it takes to play at that level. It was Larry Brown who first indoctrinated us to Carolina basketball." Grubar confirms, "You could tell he was going to be a great coach. He busted your butt, but you knew he still loved you. And all the assistants were so good at not overstepping their bounds. They really built Coach Smith up."

Well, except this one time . . .

As the season approached, the Athletic Department proudly threw open the doors of the school's brand new Carmichael Auditorium, and thousands of students streamed in, bubbling with anticipation of Bobby Lewis and the new cat replacing Cunningham previewing their skills against the freshman squad. The house was packed, the crowd was eager, the ball was tipped, the tussle began . . . and the unthinkable happened: The freshmen won. Those faces still so unknown they could have been rounded up at Sutton's lunch counter actually beat Lewis the star and Miller the show horse, leaving unsettled fans with whipsawed expectations: Were the freshmen really that good? Was the varsity really that bad?

"We had six recruited players with size, one for each position, and Larry Brown had us so pumped up to play . . ." explains Grubar, almost apologizing for the win. Joe Brown's alibi was, "The varsity didn't have a deep roster. And we had a very tight-knit team, a very unselfish team. We all averaged in double figures that year. But that didn't sit very well with Coach Smith. Larry Brown told us Coach chastised him for coaching to win that game and messing up the overall bond between the players. I'm not sure they liked us that well at first."

Miller concedes that losing to the frosh so publicly was a slap that left him with mixed feelings. "You look at it two ways: You're embarrassed that you lost, but I guess we got some good kids coming in. I didn't get too excited about those kinds of games, though. There wasn't the intensity that you had to win at all costs." Miller may have sloughed off his chagrin, but Grubar notes the next time the varsity scrimmaged against the freshmen—with no one around to witness it—"They just destroyed us."

*

Meanwhile, Larry realized the fun part of "play hard" was also going to be a challenge this year. The coeds were wearing miniskirts and Dylan had gone electric with "Like a Rolling Stone." But Billy was in Philly getting paid by the 76ers, Lewis was doing right by his mom and his girl most weekends, and some of Larry's '68 classmates were sensing they'd better study more than basketball to one day make a living. So, for Larry, bad influences were hard to come by.

Recalls Lewis, "When we were there, Coach Smith knew where Larry and I were twenty-four hours a day, every single day. He knew what classes we were in, he knew every night we had study hall where the alumni would sit and make sure you did your work. He'd watch us like a hawk. 'If you're not doing well in something, we're going to get you a tutor.' "

Well, yes, but although Larry was often seen in Wilson Library, he also studied his own way, as related decades later on the Carolina message board: "Larry was good friends with my suite-mates in Morrison and many times they would study together. I can still see him walking in the suite with four six-packs ready to do some serious studying."

"We did have a good time," admits Tom Gauntlett. "You could drink beer there at eighteen, and we all did. I don't know how much of that Dean knew—he wouldn't have been happy. I think he must have known, because on New Year's Day everybody would be throwing up and dragging, and he'd run us two or three sessions."

Adds Gauntlett's roommate, Lewis, "Larry was a character—he was a little wild, he was free-spirited, he was a fun guy—but he was respectful of older people, and we did not get in a lot of trouble. We both did well in school, and we both knew wherever we went somebody's going to pick up a phone and make a call to Coach Smith. Larry respected Dean Smith very, very much. We got into a few little things, but it was nothing that was publicized."

In other words, Larry was still good at not getting caught . . . such as that night in the parking lot behind The Shack. Still plagued by parietal hours limiting visitation between the sexes in dorms, Larry and his girl of the moment resorted to making out among the cars— "And me, being a gentleman, I sat on the gravel so she wouldn't have to. That was nice of me, wasn't it?" Eventually they realized she was late for curfew and sort of hurried back at her residence right off Franklin Street. "I was boosting her in through a window, when one of the house ladies looked out and called, 'Young lady! Report to my office right away!' And me being there wasn't doing her any good, so I disappeared."

\*

The Larry Miller era of Tar Heel basketball opened out-of-town that December, at Clemson, which was just as well when early concerns were borne out in a solid loss. Larry admitted to first game jitters, conceding he didn't feel aggressive despite contributing 17 points and 12 rebounds.

That changed, however, in the second game of the season. Miller reportedly sparkled in his and the new Carmichael's home debut together, battering William & Mary and delighting 7,000 fans with 22 points and double-digit rebounds in support of Bobby's 34-point onslaught. Finally playing with comparable talent, Larry could happily say for the first time in his life, "I guess I'm not the big gun out there this year."

Two days later, he scored 12 of UNC's last 14 points to sew up a win on the road at Ohio State. That led radio play-by-play man Bill Currie—the "Mouth of the South"—to marvel, "People, this performance by Larry Miller is the most amazing one I have ever seen for such a short amount of time. Tonight he pulled his team from the very brink of defeat."

Recalls Gauntlett, the team's point guard, "We went to all the freshman games so we knew how good Larry was. Basketball-wise, he was really strong for a guy his size with tremendous desire—he would do anything to win. Even when he went out to play 3-on-3 games with us, he'd kill you to win. A tremendous competitor. All through his career he was a lot stronger than the guys he was playing against. Because back in the '60s you didn't see a lot of 6'9" guys that were big the way they are now."

The team's playing style hadn't changed, though, because they again didn't have the size to complement two big scorers, leaving Larry to take over Billy's position fighting for rebounds. Comparing them, Bobby says, "Larry wasn't as dominant as Billy inside—but he could do everything. I scored a lot of points that year with Larry right behind me."

Wrote John Montague, who saw these early season games, "Neither holds the game in the palm of his hand like the dynamic Billy did. Lewis and Miller are players who fit into the "team" pattern. Lewis is the shooter, Miller is the hustler . . . a swashbuckling hustler with cat-like movements on the court" who repeatedly stole the ball and fed Lewis with passes.

When Peggy and Julius Miller came down for a game, they were greeted by "Welcome JJ and Mrs. Miller" on the marquee of the Holiday Inn on Fordham Road. Tommy Lloyd was always part of the gang when the Millers visited, and he helped Larry out by getting his parents to and from the games. Afterward, they'd fill up a tub of ice with beer at the hotel and party into the night.

On December 16, 1965 Bobby Lewis lit up Florida State for 49 points, besting the UNC single-game record of 48 set by Cunningham the previous year. Normally a shooter hitting 72% would be triple-teamed, but Miller kept the Seminoles honest, hitting at 60% for 20 points and 10 rebounds himself. Over the next twenty years that Carmichael served as the home of the Tar Heels, and thirty more years following the team's move to the Smith Center, through the advent of the 3-point shot and the quickened offense of the shot clock, Lewis's single-game scoring record that day has still never been equaled.

Two days later, the team played their last "home" game before the holiday break, beating Florida—but this time, oddly, in Charlotte—with Coach Smith cleverly taking advantage of an anomaly in the NCAA rule book: Schools were allowed to pay the cost of their players' transportation home and back from any game that was off campus. Therefore, Smith always scheduled the Heels' last game before Christmas on the road (although often in-state) so he could fly his charges home at no cost to their parents. And after Christmas he'd fly them back to an off campus site like Greensboro, always working the holiday schedule around that rule. Jim Heavner confirms, "If the rule permitted it, Dean would sit right on the edge. You couldn't give players money, but we would stay at the fanciest hotels—and for cheap rates because they wanted us."

*

Sure enough, after the holidays the coach flew his team back into action in Greensboro, where they throttled Princeton. Then it was home to campus for a multi-game stand that soon had them boasting a sweet 9-3 record and rising optimism. Lewis and Miller were proving to be such a lethal combination that sportswriters along Tobacco Road began calling them "the L&M Boys" after the local Liggett & Myers cigarette giant in Durham.

Lewis acknowledges that he and Larry were very close, and drank a lot of beer together. "But we were competitive to the extent that we respected each other, even though both of us had an ego—which you have to have, because you're challenged every time you step on the court. The other team is trying to stop *you*. But we had an attitude that we had to play together to win, and we were both smart enough to understand that."

And then the Tar Heels ran up against Duke—top dog in the league—toppling them into a slide of frustration. Trading 3 wins for 6 losses over the next several games, Larry struggled to explain a loss at Maryland, calling his own performance "subpar." A few losses later, against VPI (now Virginia Tech), the Heels couldn't overcome the other team's height, leaving Smith to grasp at straws: "Except for the shooting, this is one of our best games."

So now the dissention began. Tom Gauntett recalls, "When we were freshmen, Dean Smith wasn't anybody; he was just another coach who hadn't done anything yet. And in practice he was tough, not always the nicest guy in the world. He could be brutal. I had run-ins with him, and there were days I didn't like him." In fact, Gauntlett was so devoted to Coach Rosemond that he actually thought about transferring to Georgia with him. "But he said, 'No, you stay at Carolina.' He was really loyal to Dean."

Gauntlett testifies that Miller, by contrast, never gave Coach Smith any trouble, even in practice. "Larry was quiet, he just played hard. He was very coachable. Now, Bobby would go off once in a while in practice. Christ, one time Coach was yelling at him, and Bobby got so upset he ran into the locker room and turned all the lockers over! He just lost it. Because he was a tremendous competitor, like Larry."

Miller may have behaved, but he wasn't happy either. "I thought when I signed we had All-Americans here and there, but when you get to a different level . . . Even though we had a good freshman team, some of the guys never panned out. I can't tell you the exact time, you were always hoping, but it wasn't too long before you knew they weren't going to be major players. I think Bobby and I talked about it casually, going somewhere else if something didn't happen. We were so disappointed that year, knowing we needed help when you could tell we didn't have it. But that was just frustration. I wasn't used to losing that much."

Nevertheless, *The Daily Tar Heel* recognized Larry that winter as a showman "whose play has brought more people to their feet than all the tacks that have ever been placed in the teacher's chair." In mid-February there were signs of a turnaround when Miller's 15 second-half points sparked a 23-point comeback against NC State that fell just short. Then the team finally righted itself at the North-South Doubleheader in Charlotte, scoring 2 wins on a weekend that vaulted them from fifth place in the league into a tie for second.

These games served notice that, if Larry didn't quite "hold the game in the palm of his hand" as Cunningham had, Dean Smith had at last found the answer to winning the boards in the thick of battle against foes many inches taller. Gene Warren of the *Greensboro Daily News* wrote, "Although teammate Bob Lewis scored 26 and 33 points during the two days, the other half of the L&M combination became the more widely hailed at Charlotte." In the first game, a revenge win over Clemson, the allegedly undersized Miller controlled the boards with 17 rebounds, leading Smith to say "Miller's rebounding and defense helped us more than anything."

The next night, Larry hit 10 of 12 shots and 7 of 7 free throws in a balanced team win against Frank McGuire's South Carolina squad that also got 17 points from both Tom Gauntlett and center Bob Bennett. Writing that the "the golden sophomore won new fans at Charlotte," the *Daily News* reflected a dawning recognition of Larry's ability to break a game open by imposing his will far beyond his stat line—now anointing Miller as "perhaps the true rock upon which Carolina's ACC tourney hopes must be built."

*

In the 1960s, when Tobacco Road was the center of gravity for the Atlantic Coast Conference, the league tournament was a much bigger deal than the more remote NCAA gathering. The national tournament only had slots for twenty-two conference champions, so in effect not winning the ACC was sudden death for your season. You could dominate the league all year long, have a couple of guys catch the stomach flu on the wrong weekend, lose to the last place team in the league and be out of luck. UNC hadn't won this tournament since 1957, when Lenny Rosenbluth's team went on to upset Wilt Chamberlain and Kansas for the national title—Billy Cunningham never played in the NCAAs—so nearby Duke's three recent wins and two marches to the Final Four still stung.

"I told my parents they could come down to one game a year," Larry remembers, "but not the ACC Tournament. That was too much pressure. I couldn't spend any time with them in a three-day tournament—it's too intense. I couldn't sleep, I was in knots, and three straight days of that . . . I don't think anybody outside of that area understood what that was. Everything else was gravy." Instead it was Tommy Lloyd in Larry's seats at Raleigh's Reynolds Coliseum when the Tar Heels faced off against Maryland that March.

Everyone knew what the Heels brought: Bobby Lewis, whose 27.4 scoring average led the league, making him First Team All-ACC and a Third Team All-American, and Larry Miller, holder of the fourth-best scoring average and the third-best rebounder in the league. Larry's powerful performance was only good enough for the sixth-best vote total from ACC sportswriters, though, and Second Team All-ACC honors.

After the Maryland game, Larry said, "I didn't feel much different before this one than I do for a regular game. There was just one thing that was different. See, I wasn't chosen on the All-ACC team, and they told me before the game it was because I didn't play very well up at Maryland and the Washington writers didn't think I was good enough and didn't vote for me."

Big mistake.

In an echo of the Hershey game against Steelton High—the fools who provoked Larry by chanting "Mil-ler-*Who*? Mil-ler-*Who*?"—Larry set out to prove to the D.C. doubters he could play . . . and their Maryland team paid the price. Instead of doing yet another one-night stand in the tourney, Carolina survived what *Charlotte News* writer Ronald Green dubbed "a bloody, bruising battle" to begin a new era with a 77–70 win. "Miller won it. The 6'3" Big Cat from Catasauqua got in there in No Man's Land under the boards, bumping, clawing, biting, kicking, and elbowing with the bigger Terps and wrestled down 14 rebounds. Carolina is not supposed to be a great rebounding team, but Miller made them one last night. Along with that he scored 25 points with swashbuckling [there's that word again] drives, twisting layups, and delicate tap-ins while being battered about the head and body.

Six-foot-three-inch sophomores are not supposed to play like 6'8" seniors, but Miller did."

After the game, describing his schoolyard play in the Lehigh Valley as "all pushing, shoving, fighting and shooting," Miller told the *New York Times*, "You learn fast how to take care of yourself. It's a matter of survival in the jungle . . . I love it when it's rough. It doesn't bother me. If they foul me I get a chance to score. If they hang on me I still get a chance to score . . . There's no tomorrow . . . Why save yourself?" This made for a different, ferocious Carolina added to the normal 23 points knocked in by Lewis, who flopped down next to his buddy in the locker room saying, "You're the greatest, Larry, but you're big enough to hack it. I'm skinny and I'm bushed."

That win earned UNC a second round game against Duke, a contest of coaches' wills which became known as the infamous "stall-ball" game. Larry explains, "We weren't that good, and Duke had a better shot at going further that year, so we played the 4-Corners. What people don't understand is the 4-Corners was designed to be an offense, not a stalling tactic. Playing the 4-Corners up at Ohio State, when Bobby or I got in the middle we'd have someone bigger on us so we could drive. I think Bobby had 36 and I had like 32 in that game because we were shooting layups or easy jumpers. That's how it was designed. We scored 82 points from that offense."

Unfortunately, Vic Bubas knew better than to come out and chase the Heels (leaving gaps in his defense), resulting in a lot of players standing around in this era before the shot clock as boos rained down from the stands. The Tar Heels actually led the game, 19–12, but eventually succumbed, 21–20. What Larry couldn't know that night is this was the last ACC Tournament game he would ever lose.

\*

The Tar Heels' season record of 16-11 was hardly better than the previous year's 15-9, but this campaign offered flashes of hope by setting new records for the offense. The team's season average of 80.9 points per game was a new school record, and so was their overall 51.7% accuracy rate. Their 127 points against Richmond were an all-time high. Individually, Bobby's 27.4 ppg led the ACC (and remains the second-best all-time at UNC to Lenny Rosenbluth's 28 ppg in 1957)—and he wasn't hogging because Larry was right behind him with 21. In fact, the L&M Boys' combined average of better than 48 ppg is still the highest average by two UNC players in a season to this day.

Still, the boys had fought nobly but lost . . . and they were tired of it. As everyone suspected, a two-man band was not enough in the ACC, and the '69 class's 15-1 freshman record was unreliable, still untested in varsity competition. Larry and Bobby knew the program needed another star, and that spring Coach Smith was hot on the trail of a remarkable talent who checked all the boxes . . . plus one that would make history.

Bobby Lewis had grown up playing against every black public school in Washington, so he'd experienced reverse-culture-shock as a white boy finding no black players on southern courts. He was aware that Coach Smith was trying to integrate the team with players like Willie Cooper. "But in those days, to be accepted, you needed a superstar—somebody people didn't see as 'black.' You needed a Charlie Scott."

*

Charles Scott was already an inspiring story, a Harlem kid who had taken care of himself since he was eleven, talented enough to play summer league games with Lew Alcindor, and also bright enough to test in the top 4% of applicants to New York City's brainy Stuyvesant High School. As a freshman there, he noticed that older playground hotshots were finding a path to college scholarships through the nation's oldest African-American prep school, Laurinburg Institute in North Carolina, founded at the request of Booker T. Washington. So Scott without parental help gained himself admission, and eventually became his class valedictorian.

Here was a slam-dunk recruit whose combination of high-flying skills and the smarts to handle any curriculum in the country made him a natural to become some lucky white college's Jackie Robinson. The early favorite was

Davidson's Lefty Driesell, who gave Scott jobs at his summer camp, made him feel wanted, and offered an early scholarship. But the small village found a way to offend Scott's Laurinburg mentor, who also wanted Charles to consider larger schools where he could have a bigger impact. Among them was UNC, and when Assistant Coach Larry Brown scouted the kid he was dazzled by Scott's speed.

By now Dean Smith had learned an angle on recruiting that other coaches often missed: Instead of throwing a high school kid to his brightest stars, who would soon be graduating, he understood youngsters wanted to meet the guys they would actually be playing and living with. Bob Lewis was all-in on Scott—"He was black, he was from New York, he could win games, *and* he was a great person"—but Lewis would be gone before the recruit reached the varsity. So when Scott made his official visit on UNC's annual Spring Jubilee weekend in late April with concerts by the Temptations and Smokey Robinson and the Miracles, "Coach Smith had me go around with Dickie and Larry because they were guys who would be there. And Larry was from Pennsylvania, not from the south, so that was an even more at ease circumstance for me."

Miller remembers that first dinner at the Ranch House with Grubar, Joe Brown, Scott and his adviser. "I swear, during the whole dinner Charlie never said a word. He just nodded his head. He seemed to be kind of a quiet guy. We didn't really think he could talk. But then, when you get him alone, you can't shut him up."

Scott now laughs at that recollection, explaining "When Larry met me I didn't have my two front teeth. I lost them when I was eleven years old. That's why I was so quiet; I was embarrassed about my personal looks. That was part of my insecurity. But then Coach Smith took me to the Dental School and that made a big difference in my personality."

Miller confirms this was one of the nice benefits at UNC, where volunteer patients were part of the teaching process. "Our manager was a dentist and so was Jim Hudock [the former captain], so we had a great connection there. I had all kinds of problems, because I'd shot up from 5'9" to six-foot something, and when that happens the calcium goes to your bones instead of your teeth—so you get more prone to cavities. So they sent me over there to get work done, too."

Scott had seen a freshman game, and sizing up 6'11" Rusty Clark, 6'8" Bill Bunting, and the 6'5" Grubar he recognized this could be a great team. But how would they all get along together?

Grubar recounts, "I'd never seen Charlie play, but Coach Lotz said, 'This kid can fit in really well with us,' so we took him to a fraternity house. Can you imagine, a black kid and I took him into the KA house, which I think was the most southern house on campus? I called ahead and said, 'Now I know you guys love basketball. If you want us to keep winning, you'd better be really good to *this* guy.' And they were. But it was hard as hell on Charlie. I can't imagine going to a school where there are sixty black students and everyone else is white."

Scott concedes that, after three years in Laurinburg, he was wary of potential southern teammates like Clark who was from Fayetteville and from money. "Not that he did anything to make me feel that way, but from the outside those were the type of people I was more worried about, who'd never played with or against a black person in their lives. But the fact that the two stars—Larry and Bobby—were from up north probably meant a lot to me subliminally, because they were used to being around blacks. I knew Bobby used to play around Dave Bing all the time. So for them this was not a new thing. And Dick made me feel comfortable, too. But the key had to be Larry—because if the star didn't want me, I wasn't coming."

Miller, ever the pragmatic battalion commander, pulled Scott aside on that visit and pitched him, "If you come here we've got a shot at the national title. We're going to win a lot of games. And you're not going to have to worry about anything. You're with us. There's not going to be any problems."

That sold it for Scott: "There was no apprehension in him, and that was a comfort to me. By the time I got to the varsity it would be his senior year, and this point I did understand: That the spotlight would be challeng-ing—just from me being the first black varsity athlete at UNC—that was going to take a lot of attention away from him. But Larry was very open to it, which made me feel comfortable about coming.

"I didn't have a family. I was just an eighteen-year-old who was looking for people who liked me. And Dickie and Larry showed that they liked me. That's as simple as it could be."

*

Once Scott was in the fold, Larry's outlook lifted. But Charles wouldn't reach the varsity until the year after next, and meanwhile the Class of '69's impact would remain unknown until they faced enemy fire in the fall. With recent letdowns in mind, Larry's eyeball assessment was unsparing: "If you looked at them on paper, none of them was a monster physically. Dickie was a big guard, but not a big leaper . . . and Rusty was tall but not fast . . . and Bill Bunting was tall, but real thin . . . so nothing jumped out. Whereas Charlie Scott was 6'6" and a guard, and he could jump. You could see what he could do, so you know he's going to play. But the others . . . we were hopeful, but it wasn't apparent."

*

That summer, Larry again remained in Chapel Hill for a couple of weeks to work at Coach Smith's basketball camp. There he impressed his charges, including Ron Green Jr. whose dad worked at the Charlotte newspaper. "One day they were taking us on a tour of the campus, and I remember Larry leading us by Carmichael in the sunshine and teaching us songs about Carolina. That was pretty cool."

Miller also worked a second job doing hard labor at Triangle Brick which, at $50 per week, was like being paid to work out—but the job was brutal. "You started work at 5:30 in the morning—that's the cool part of the day—and I got the tough jobs, lifting bricks and loading them into the kiln, while the owner's young son swept up. Did that until 2:30 in the afternoon, when I'd go to work at the basketball camp, and after that I'd go out drinking beer until 1:00 in the morning. Slept a couple of hours, and then I'd be back at the kilns at 5:30 again. That's when my father told me not to burn the candle at both ends—'You'll burn yourself out'—but I did. I worked really hard, and then I played. I was burning that candle at four ends all the time. But I only did that for a couple of weeks. More than that and I would have been dead."

\*

Back home in Catasauqua after basketball camp, Larry returned to his open-ended job at Buff's service station, swapping his labor and stories of Chapel Hill for good pay. He always found time for conditioning, though, running five miles a day through the last six weeks of summer, and playing pickup games and scrimmaging at the old playgrounds and deserted school gyms. Sometimes at Allentown's Community Center he would run into Scott Beeten, a year younger and about to start Penn, who was destined to become a coach and a lifelong friend. There in the steamy gym the two would go at each other, first man to 100 points. And this year, anticipating rebounding help from the Class of '69, Larry worked on his long-distance marksmanship.

One day the phone rang on Wood Street, and it was Bob Nemeth who had heard Larry was home. Nemeth was about to begin coaching at Northampton High, had noticed Carolina players all wore wristbands, and wondered what was the story on that? Larry told him that Coach Smith had seen tennis players wearing sweatbands on their wrists and ordered them for his team to improve ball control in sweaty hands. So Nemeth promptly ordered them for his own team to wear in practices and games, basically as a way to mold his team together. Even before Coach Smith was a proven winner, attentive coaches were following his lead.

Later in his twentieth summer Larry heard about a big, 30-keg party just over the state line in Mountain Lake, NJ. By this time in August he had long hair, sunglasses, and no fear of the Pagans motorcycle gang he found gathering there. The Pagans were (and are) one of the Big 4 outlaw motorcycle clubs, along with the Hell's Angels, Outlaws, and Bandidos, and on this afternoon one of them turned out to be a buddy of Larry's.

"He loaned me his bike to ride, and even gave me his colors [the club's identifying patches], which is a really forbidden thing. So then I'm cruising along the highway looking like Easy Rider and I come across a car accident. I park the bike and, lo and behold, it's one of my friends from Catty, and I ask 'What's going on here?' I can see he doesn't recognize me, he's been drinking and this is probably his fault—so I just take charge: 'Let me tell you both, this is what we do. We're going to clear this highway, got it?' And they all nod, 'Yessir!' right away. 'So write your names down real fast, because we don't want any cops involved, right?' 'Yessir,' again, 'Yessir.' I mean, it's amazing how quick they obeyed me—because I had those Pagan colors on. So they swap information and the other guy takes off, and then I tell my friend who I am. And that's how I got him out of trouble. There's a lesson for you: When you're in a situation you can control—take charge."

# CHAPTER 6

# MEET THE BEATLES

Crowning a hardworking summer, Larry rolled into Chapel Hill for a new year with a new haircut and a new car—this one a beautiful, green '67 Buick GS400 convertible, essentially a sport model of Tommy Lloyd's car pumped up on steroids. He'd customized the trunk with a traveling record collection, so wherever he landed that crisp autumn season the good times could roll— which earned him a reputation as "Instant Party." Listening to whatever soul or psychedelic vibe was in the air, dancing the frug, the jerk, the bugaloo and shingaling (contortions containing various elements of Larry's typical 3-point play), he made the rounds of dorm and frat parties with his football and basketball buddies . . . All but one.

Charles Scott was already settled in Avery when Larry arrived and did his best to make the freshman feel welcome. And Scott did appreciate that: "Larry was the star of the campus when I was there. He could do no wrong— everybody loved Larry—so I just tried to stay in his shadow." But all first-year players were still scheduled out of rhythm with the varsity, and being one of only sixty black students on the big campus inevitably left Charles to find his own lonely path. Because, even as Larry and the team felt he was always invited along, Scott often knew better than to go.

"Larry and Dickie hung out with the KA's, who were probably the most bigoted frat on campus—but also the most partying one, that's why they went there. But I understood that, no matter how much *they* accepted me, wherever I went there'd be no other blacks but me—and I would be a discomfort to everybody else. Larry understood that some circumstances wouldn't be as conducive for me. What was normal for them would be abnormal if people were seeing me do that."

Recalling Scott's first months on campus, Joe Brown says, "I was from a small town in western North Carolina, and with high schools being segregated then I had not had much interaction with African Americans. So it was kind of a big deal when Charlie came, but it didn't seem like such a big deal to us. I don't think we ever said anything to Charlie about this, but there was one restaurant in Chapel Hill that we used to go to a lot, and the owner told us, 'Don't bring him here.' So we just never went back. I don't think Charlie had ever been there before anyway, but we just didn't go there anymore. As a human being it doesn't sit right with you. But I don't think any of us could really apprehend what he was going through; it's hard to put yourself in that situation."

Eventually, Scott found a more welcoming social life on weekends down the road at Durham's historically black NC Central University. But daily life was a different matter. "To be honest with you, Larry Brown was more important to me than Coach Smith. When I got out of class—when most kids went to the arboretum—I went straight to the back of the basketball office and talked to Larry Brown. That's the absolute truth; he was the only person I could talk to. If it wasn't for Larry Brown I wouldn't have made it through my first year at Carolina."

*

Meanwhile, "Mills" as his teammates came to call him, spent much of that fall getting to know the sophomores who were just moving up to the varsity. "Everybody liked Larry," says Gauntlett. "Great guy, but Larry could be kind of a loner." One of those sophomores, Joe Brown, agrees. "He was somewhat of a private person; you didn't always know what he was doing all the time." But Brown got a glimpse behind the curtain one night as he and Miller headed home from a road trip to the Women's College in Greensboro. "Larry was driving my car and I fell asleep. When I woke up, we were in the middle of nowhere, going around these curves in the dark, and all of a sudden we come up on this honky-tonk. The parking lot is full and you can hear loud music, it's probably 2:00 in the morning, and the tables are full when we walk in—and the music stops. Everybody stops . . . and stares at us. And I'm thinking, 'Omigosh, what's this going to be?' And all of a sudden about twenty people throw their arms up and yell, 'LARRY!!' Because he was a regular! We sat down, ate and had a good time, and everybody knew him. And I couldn't get back to that place if I had to."

*

Larry was now widely recognized as a Big Man on Campus—but, unfortunately, not recognized by everyone. One night in early October, he was standing in line at a Chapel Hill restaurant when a guy cut right in front of him. Larry tapped the fellow on the shoulder to discuss this, but was rebuked, "Get your hands off me or I'll smack you!" (We know where this is going, right?) Larry retorted, "You say that one more time and I'll smack *you*" . . . and it went from there. In Larry's retelling, "He did . . . and I did . . . and I knocked a couple of his teeth out. It hurt my hand worse than him. I put my hand in my pocket, but I had to go to the ER—and it was right before the season started. The next day I went to our first practice, and my hand was swollen up bigger than my head. So Dean kicked me out of practice for doing something stupid. Which I did."

An exchange of correspondence with the victim over the following six weeks led to a new crown for the victim's fractured upper central incisor at a cost of $200 from Larry's wallet. By then, the basketball season was under-way, leading the punchee to close his invoice letter, "Congratulations on the season so far. You looked great against Penn State." At least he knew who Larry was now.

*

As the season approached, this year's Carolina media guide dared to be far more optimistic than in previous years, proclaiming this team was "packed with height and hustle" and that Lewis and Miller were "perhaps the best one-two punch in college basketball." Not only was Bobby a certified scoring machine, but by now the promise that Miller was recruited for had been assayed as 24-carat gold. Some in the press even thought that, although Lewis was the team's top scorer, it was now Miller who was the more valuable player for the scrappy attitude he brought to the court. Harry Lloyd of the *Charlotte Observer* wrote, "Miller looks like a carryover from basketball's Pleistocene period . . . having the muscles to overpower a smaller man and the speed to leave a larger one behind . . . and his defense is the kind a bayonetted para-troop patrol would play." Coach Smith noted, "Larry plays the kind of game that isn't represented in the box scores. It takes a real student of basketball to appreciate everything he means to our team."

The big change, of course, was the quality of the sophomore reinforce-ments, chiefly the big men, 6'8" Bill Bunting and especially 6'11" Rusty Clark who had averaged over 20 ppg as a freshman. Smith relished these lineup additions, hoping that, for the first time, he would have the team balance he had always wanted. "We'll be a completely different kind of a club this year," he promised. "Now we can play without gimmicks and we won't have to hold the ball on anybody." The new rebounders meant Miller's role would change to make him even more dangerous, no longer having to fight through thickets of taller men to get his shot. "With more height this year, I'll probably play less inside and be running a lot more. I'm working on my jumper from the top of the key." But the newcomers would also create a ripple effect of position changes that, not for the last time, the coach would have to manage carefully to avoid putting team chemistry at risk.

To make room for the big men up front, Smith took the bold step of moving his hottest scorer to the backcourt, where slender Bobby Lewis became more of a playmaking guard. "And it was the right thing for me, too," Lewis concedes, "because when you go to the pros, and you're 6'3", you'll have to play guard. So Larry became more the star of the team then—which he deserved to be, because I would be leaving and he'd be coming back for another year. It was fine for me to drop back, because he had a fantastic year and the new guys were scoring, too."

Also forced to adjust was Bobby's roommate, the off guard, Tom Gauntlett: "We'd seen the freshmen play, so we knew the guys coming up were good—Grubar and Rusty especially. Bunting came along a little later, but he had the size and could run. It was just a matter of getting everyone to accept their roles." Smith and Miller had seen enough of Grubar to know he was an excellent point guard who could distribute the ball, and nobody stole the ball from him. He could also hit the outside shot. So when the musical chairs of preseason practices stopped, it was Gauntlett who was the odd man out.

"Coach Smith called me in right before the season and said, 'I'm going to move you to sixth man and you have to accept it, because we're better off not having all 6'4" guys running around.' And I said 'I'm fine with that.'" Nowadays, Gauntlett admits this was a tough pill to swallow for a senior co-captain who'd been a two-year starter . . . one whose scoring the previous year remains linked to this day with Bobby and Larry for the highest season combination of three players in UNC history. "Larry probably cost me my starting role, because I played the same position and when the new class moved up I got bumped. But that was legitimate—Lewis and Miller were All-Americans—they were better than me. And I got to play a lot and it was still fun."

Also not starting at this point was Joe Brown, the 6'5" sophomore guard who says all the Class of '69 players liked and enjoyed each other, and he never minded drawing perhaps the team's most thankless assignment: "I had to guard Larry—well, I *tried* to guard Larry—practically every day in practice for two years. And that made me a better player. He never stopped moving."

In Dick Grubar's mind, "We were the beginning of the Carolina Way. That's when Dean was able to institute what he wanted to do—not only on the court but off the court—and we accepted it and went with it. We knew we were there to be real college students. Rusty was excused from practices when he was going to Chemistry labs. How many coaches back then let a player do that? So we knew there was more to it than just being a player."

Coach Smith was known to say, "The ACC isn't a sophomore league," to preface his admiration for Larry earning a starter's role the previous year. Now—with Grubar, Clark, and Bunting—the coach was starting three of them. No one knew how these rookies would perform under the glare of the ACC's biggest stages—least of all Larry and Bobby—but the answer came quickly.

*

Starting off against Clemson as usual, Larry laid back in the first half while the sophomores found their rhythm, and then blitzed the Tigers for 18 second half points in a solid 11-point win. Then the new roster turned lethal, scorching Penn State by more than 30 points and Tulane by a margin of 23. These were not great basketball powers, though, so the question remained: How good were the Tar Heels really?

All was revealed when they traveled to Lexington to play mighty Kentucky and their famous Coach Rupp. Kentucky was basketball royalty, had won its first twenty-three games in a row the previous year, and beaten Duke in the Final Four before being upset by Texas El Paso in the championship game. That 27-2 team had been led by Pat Riley—and he was back for more.

Heavily favored in their own Memorial Coliseum over the inexperienced Tar Heels, Kentucky was bushwhacked for a 64–55 loss, called by the *Charlotte Observer* "the thud heard around the basketball world." Larry's game-high 24 points and 10 rebounds were no shock to anyone, and Bob Lewis's 10 points on few attempts were modest. But Clark's 11 rebounds to go with 10 points and another 9 boards from Bunting controlled the game—and the front line's ability to frustrate Riley into just 2 made field goals in 16 attempts before fouling him out was fatal to Kentucky's chances. Overall, the new UNC shot over 60% to Kentucky's 38%, out-rebounded the Wildcats 41 to 24, and shot almost twice as many free throws—making it clear that, on this night at least, they were the big boys in town. Said Rupp afterwards, "We expected trouble from Dick Grubar and Bob Lewis, but I didn't think Miller would beat us"—which doesn't say much for his scouting reports.

*Miller blows by Pat Riley in the upset at Kentucky*
*as Bobby Lewis looks on.*

The win was a tonic for the sophomores like Grubar. "That gave us younger guys the confidence that we were good enough to win anywhere. Bobby sacrificed his game a little, but he could be an awesome scorer, and Larry did it all, so even though we were highly recruited, Rusty, Bill, and I could sort of take a back seat our sophomore year because they didn't need us to be stars. We knew if we all played the game the way we were supposed to, we could be pretty good. And that was comfortable." The team was so elated that they repaired to their hotel for what would become one of the most infamous parties in Tar Heel lore.

To this day Grubar says, "I think that party brought us together even more. At the time you got post-game meal money, and we all put our money in together and stayed at the hotel because Larry had an amazing way of always having girls around. He'd gotten them invited over—girls from Kentucky!" Asked how Miller produced instant coeds in enemy territory, Grubar just laughs. "Who knows how he did it! I'll never understand all the things he was the ringleader for over the years. I never knew how he pulled it off. All of a sudden people would be showing up, and you'd be thinking, 'Whoa, this is going to be pretty good!' "

Joe Brown confirms there was a lot of drinking and girls. "It was not a quiet party. It was a huge party. Eventually Larry Brown came down the hall to one of our older players and said, 'You've got to do something, it's out of control in there.' Of course Coach Smith stayed in his room—but we practiced pretty hard the next day."

Miller, himself, remains pleased he planned ahead for that night to remember. "Not only did I get the girls, but my teammates all drank different brands and I had the beers and everything all set up ahead of time. I don't remember how I got the girls—I must have had a connection down there—but we had such a good time that they actually came up to see us later in Chapel Hill." The larger question is, how did Larry know the Heels would upset the national runner-up and make the whole setup worthwhile? "I guess I had to know we were going to win . . . but I don't know how I knew that."

By the end of the night, not only had the team proven their mettle on the basketball court, but with the spoils of victory sitting in their laps, the play-hard Tar Heels had also won the after-party.

*

But they lost the morning-after. Next day, Coach Smith sat the team down at Carmichael for some straight talk that Larry still remembers: "He said, 'About what happened in Lexington . . . You all know who you are, and if that happens again—and I don't care who you are or what kind of scholarship you're on—you're gone! Understand?' So that's when I changed my party strategy."

Partying hard was always a challenge in the confines of Chapel Hill because Coach Smith had eyes and ears everywhere, as Joe Brown can attest: "Coach knew what was going on with us, no matter what. There was nothing that happened that he didn't hear about. I remember one night I went out to get something to eat, and I'm driving down Franklin Street and didn't realize I didn't have my lights on—and I got a ticket. Well, Coach Smith knew about it by 9:00 AM the next morning, and asked what I was doing out at that hour."

Grubar, however, confides the team did have one refuge from the long reach of the coach—former captain Jim Hudock's cabin out in the country with a hidden key. "We were very good at not being where a lot of people were after games, because if we did whatever we wanted to do it would be a problem. And he gave us a place where a handful of players could go and have a good time, and not have to worry about somebody reporting back to Coach."

*

The Kentucky win pushed North Carolina to #3 in the country, and with their confidence sky-high now, the Tar Heels crushed December with 9 straight wins by an average margin of 23 points. They clobbered New York University in Greensboro so badly that Smith pulled his starters with 10 minutes left in the game and an 80–44 lead. By that point Miller already had 27 points and 18 rebounds—he only needed 6 more points to break his career high, but any more would have been just cruel. Smith gave much of the credit to Clark and Bunting's work around the basket so that "Larry is able to play with more abandon." Miller exulted, "The opposition can't stay with me when they have players like Rusty and Bill to look out for."

And now sportswriters like Gene Warren of the *Charlotte Observer* were not holding back: "While Bob Lewis is a swan on the basketball court with his dexterity and polish, Miller is a player of power . . . On the fast break, he's thunder and lightning, a spinning turbine of determination . . . The tiger of the Tar Heels is snarling as Carolina makes its big move under Coach Smith."

The team's reputation preceded them when they arrived at the Tampa Invitational tournament, along with Columbia, Florida State, and The Citadel, featuring a 5'11" point guard named Pat Conroy. Thirty-five years later, the visceral impression the Tar Heel stars made on the writer of *The Prince of Tides, The Great Santini, Beach Music,* and other Southern classics was still full upon him at the writing of his memoir, *My Losing Season*:

*"Before going into the locker room to suit up we watched the Tar Heels warm up. I studied two players and two players only. I had seen the ethereal and vastly gifted Bobby Lewis play for St. John's in Washington, D.C. He had extraordinary leaping ability and moved on the court with all the presence of a young king. Then my eyes moved to number 44, Larry Miller, who fired jump shots from the corner, a darker, more brooding presence than the sunnier Lewis. They were the stars of the tournament; the true stars of basketball have all eyes in the building studying their every move because of the sheer magnetism of their great gifts. I turned to the invitational rosters and found the names of Bob Lewis and Larry Miller, then with my finger I went down the page and saw my own name printed along with the other Citadel Bulldogs. In one night I had tied my destiny to the lives of two legitimate All-Americans and it thrilled me to see my name listed on the same page as theirs . . . "*

*Miller and Lewis, together on the same basketball court, blended like balsamic vinegar and the richest olive oil. Miller's darkness matched Lewis's lightness and speed on the court and their congruent talents made everyone around them better basketball players. Bill Bunting and Dick Grubar and Rusty Clark had to raise their own games to a higher level and that was part of Lewis's and Miller's genius—they wove their brilliance through the moves and passes of their teammates, wonderful basketball players all, but mortals like me.*

*So hello, Bobby Lewis, and hello, Larry Miller. I salute you from the secret place to which lost nights go. I tell you how splendid the two of you were that night and the next night and all through that long season. I have never forgotten the dark fire of Larry Miller or the breathtaking swiftness of Bobby Lewis and I did not deserve to be in the same building with them."*

Happily, Conroy's words are better remembered than the victories as, many years later, Lewis—already a fan of the author—read *My Losing Season* and returned the compliment as only one fan can to another: "I read it to my mom."

What the famous writer and Bobby's mother never knew was that Conroy's kind thoughts might have been Larry's epitaph if his hijinks later that night had kept him forever young, along with James Dean. As Larry tells it, "We found out there was a girls' school up on the thirteenth floor of our hotel, so naturally we all made our way up there. We were partying with the girls and—I don't know how we got out there—but me and one of the guys were sitting on the window sill with our legs dangling outside, and a glass bottle fell down on the hotel awning and the street. I don't know why we were being so stupid. That could have hurt somebody, and the next morning we walk out and we're crunching over this glass on the ground. But sitting in that window, if one of us falls . . . we're going to grab the other guy, right? I still wake up from bad dreams about that one. It's like walking up to Death's door and asking, 'Hey, you want to pick me up?' "

*

From Tampa, Coach Smith's scheduling magic flew his charges home for the holidays, then bounced them back to Greensboro a week later for a 101–56 slaughter of Furman. Then it was down to Charlotte for a solid 23-point win over Ohio State, before returning to home sweet home, Carmichael Auditorium . . . where they stubbed their toes against Princeton. Beginning the new year with a 10-point loss startled everyone (although Clark's absence with a virus and Bobby's 4 fouls in the first half were atypical), and two days later third-ranked North Carolina found themselves on the verge of losing a seesaw dogfight to Wake Forest in Winston-Salem, suddenly in danger of entering the meat of the ACC schedule with back-to-back losses.

The Heels were down by 2 with 35 seconds left, before Rusty Clark tied it with 17 seconds to go. But that left Wake Forest in possession of the ball, the final seconds ticking down, waiting to take the winning shot. Suddenly, Grubar deflected the other guard's dribble off his leg, Miller knocked the carom ahead of him and, with 7 seconds left, gave chase down the sideline with the hounds of hell in hot pursuit. He never seemed quite able to get control of the ball, and by the time he caught up, two Deacons were defending the basket. Somehow twisting through them, he spun up a desperate, underhanded layup with "English" guiding it off the backboard, and as the final second ticked off and the ball fell through the net, Larry kept running full speed ahead off the court in a whirlwind finish. "Whatever got in my way was going to get knocked over," he remembers. "Jack Williams, our PR director, tried to shake my hand and I just flattened him, ran to the locker room and it was locked, and I busted the door down. I had so much energy if a little kid had been there I would have run him over—because I was *gone.*"

People who were there testify that half the crowd leapt to their feet, cheering what has since become known in the Miller canon as simply "The Shot." Ronald Green, sports editor of the *Charlotte News,* called to mind the cellist Pablo Casals's exhortation to a student, " 'Do not play the notes, make music.' Most basketball players play the notes . . . Larry Miller, though he is built more ideally for heavyweight fighting, makes music. In his own way, he is an artist but his artistry is swift and violent, like bullfighting."

Later that week Jack Williams put his own experience somewhat less elegantly: "It was like Bronco Nagurski bumping into Don Knotts, and I've still got the bruise to prove it."

Four days later, in Durham, Miller stuck it to Duke with the same dagger. Duke star Bob Verga's shot had just tied the score with 16 seconds left when Larry drove the length of the floor, passed off to Clark, then caught Clark's return pass to spin up the same underhanded layup for the same knockout punch that had just slain Wake Forest. Said a relieved Dean Smith moments later, "I stood wanting to call time-out. Then I saw Larry breaking and quickly hid my hands . . . That layup of his is very difficult to block—especially with Larry's strength."

Later, Miller harkened back to Catty explaining why he always wanted the ball at the end of games: "We lost my state high school final when I brought the ball down the floor and passed off to one of my teammates for a layup and it went through his hands. It was kind of a lesson I learned—and it stuck with me."

The memorable, floor-length winning drives in consecutive games spurred Gene Warren to write, "Miller took the Tar Heels by the seat of their pants and propelled them through the door to victory." Those two signature performances four days apart were enough for the *News & Observer's* AJ Carr to call Larry "Batman in shorts and sneakers . . . When it comes down to the point of life or death, win or lose, there's no better man to have around than Miller. He wins."

*

Even as the Heels got used to winning on the court, they were caught off guard to find themselves winning big-time in a brand new arena—television. Back in 1957 an entrepreneur named Castleman D. Chesley had cobbled together five North Carolina TV stations to broadcast the Tar Heels' Final Four victories from Kansas City. That had evolved into the ACC Basketball Network—the first conference basketball TV network in the country—broadcasting a single game every Saturday afternoon at 2:00, produced out of an old converted Trailways bus.

Recalls Jim Heavner, "That game began to get big ratings because TV options were so limited then—you might get a 50-share. It was absolutely appointment viewing; you would work your whole day around it. And I believe putting the games on TV not only made the games iconic, but also made the arenas themselves more iconic. It makes people want to come see in person what they've seen on TV."

The more the Heels kept winning that winter, the more they appeared on Saturdays, and with TV exposure came a whole new cohort of fans from rec room couches all across the state—teenage girls. It was they who recognized before anyone else that the startling Miller and the dreamy Dick Grubar were the Lennon & McCartney of the Tar Heels, and the handsome, fun-loving, chart-topping team was becoming The Beatles of North Carolina. While Pat Conroy was admiring the grace and power of Lewis and Miller, the girls watching TV close-ups of Larry on the foul line cared less about the score than what color his eyes were (blue).

"When Dick first came on the scene and we started winning, that's when all the girls started hanging out," remembers Larry, passing the praise to the open man. "Once we got successful, the number of people waiting around for autographs was amazing." As the season went on, boys began showing up in elementary school wearing sweatbands on their wrists, puzzling their teachers. (To this day, former Raleigh *News & Observer* columnist Barry Saunders recalls a teacher snapping at him to "Get those wristbands off! You ain't no Larry Miller!") When middle school girls started trading their first kisses to young swains for cheap jewelry, they asked for necklaces with St. Christopher medals. And then the letters started coming.

"There were so many, you'd try to look at them all but it was kind of overwhelming," recalls Grubar, apparently still in disbelief. "You think you're just a ballplayer, and all of a sudden you're a so-called 'matinee idol'—Larry and I, both—as many as one got, the other would get. I have no idea why people chose us, but they did. And not both of us—they chose one or the other—whoever they liked better. It was pretty amazing stuff you'd get, from underwear to bras . . . everything. Most of them didn't expect a reply, but if they asked you to sign something and enclosed a stamped envelope, I had no problem with that . . . but I didn't have any money in college for stamps."

\*

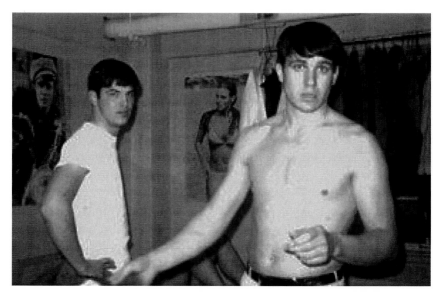

*Matinee idols Grubar and Miller, hanging out with roommates*
*Marlon Brando and Ursula Andress.*

Following the Wake and Duke games, North Carolina played their third game in a row against an in-state rival. NC State, at the eastern end of Tobacco Road in Raleigh, who shared the same media market as their more celebrated neighbors, had gotten a bellyful of the media gush over the Tar Heels, and were sick of it. Still winless in the ACC, on their way to a miserable 2-12 year, the scrappy Wolfpack came into the happy new Carmichael with a chip on their shoulders and ready to fight—literally.

There are many versions of this confusing brawl-game, but everyone agrees with Larry's recollection that "tensions were really high that game—it was particularly nasty." As recalled by Carolina message board member "fishnheel": "Moo U tried to rough up Lewis during the last minutes. Two State players, one in front of Lewis, the other in back, while Bob was the middle man in the 4 Corners, kept elbowing and punching Lewis. That led to a bench-clearing brawl." Remembering his part, Larry says, "I was on the bench—that was the only game I fouled out of in my whole time there—so I wrapped a towel around my injured fist and came off the bench looking for Dick Braucher, who I knew from Kutztown, to make sure he didn't start anything. And suddenly there's a tap on my shoulder and he was behind me saying, 'Let's not get involved, Larry.' Well, okay, my hand was still injured from hitting that guy before the season—it cut my tendon to my forefinger on my left hand—so it was still a little tender."

Adds Tom Gauntlett, reporting how the 79–78 victory was won in the waning seconds: "Lewis was on the foul line, shooting a free throw with 5 seconds left, when this guy Trifunovich spits on him. He *spits* on him! And Bobby just takes a breath and makes the second shot, and he waits as the clock runs out so it's final—and *then* Lewis punches him. We're all running off the court, and somebody says, 'Hey, Lewis is still out there!' So we all run back and now everybody's swinging. Everybody got into it, the football players came down on the floor, it was a brawl. We hated them as much as Duke, the rivalries were incredible."

Another eyewitness remembers a footballer fondly nicknamed "Marion the Barbarian" jumping into the State huddle and punching a 6'8", 230-pound center who was one of the two goons harassing Lewis. "It is the biggest fight I have ever seen in a game—and it happened twice."

In the end, though, order was restored: State was still winless, North Carolina had defeated each of its Big 4 rivals, and Tobacco Road had a new boss on the block.

*

That winter, Larry got a ride home from fellow Pennsylvanian Gauntlett, with a scrappy freshman guard from Newark tagging along. Jim Delany would one day become the hugely influential Commissioner of the Big Ten Conference, but in those days he was just another 5'11" kid to scrimmage against. "Larry was an outgoing, fun guy with a big smile on his face," Delany recalls, ". . . as much of a celebrity as you could have at that time in college. Whatever Joe Namath had in Q-rating, Larry had the same thing in Chapel Hill."

*Miller puts a NC State player in his place.*

What impressed Delany most, though, is how the hotshot treated the little guy—him—when Gauntlett dropped them off at the Miller house on Wood Street. "It was in a snowstorm, and I had to stay overnight. The thing I remember is Larry wouldn't let me sleep on the couch in the living room. I was just a freshman, only at Carolina a few months, but Larry put me up in his room and *he* slept on the couch. And when his father got up in the middle of the night to go to work at Mack Truck at, what—3:00 or 4:00 in the morning?—I remember his father yelled 'Larry!!' And Larry was out there in the dark, helping with the snow to get his father's car out. Then the next day Larry gave me a ride to New Jersey. But I'll always remember the impulse that he had, to look after me."

Larry's exploits were still followed so avidly in the area that the previous year 600 people had traveled to New York City to watch him play against NYU at Madison Square Garden. That led Assistant Coach Lotz to marvel, "I can't believe that one boy could hold so much interest in his home town." Now someone had finally decided that, if the townsfolk couldn't get to every game, it was time to bring the games to the town. So they collected $4,000 worth of advertising to coax an Allentown radio station to broadcast the Tar Heels into the Lehigh Valley. "That was the winter they started piping in games from one of the Carolina radio stations," recalls Don Canzano. "I was a senior at Kutztown, and I was laid up with a strep throat when that first game came on, and I had a bucket on the side of me with disinfectant. It was a horrible thing. But at least I got to hear Larry on the radio. And that was the start of the Carolina fan base way up here."

After exams, as the surging Tar Heels cut a swath through the ACC, their gaudy 16-1 record drew the attention of America's foremost arbiter of athletic fame, *Sports Illustrated.* The magazine assigned its ace, Frank Deford, to herald the program's return to national prominence, focusing on the "Tobacco Rogues," Lewis and Miller, who were slated for the magazine's cover wearing blazers and ties in front of the Old Well. Leading off with a rib that UNC was now quashing "L&M" references after complaints from rival tobacco companies (i.e. donors) who felt this was an unfair plug for Liggett

& Myers, Deford characterized Lewis as the soft pack of the team and Miller as the hard, flip-top box. Then he went on to profile Coach Smith and the world of Chapel Hill.

*The L&M Boys show presidential candidate Senator Hubert Humphrey around the Chapel Hill campus—and this time Miller is the fan scoring an autographed photo.*

But gradually one senses Deford hedging on the coronation, remarking that Lewis's new role on the team has made him "so smitten with playmaking and the general joys of selflessness that by last week he was just about killing the team with kindness . . . taking only nine shots." And Miller is quoted conceding, "Too often I relax and get carried by the tempo of the game rather than dominating." Deford is fair in analyzing the team's weaknesses—poor free throw shooting and a passive approach against zone defenses—but in faint-praising Carolina for staggering to conference victories, even while prodding the L&M boys to belay the team play and use their vast skills to the utmost, the article gives evidence of a revision . . . and the reason is apparent: During its preparation, Carolina did what cover boys must never, ever do—they lost.

*The Old Well, a campus landmark, is the background for blue-blazered Lewis (left) and Miller.*

The Sports Illustrated cover that wasn't to be.

In falling by 2 points at Georgia Tech, the Tar Heels had also fallen victim to the most notorious urban legend in all of sport—the *Sports Illustrated*
cover jinx—losing their grip on the top rung of the glory ladder when track
star Bob Seagren pole vaulted over them onto the cover with a story titled
"He Sizzles at the End of a Swizzle Stick."

✶

Now came the grinding work of fighting to the finish line. They ricocheted between convincing wins over NC State and South Carolina . . . an upset by Clemson . . . a 1-point win at Maryland . . . a 32-point beat-down of Virginia Tech . . . followed by their worst loss of the season at South Carolina. Coach Smith was becoming concerned, and one player admits, "We were thinking, 'Uh-oh, what's going on?' "

Those concerns were temporarily swept aside when Carolina thumped Duke in the final game of the season for a sparkling 21-4 record that gave the young Dean Smith his milestone first ACC championship. That triumph would be fleeting, though, if the team that seemed so powerful early in the year didn't address its unsteady mojo and bear down for the big prize—the ACC Tournament crown and national recognition beyond.

"The ACC Tournament was crazy," recalls Dick Grubar of his first appearance there. "In the press in North Carolina—whether Charlotte or Greensboro or Raleigh—the ACC was splashed across everywhere. There was so much interest you could sell a $15 ticket for $500—that was a lot back then." And the top-seeded Heels were all too aware that if their late season swoon continued they were ripe for an upset.

It almost happened. Opening against bottom-seeded NC State, the Heels were lucky this was the league's first tournament held in neutral Greensboro, rather than on State's home court in Raleigh. In a hard-fought, low-scoring game, at a pace controlled by NC State, Larry only managed 14 points and very oddly did not sink a bucket at all in the second half, so blanketed was he by State's zone defense that no one could get him the ball. Somehow the Heels managed a 3-point win. Equally inauspicious for Carolina was the earlier game in which confident Duke had blown past Virginia by 21 points on the strong play of Larry's pal Bob Riedy who said, "This tournament is like a guy trying to get through an alley with seven men at the other end trying to stop you."

The following night, the Heels' hangover went from bad to worse against Wake Forest, shooting only 31% in the first half. When Rusty Clark picked up 3 early fouls and spent too much time on the bench, Lewis hit only

2 of his 10 shots, and Miller hit only for 1 of 6 with no rebounds, it was a recipe for disaster. Sleepwalking into the locker room at halftime, it seemed the Tar Heels had lost interest in winning. Said Miller after the game, "I was in a daze . . . At the half I wondered to myself what I was doing in this game and it came to me that I was doing absolutely nothing." Meanwhile, in the locker room down the hall, poor Wake Forest holding a 38–34 lead must have been so hopeful. In the end, though, Wake coach Jack McCloskey was left to lament, "We got in trouble when Larry Miller came out in the second half."

"Larry was truly a man on fire," reported Gene Warren, "blazing away for 29 points in the second half alone . . . He was devastating." Dick Grubar, almost consoling Wake, said "Nobody could have handled Miller in that second half. He's the best in the country."

Said Dean Smith of Miller's startling comeback, "It was purely determination. I've never witnessed anything like it."

It was also infectious. Clark, playing with 4 fouls, began dominating the boards and blocking shots and the other Heels woke up, too. Said Bobby Lewis later, "As soon as Miller started to go, we just snapped out of it. I don't know what it is, but if one guy gets hot we all begin to click. We needed something like that to pull us together."

When Larry trotted off the court with 20 seconds left and a 10-point lead, the crowd erupted to its feet, and the press in the locker room later reported "he was swarmed like they crowd around a World Series hero or Master's champion."

Summarized John Kunda in the hometown *Morning Call,* "There was never a 20-minute performance in Atlantic Coast Conference tournament history like the one Larry Miller turned in Friday night . . . This game made Miller a legitimate All-American."

*

The next night was the biggest night of the season from the moment it was etched on the ACC calendar. Everyone on the court knew this was the biggest stage of their basketball world, and the Tar Heels were eager to play for the highest stakes of their careers. Nevertheless, the reigning champion Blue Devils were able to convince many of the press that it was the season champion Tar Heels—two-time winners over Duke but still disrespected—who were really the underdogs. That served to put a chip on offended UNC shoulders, none more so than those of Bobby Lewis who prepared for his last-ever ACC contest by clipping Smith Barrier's *Greensboro Daily News* story predicting "The ACC: The Winner Duke" and taping it on his locker.

As some Tar Heels played cards or tried to rest that March afternoon at Greensboro's Sedgefield Inn, Larry Miller was already pacing like a tiger in a cage. "The day of a big game in high school I couldn't stand to talk with people," he told Bill Hunter. "I wanted to go off somewhere and be by myself. I've settled down some now, but I still get awfully keyed up." Then Miller noticed a group of kids lingering by the door of the Inn, autograph pads and pencils in hand but too shy to come inside, and reflexively he made a team play. Walking outside, he offered to help and then took their pads inside to get them all signed. At that point reports Hunter, "One of the kids turned to the others and said, 'That sure is a nice man. I wish the players on the team were as friendly as he is.' The kids might not have recognized Larry Miller . . . But no one in the Greensboro Coliseum Saturday night had any trouble picking him out. He stood out like the Empire State Building."

Larry started quickly and Bobby did, too, the one-two punchers connecting all night long as the team that had struggled through a swoon refused to choke on this night. Bobby poured in 26 points, capping his ACC career in a burst of glory with 13 points in the final 9 minutes. But it was Larry who played with nearly unconscious abandon, hitting 13 of 14 shots from the field for 32 points with 11 rebounds in a performance many experts hailed as one of the greatest in Tournament history—and he did it playing the last 11 minutes with 4 fouls.

Coach Bubas at courtside must have rued watching Miller perform just as he'd imagined since seeing the boy at fourteen, but now wearing the wrong shade of blue. When it was all over, Lewis was clutching the winner's trophy after an 82–73 victory, telling the press, "I've been waiting for this a long time. I wanted this very much—more than anything in my life." Moments later, Larry was declared the Tournament MVP and no one argued, including Bubas who visited the Carolina locker room to congratulate him. After this night, fading Duke would not win their next Tournament title for another dozen years, during which Carolina would win five more.

"That was a special game," Lewis recalled many years later. "We had never gone to the finals before, because Duke always beat us. So I think that was the biggest turnaround for Coach Smith and Larry and me—that we had finally gotten over that hump. That run starting in 1967 is when Dean Smith became a big-time coach along with Rupp and Wooden."

Just as he'd come on strong at the end of so many close games, Larry was UNC's "closer" on the season, hitting 24 of 29 shots in the final three periods of ACC play. It was no surprise, then, when a few days later he was named the ACC Player of the Year. In taking over the tournament, Miller had led Carolina back to the NCAAs for the first time in ten years and won Dean Smith his first-ever ACC and Tournament championships, kicking down the door to all the unsuspected glory and memories to come.

"I was so in the zone that night, I was somewhere else. Everybody has that power, but tapping into the source . . . it's hard to turn on and off. It's a different frequency in your brain. That game was so intense, I was so drained afterward, you could have shot me and I wouldn't have felt it. In those games I went from something . . . to something else."

After the crowds melted away and his teammates headed for well-earned rest, Larry was still surfing on adrenalin, more awake than anyone in America. "When we got back to Chapel Hill after the game I had so much leftover energy I didn't sleep much that night. So the next afternoon, Sunday, all I could think to do was get in my car, put the top down, crank up the music—'Groovin' on a Sunday Afternoon'—and drive . . . all the way out to Greensboro and back."

*

*Miller cutting down the net after the Heels win the first of
Coach Dean Smith's thirteen ACC Tournaments.*

*Miller, with co-captains Lewis and Gauntlett, sharing their long-awaited championship trophy.*

Staff Photo By John Page

**Larry Miller And His ACC Awards**

# *Unanimous: Larry All-Everything*

*Bobby Lewis hugs Miller holding his Tournament MVP award.*

The NCAA Tournament that followed began as an afterthought. In ancient days before splashy media money, the broader tournament was just too remote from fans not knit together by national exposure. Dick Grubar, for one, was underwhelmed. "Winning that ACC title was exciting, and having the chance to move on to the NCAA. But when you got there, it wasn't the same level of interest you had in the ACC—maybe because the community it was held in just didn't care. In College Park, Maryland the local paper covered the Eastern Regional on page 5, and anyone could always find a ticket."

The Heels found motivation when their Round of 16 opponent turned out to be Princeton, the first blemish on their record back in January. This time, Clark was not ill, Lewis wasn't whistled four times in the first half, and Carolina won to move on.

Next up was Boston College, still coached by the great Bob Cousy. Larry's Allentown pal, Scott Beeten, went down to witness the win that would bring Dean Smith to his first-ever Final Four—but he most remembers the stir that Larry caused off the court. "I saw Larry at his hotel before they left for Cole Field House, and I remember him walking out of his hotel room, because people started screaming for him. He was almost embarrassed by it, but it reminded me of Catty, when people lined up during snowstorms to get into a high school gym that sat 900. Larry had charisma."

Unfortunately the following weekend's national semifinal in Louisville against Dayton was the end of the road. Bobby Lewis concedes, "Neither Larry or I played very well, because they really keyed on us, which was smart." After the team lost the third place game to Houston as well, though, Tar Heel fans just happy to be there amused Coach Smith by proudly chanting "We're Number 4! We're Number 4!" Rusty Clark, for one, wasn't content with that, later telling Pat James of *goheels.com*, "We thought we were a better team than fourth in the nation, but for a bunch of sophomores and guys who hadn't been there before that was not all bad."

In fact, what the departing Lewis, the rising captain Miller, and the Class of '69 couldn't know yet was that this season's accomplishment would only grow more momentous over time. This turnaround year was the first of

Dean Smith's thirty seasons with 20 or more wins, and beginning here the North Carolina basketball program became so dominant that it would never finish worse than second in the ACC for nineteen years in a row.

*

After the tournaments, evidence of the Tar Heels' surging popularity began showing up on the playgrounds, as boys all over the state now played with St. Christopher medals dangling from their necks whether they were Catholic or not. No longer pretending to be three-time-loser Duke stars, they punctuated boisterous pickup game antics by claiming to be Bobby, or Dickie, or Larry. Meanwhile, teen girls were now identifying themselves as either "Grubar girls" or "Miller girls."

That spring, Larry had been invited to play for the USA in the summer World University Games in Tokyo, considered a prelude to next year's 1968 Olympics. At first he was hesitant about not working at Buff's, but Coach Smith pressed him to do it. So Larry went home to Catty that summer to earn what he could at the gas station before flying out to San Francisco where the team gathered for two weeks of practice. While there they checked out the hippies in Haight-Ashbury, noticed the presence and huge impact of psychedelic bands, and got a peek at the sex industry on the naughty side of town.

Then it was off to the Far East for a couple more weeks, where the team easily went 7-0, winning a gold medal. "It was a fun trip," Larry found. "That's when I learned how good Wesley Unseld was; he was on that team. We stayed in the Olympic Village, where the previous Olympics were, and went on tours and up the Tokyo Tower. And I met a couple of girls over there, so it was nice. When it was over I flew straight back home from Japan, and I saw the sun rise two times that day.

"That took up most of my summer, and by the time I got back it was August and almost time to return to school. But Dean absolutely had an ulterior motive: He wanted me to do that trip because he knew if I went home for the summer, I'd come back to school in not so good shape."

What the Coach couldn't anticipate was that his plan nearly backfired and hobbled his star before Larry's final Carolina season even began . . .

**LARRY MILLER**

Catasauqua, Pa.

Position: Frontcourt

**44**

Height: 6-4
Weight: 210
Age: 21
Class: Senior

You name it and he does it in All-America fashion. His name is Larry Miller and he was the Atlantic Coast Conference Player of the Year in 1966-67 . . . Voted first team All-America by the Basketball Writers' Association of America and by the Helms Foundation . . . Always at his best in the clutch, he hit 13 out of 14 shots in ACC title showdown game with Duke last season . . . His miraculous last-second shot against Wake Forest was rated one of greatest plays in the nation last year . . . Larry averaged 20.9 points a game as a sophomore and upped his mark to 21.9 last season . . . He had 277 rebounds as a sophomore and 299 last year . . . Quick as a cat, Miller maneuvers well under the boards without drawing many fouls . . . Has the ruggedness to battle players much taller under the boards . . . He's a southpaw shooter and is deadly from inside or out . . . An excellent ball-handler, he can adapt to guard if the occasion demands . . . Scored a career high with 38 against Virginia in Chapel Hill last season . . . Coach Smith rates him one of hardest workers on Tar Heel squad . . . Expected to be an outstanding team leader in his senior season . . . His teammates have great admiration for him, call him "Mills . . ." His opponents call him nothing but trouble.

**PERSONALITY CHART**

Hobby: Dancing, records, recording music, sports cars
Post School Ambition: Owning business in entertainment field
Favorite Film or TV Star (male): Paul Newman
Favorite Film or TV Star (female): Elke Sommer, Ursula Andress
Favorite Food: All foods
Favorite Sport (other than basketball): Football
Sports Star You Most Admire: Arnold Palmer, Jerry West
Biggest Sports Thrill to Date (either high school or college): Winning ACC Tournament

*Now a national cover boy. "His teammates call him 'Mills' . . .*
*His opponents call him nothing but trouble."*

CHAPTER 7

# ALL-EVERYTHING

Larry Miller was having a dream. In it he was driving a car, but this was not the old nightmare of tipsily tearing down a dark dirt road with another man's wife in a borrowed Corvette. In this dream he was simply driving home from an all-night diner in Durham well past midnight, falling asleep at the wheel . . . unaware he was slowly veering off the road . . .

"Then I woke up—and I *was* driving! Going like 50 down the highway, I was already on the grass, aimed straight at a bridge buttress, and I swerved away just in time. So someone up there was looking out for me. My roommate Ralph Fletcher, who was asleep next to me, slept right through it, but that night we almost died. Those are the ones you have nightmares about." (But better when they actually *precede* the event.) In that moment, the story of the Tar Heel season did not change in the blink of an eye, but this was far from the last time Larry would flirt with death in a car. As admired as he was for living with as much abandon as he played, nothing gave Larry Miller worse nightmares than himself.

✳

Practice and playing in the Tokyo games came at a cost for the Carolina captain when he aggravated a recurring abductor muscle tear in his groin, right where the top of his leg joins a more tender area. "It was very painful," he recalls, "and if you're a basketball player, your first move is right from there—I couldn't move quickly anymore. So they sent me to the hospital, and there's a very unique treatment. It wasn't pretty. First they stuck a small needle in there to deaden it, and told me to relax. Right. But then they pulled out a bigger one. So they inserted this big needle to search for the tear, and he's wiggling it all around asking 'Can you feel that?' and I'm saying, 'Is this a joke??' After what felt like an hour, he says, 'Okay, now we'll do the other side.' And I said, 'Oh, no, you're not!' I got a lot better after that."

✳

The 1967–68 season shaped up as a reward for the Tar Heel faithful, still floating on the adrenalin rush of last year's surprising 26-6 breakthrough. Now, with four starters returning from the fourth best team in the country, joined by a deep bench and the intriguing Charles Scott, everyone knew this team widely favored to repeat as ACC champs would be good . . . so good that the only luxurious question was, *how* good?

Those inclined to caution could point to what Coach Smith called "probably the most difficult schedule in the school's history" and the loss to graduation of the second leading scorer in Tar Heel history. Even Smith, though, admitted the depth he had built would now allow the Heels to play or attack any type of defense, and with the Class of '69 a year older and stronger following Rusty Clark's summer workouts with weights, and Miller still nothing but trouble for opponents, the only wild card was enticing: Charles Scott.

Dick Grubar knew what was coming for the rest of the league—he had to guard Scott in practice: "He was one of the quickest guys I've ever seen."

In fact Coach Smith, realizing he was loaded with depth and team speed, promised this team was going to run all night long. One ACC preview guide, well aware of Miller's MO of late-game heroics, called him "200% muscle waiting to be juiced up by a close score." But Larry was so confident that he predicted not many games would be close at all, that he'd be playing fewer minutes because, "We're tall, fast, and strong, and we have ten guys who will play a lot."

The only cloud on the horizon was far, far away, on the other side of the country and the regular season, where Lew Alcindor blocked out the sun. UCLA had won last year's NCAA Championship by brushing aside every opponent by 15 points or more, and it was gospel that this year everyone else was only fighting for second place. Even Larry seemed resigned to the obvious, saying "I wish it was a normal year, so we could have a real chance at it because I've always wanted to win the ultimate championship."

*Joe Brown, the "6ᵗʰ man" who battled Miller every day in practice,*
*with future Big Ten Commissioner Jim Delany catching the sun*
*outside their dorm at "Avery Beach."*

*Sophomore Eddie Fogler, with senior Miller in practice jerseys.*
*Recalls Miller of the class of '70, "They were all quiet kids . . .*
*unlike the rest of us."*

All 8,500 seats at Carmichael were sold out for the season, and the team was so popular that students now dropped by just to watch them practice. Miller, the senior captain, was the main attraction, of course. Maintaining his boyhood routine of putting on a 25-pound weight vest, he led the team in jumping rope—50 hops on each foot alone, and then another 150 on both feet—before strapping weights to his ankles and running up and down and up and down the steps in the stands with the vest still on. This not only prepared him for prime time, but set the bar for his teammates as well, earning Coach Smith's admiration that, whatever his off-court antics, "He's the most dedicated player I've ever seen."

To this day, Dick Grubar marvels, "Larry was such a leader he was always out in front of everybody. Anything he would do, he would do it so wholeheartedly that if you were there you would try to keep up. But there was nobody who could keep up with him—on anything! Whether it was basketball, getting in shape, or partying, he could do it all. He could drink a few beers, and then show up at practice, and we'd have to run and run and run . . . and he would be first. He'd *always* be first! He'd run the hills before preseason, and he could force himself to do things that killed a mere mortal like me—there's no way. You'd be dead and he'd keep going. He didn't have some physical attributes that other players did, but if I had to pick, he would *always* be my first guy. And we all fed off him."

*

When the Heels' winning ways began attracting attention, attention-seekers began coming to them. "There were always people coming through there," Larry recalls. "Anytime someone important came to town and wanted to curry favor with the students they'd want to meet us." The players met NASA astronauts, in town to get acquainted with the real stars at Morehead Planetarium in preparation for their space flights and also to promote NASA's mission. Presidential candidate Hubert Humphrey had stopped by to campaign for young voters the previous year, and Larry met him, too. But the photo op he was most suited for was escorting Hollywood honey Yvette Mimieux around the Chapel Hill campus. The mouthwatering starlet of "Where the Boys Are" and "The Time Machine" was in town shooting scenes at the ATO house for a movie called "Three in the Attic"—about a college lothario who is kidnapped by three girls he's tri-cheating on, who lock him in a sorority attic and take turns trying to kill him with constant sex. (So a typical weekend for Larry.) Miller confesses the brief meeting of movie star and All-American boy was photo fodder for the local papers but there was no hint of a real liaison. "But it didn't hurt my résumé any."

*

The team woke up slowly in their first game of that year, trailing Virginia Tech by 7 points at the half before someone remembered the season had started, and Larry finished with 30 points, 9 rebounds, and 6 assists. More important, though, Charles Scott scored a strong 18 points, proving himself more than a token as UNC's first black varsity scholarship athlete.

The next game was a runaway with balanced scoring against a weak Kent State team, distinguished by one heroic performance—from the opposition. Recalls Joe Brown, "They had a guy, Doug Grayson, who hit his first 16 shots in a row. We tried all sorts of things to slow him down, and I finally cooled him off in the second half—but fifty years later his streak is still an NCAA record."

## They're Stars In Different Fields

North Carolina's basketball ace Larry Miller chats with actress Yvette Mimeux in Chapel Hill, N.C., during break in filming of American International's 'Three In The Attic" in which Miss Mimeux stars.

The next game, against Vanderbilt in Nashville, matched up Scott against another barrier breaker, Perry Wallace, who was the first African

American scholarship athlete to play varsity basketball in the Southeastern Conference. Joe Brown's stellar play had earned him a start in this game but . . . "We lost because the chemistry was different with me starting. So Coach Smith told me he liked my energy coming off the bench, and Bill Bunting went back into the starting lineup—and we won the next twenty games in a row."

The Vanderbilt loss, in spite of Miller's 21 second-half points, startled the Heels, but Coach Smith almost seemed to welcome it, telling reporter Ken Alyta: "I hate to say any defeat is good, but we had won our first two games rather easily and perhaps we were too complacent. That game really woke us up. It helped us beat Kentucky three nights later."

The Kentucky win, and the next one over Princeton—their second in a row against Top Ten competition—were both in Greensboro. That meant Coach Smith could once again fly his boys home for the holidays, until they reunited in Portland, Oregon for the Far West Classic. Knowing he was losing his team for twelve festive days, Smith eyed Larry as he admonished, "Take care of yourselves when you go home."

Larry's response: "You know me, Coach—of *course* I will!" (You can almost hear him crossing his fingers behind his back.) Smith could be forgiven if he raised an eyebrow at this player who signed his letter of intent while drinking whiskey . . . who missed opening day of basketball camp while hitching up from the beach . . . who arrived at his first junior practice with a swollen hand. Yeah, he knew Larry alright . . .

In fact, Larry had a grand time celebrating Christmas as only a man tanked up on Catty cheer can: "It was snowing, and my friend Warren had a motorcycle with a sidecar, and he drove me around town with a girl I was dating at the time. We called her 'Mrs. Claus' because she had a big fur coat on. We went riding all over town, greeting people at Midnight Mass and various parties—we had people dressed as elves following us—freezing our asses off and visiting kids and their families and spreading the cheer until 3:00 or 4:00 in the morning . . . so I got a little chilled."

The following morning, Larry had to fly out to Portland to play three West Coast teams in three days—and of course he was sick as a dog. Nothing was improved when the airline lost the team's luggage and the fifth-ranked Heels had to practice privately in their underwear. *Sports Illustrated* even razzed them as "The BVD Boys," with the fan-mag revelation that Larry not only loved sports cars but also wore plaid undershorts (bvds). What began as a cockeyed adventure, however, became a notable milestone for Larry's senior team when The Far West Classic brought severe tests of the team's resilience both on and off the court.

The West Coast teams fought hard in this tourney because, living in a neighborhood patrolled by Alcindor, this was the only championship they had a shot at. The first night's game 3,000 miles from home, a win over Stanford, left the *Oregonian* somewhat oddly praising Larry for being inconspicuous in doing a little of everything—if leading the team with 27 points was "little"—while noting the game turned in the second half when Rusty Clark asserted himself on the boards.

The second night meant trouble, then, when the Tar Heels had to face an undefeated Utah team with the entire front line of Clark, Bunting, and reserve Ralph Fletcher out with food poisoning—leaving Joe Brown matched up against the Utes' seven-foot center. "I had pretty good hops then and was fairly strong," Brown recalls, "but we were down 17 points in the second half, and everybody on the east coast turned their radios off and went to bed. There wasn't a lot of television back then. So thank goodness Larry had the game he had in the second half." Miller remembers turning to Grubar at one point saying, "Well, Grubes, we might as well enjoy ourselves, because we're getting our ass kicked."

Up in the booth, though, announcer Bill Currie knew better: "Fans, have no fear. Miller's going to get mad in a minute and Carolina is coming back." Sure enough, the Heels bore down on defense, and new sensation Charles Scott scored 12 relentless points to whittle the Utah lead, finally putting Carolina up by 2 with 8 seconds left. A Utah guard then sank the tying bucket as time ran out . . . but the refs waved it off because he'd stepped on the base line. Miraculously for an era before the boost of a 3-point shot, UNC climbed out of the hole and escaped with a win.

Facing off against hometown favorites Oregon State in the finals, Miller had a quiet first half as Scott again did the scoring. And then, in typical fashion, Miller erupted in the second half, stealing a pass, making 2 free throws, then stealing the ball again from an OSU sub right under the OSU basket. Larry wound up with 27 points in that second half alone (33 overall), seizing the championship for the favored Heels. It was after this game that the Oregon State coach famously marveled, "I've seen a lot of college teams that couldn't beat Larry Miller and four girls."

And yet, in the flush of celebrating the win, Coach Smith received a tip that alarmed him: Before Miller's dominant closing onslaught, early voting had made Charles Scott the tournament MVP, and now Smith suddenly worried that, for the second year in a row, he had to stave off potential dissension. Rushing to chide the other coaches into a hasty revote, Smith got the MVP trophy awarded to Larry instead. So now the coach had another problem.

Charles Scott: "After the game Coach Smith pulled me aside and told me, 'When you get home, you're going to hear that Bill Currie announced you as the MVP—but I went to the committee because I believe in seniority, and when you're a senior you'll get all you deserve.' That was the one time I felt cheated out of something I earned by Coach Smith. And if the coach hadn't told me, I probably wouldn't have heard about it, because black people didn't listen to Carolina basketball at that time. But as I got older—it took me years to come to this conclusion—I think Coach Smith was really aware of team chemistry. And this was early in the season; it could disrupt the team. Remember, there were still people who didn't want me to be there—alumni boosters and donors at that time—and this black guy is taking over our team from an All-American ACC Player of the Year, and he wins the MVP? You're talking not that long after Jackie Robinson, with people warning 'Watch out, he's coming after your job.'

"At first I was disappointed, but to be honest I never worried about being the top dog. What I worried about was the team being split, with some guys for me and some for Larry. I'm pretty sure that happened with other teams that had black and white players then. But Larry was always the leader of the team to me, there was never any question in my mind—that was Larry's team. And what he did backed it up. So me being just a sophomore was the perfect scenario for us."

\*

Returning home, the Tar Heels plunged into the heart of the ACC schedule by knocking off Wake Forest, the 100th win milestone for Smith who would one day retire as the winningest Division 1 coach of all time. Later the same week they edged Duke by 3 points, then NC State by 2, and by the time Larry poured in 22 points in the first half against Clemson, the team was playing so well he was able to sit out the last 9 minutes of the game. His preseason confidence apparently justified, the Heels reached the late January exam break on a nine-game winning streak, with Larry leading the conference in scoring and sophomore Scott ably duplicating Bobby Lewis's 18 ppg for second-best on the team.

This first go-round in the old south was no cakewalk for Scott, though. Dean Smith avoided hostile lodgings and eateries on the road, but he couldn't protect Charles from being heckled on cramped courts with hateful fans right on top of him screaming horrible insults. Miller confirms that certain arenas were full of jerks, but tried to share the load by noting that he got heckled, too—that was normal, the attitude they had toward North Carolina.

"Larry and the others kept me in a cocoon," Charles remembers. "They sheltered me and they never made me feel alone. I was always one of them. They never made me feel like a black guy on a white team. And Larry's leadership was probably most important for the other guys to take their lead from him and fall in line. Because if Larry accepted me, how could they be dismissive of me? He's the star!"

\*

*Fighting off the flu, Miller was named tournament MVP*
*of the Far West Classic after a controversial vote.*

With games and team practices suspended for exams, Larry worked out on his own in Carmichael, but one day took a break for reporters with slack in their sports pages. The *Raleigh Times* was now calling Larry "a household word . . . handsome and tough," and Sports Information Director Jack Williams seemed to have his hands full with Larry-mania, saying "I've never seen anything like it. The fans love him, especially the girls."

Ronald Green of the *Charlotte News*, had already concluded, "Miller is the closest thing to a matinee idol to come along in ACC sports in a long time. He turns people on the way he plays basketball, the way he looks and the way he acts."

*Charles Scott, integrating the starting lineup between
Clark and Miller with Grubar.*

Larry admitted to Elton Casey of the *Durham Sun* that he was now getting about fifty letters a week—some with cuff links or tie pins—from fans of all ages. "I don't go steady," he testified. "I date a lot of coeds here and town girls . . . The way I feel now I'll never get married." Ronald Green caught him rakishly adding, "There are a lot of pretty girls on this campus, and I'd like to get around to meeting all of them before I graduate."

*The Sun* got a glimpse of the senior's future plans when Larry revealed that, with two months still to go in the season, he was already considering the prospects of the new ABA compared to the established NBA: "I think there will be better opportunities there . . . I don't like the idea of sitting on the bench, and I might have to do that in the NBA. I wouldn't be happy if I couldn't play regularly."

Graduating, however, would mean the end of Larry's student deferment and exposure to the draft for Vietnam—and like many of his generation, he didn't see much sense in the war. "Still, I'd be loyal to my country if I got the call to go." (In fact, the military's mixed feelings about Larry would become a saga, itself.)

Another possibility for the Business Administration major was to one day open a night spot around Chapel Hill in the off-season. (Are we surprised?) "It would be a place where boys and girls could meet and not necessarily have to have a date."

Two weeks after these fan-fodder musings appeared in the press, the reach of the Miller mystique was evidenced by an item in the *Tallahassee Democrat*, shortly after the Heels beat Florida State: "University of North Carolina got the following request from a basketball fan: 'I would like a picture of Dick Grubar and Larry Miller in their basketball suits. I would also like to have one of them without their suits on.'"

*

Larry would often hang out with football players, and one was Bo Wood, an ex-Heel who was now a pro and back to get his Master's degree. In the way of the times, Bo and his wife Suzi (now Suzi Mutascio) always left their door open at University Garden Apartments, and one night Larry poked his head in saying, "Let's go down to the watering hole." That's where they met Monty Diamond, who was not an athlete. Monty, who has a gift for making friends, remembers the night he and Larry went to see "The Graduate" which had just come out.

"We walked out of the screening and I thought to myself, 'That's what I want to do. This has theater, it has art.' Larry was a big figure in those days, and that we could be friends was a big deal for me. It meant something that here was a person who was admired by the rest of the world, but saw something in me and gave me confidence. It was a great send-off for whatever I was going to do in the future." (Monty now has production credits on over forty feature films, and his short "The World Trade Center in the Movies" has played at the 9/11 Museum ever since it opened, still showing twenty times a day.)

*

When the Heels went north to play Maryland, they were greeted by a Catasauqua crowd that included the Millers, Coach Mushrush, and a hundred more Lehigh Valley fans who not only saw Larry but watched Rusty Clark grab 30 rebounds, a UNC record that stands to this day. The #3 team in the country didn't have many weaknesses. When your star scores 17 points, with 7 rebounds and 7 assists, for your fourteenth win in fifteen games and calls it the worst game of his college career, while everyone can hear dozens of kids outside the locker room chanting "We Want Miller" over and over on enemy turf, the sky is Tar Heel blue.

Three days later, Carolina obliterated Virginia by 44 points—then the highest margin in ACC basketball history—leading the opposing coach to call them "the greatest Carolina team I've ever seen."

By the time the Tar Heels' bus headed down Tobacco Road to Raleigh, their sparkling 17-1 record left no doubt that they deserved a #3 national ranking. Meanwhile, down in the Houston Astrodome in what was billed as "The Game of the Century," mighty UCLA had fallen to Elvin Hayes' Houston team. That was the only encouragement Larry needed to start dreaming like a champion again. "This year I have so much confidence in the team it takes all the worry out . . . We are a lot better than we were last year, more experienced and a lot more versatile. We realize everybody's shooting for us, but we want to stay on top. Now we know that UCLA can be beaten, and I think this club can do it."

Lying in wait, though, was the ever ornery NC State. The Tar Heels won on points, but State didn't go down without another fight. Larry had the ball when he saw that State guard Eddie Biedenbach had kicked Gerald Tuttle while he was lying on the court. So Larry threw the ball back to the referee ("like you should"), went to pick the guy off Tuttle (lifting him off the floor), and "just gave him to the referee." Biedenbach, noted for his ball-hawking ability, was nicknamed "The Pickpocket," and next day *The Daily Tar Heel* ran a drawing of Larry lifting a black-masked Biedenbach off the ground by his jersey, with the caption "The Pickpocket is caught!"

The 96–84 victory made NC State the fall guys of another Miller milestone: His 24 points in this game moved Larry past Billy Cunningham to become North Carolina's third leading all-time scorer (behind only Bobby Lewis and '57's Rosenbluth).

It was about this time that Ronald Green wrote a story about Miller titled, "The Wild Ones." No, this wasn't a reference to Larry's black leather jacket or his motorcycle ride as a Pagan. It was a fond appreciation of his circus shots that continued to astound and delight. The paradigm, of course, was The Shot against Wake Forest that he made as a junior, but this last game caused Green to write, "Did you see the shots he made against NC State the other night? . . . Of all the gosh-awful shotmakers that have played in the ACC, Miller may be the champion. Not the best shooter, but the most creative shooter . . . Probably the most unlikely shot Miller has ever made over at Carolina was an atrocity on the spur of the moment against NC State the other night . . . Dean Smith broke into a wide grin and shook his head in disbelief when he saw it . . . There have been few players in this league who were in a class with Miller when it came to thinking up shots while strolling along in midair through heavy traffic."

As Larry was slathered with enough praise to make his teammates gag (and perhaps recalling bruised feelings on his high school team), he found ways to keep the mood light. After *The Herald* called him "Captain Clutch" in its headline, Larry came bursting into Joe Brown's suite wearing a cape and zooming around the room, like a kid playing Superman. Brown says the guys cracked up and appreciated that. "But the thing is, he *was* a superhero."

*

Larry's senior streak continued to the end of February when the Heels' twentieth win in a row, at Virginia, clinched the season title, still undefeated in the ACC at 12-0. Coach Smith didn't want to risk another party by staying overnight, so he put his boys on the bus for the three-hour ride back to Chapel Hill. Larry, however, was way ahead of him. "I took two suitcases on that trip and one of them was empty. So I had the kitchen staff fill it with a couple cases of beer and sneak it onto the back of the bus for us. Heading home we were celebrating, making a lot of noise, and at one point the driver slammed on his brakes and momentum pitched Charlie all the way forward to where Coach was—and Charlie had a beer in his hand! Some people claim Coach didn't see it, but I figure he knew what was going on—we were just having a harmless good time—and he had enough sense not to notice. And that was the only time I did that."

A day or two later, Larry got a call saying he'd just been selected a First Team All-American and was asked by General Mills to fly up to Minnesota to be interviewed for the announcement sponsored by Wheaties. When he arrived, though, the other players were nowhere to be seen, nor was the well-known spokesman, Bob Richards. "They had me talking to him but he wasn't there—they were all edited in later. It was a ten minute deal, and I was out of there. I'm only up there one night; I didn't even miss a class. But I ran into Bobby Lloyd, who I played with the summer before, and he said he knew a girl—was I interested?—and I said 'Sure.' And then—you know me—I told her 'We've got a game tomorrow night. You want to come back to Chapel Hill?' "

Suzi Mutascio picks up the story: "So Larry walks in with this girl—she had a silver metallic minidress on, silver boots, and a silver metallic hairband that had to be four-inches wide—that's why we called her The Silver Bullet.

*Initiating an old-fashioned 3-point play: "Once I went up,*
*there was no telling where I was going after that."*

She wasn't a stripper, at least we don't think so. She seemed like a really nice girl. And she only stayed around for a day or two, and that was it. I said, 'Larry, how could you drag that poor thing all the way from Minnesota?' And he said, 'I didn't drag her home—she followed me!' "

The Silver Bullet made quite an impression on the good (and bad) people of Chapel Hill in her silver microskirt, one of them radio man Jim Heavner who was idly scanning the crowd during pregame warmups when he suddenly froze like a Pointer. "I said, 'Whoa . . . What is *that?* And somebody laughed, 'That's Miller's girl.' " Miller confirms the town thought she might be a movie star or somebody famous. "Someone wrote an article comparing her to Yvette Mimieux. But I think she could travel because she was a stewardess. She just stayed a couple of days and meandered on."

The game she saw at Carmichael was the last home game of Larry Miller's career in the gym he'd helped baptize. Writing in the paper that day, Jack Williams felt it a sad occasion saying, "Perhaps never in the history of the Atlantic Coast Conference has any player had such an impact on the game as Miller . . . In everything he ever did he represented the University of North Carolina with class." The stands were packed, the crowd emotional, and when Larry's name was unexpectedly announced first in the pregame introductions the thunderous standing ovation went on and on . . . stranding him alone on the court so extra long that the adulation began to embarrass him.

But that was the high point of the evening. The game against Frank McGuire's Gamecocks spoiled the Miller celebration by one dang point, when a 59% career foul shooter named Bobby Cremins made 6 of 7 free throws in the final 90 seconds (and 13 of 16 overall) for an 87–86 South Carolina win. The next and last game of this glorious season, at Duke, also clanked off the rim with an identical 87–86 loss in triple overtime. And now the cocky Tar Heel express was suddenly fishtailing into the ACC tournament, where one more crack-up would mean sudden death.

The sting of the Duke loss may have been mitigated when that same day the Associated Press named Larry to their All-America team for the second year in a row. What's certain is that, in joining Lew Alcindor, Wes

Unseld, Elvin Hayes, and Pete Maravich, Larry would forever be part of what many people consider to this day the most talented All-American team ever.

*

The first ACC Tourney ever played in Charlotte gathered with the Tar Heels still top-seeded, but the two late losses had slid their national ranking to #5. And opening against Wake Forest that Thursday night, much of the team was so ragged in the first half that even Charles Scott couldn't find his range. The tournament was always Miller Time, though, and Larry buried 9 of his first 11 shots for 22 points in the first half alone, making it clear what the outcome would be. Said Smith after the game, "We like to think we're a balanced team, but there are times when one boy has to carry us. Most of the time when that develops, it is Larry."

Reminded of his 29-point second half against Wake the previous year, Larry joked, "I wanted to get it over with quickly this time." His 31 total points did more than push the Heels into the semifinals; they also pushed Larry past Bobby Lewis to become Carolina's second all-time leading scorer.

Like his teammates, Larry had rooted hard for South Carolina to meet them in the semis, where they'd have a chance to avenge the loss that ruined their perfect ACC record. But all he would tell the press before that Friday night game was, "I'm ready." Remembering how Bobby's newspaper clipping had fueled the Tar Heels before last year's final, he added, "I'm not going to say anything that the other team can read and get fired up about."

Larry's shooting helped UNC build a 12-point lead, but South Carolina fought back and the Tar Heels needed every one of his 24 points to squeak by the Gamecocks in overtime. (Dick Grubar's scoring in the final minutes of this win would earn him a place with Larry on the All-Tournament team.)

That set up a showdown with NC State, which had surprised sixth-ranked Duke and everyone else in North America by winning the most hideous of all slow-down games, 12–10 (at halftime Duke was up 4–2), the lowest scoring game in ACC Tournament history. (At one point, Larry's Kutztown friend Dick Braucher walked over to the Wolfpack cheerleaders on the baseline and borrowed a stick of chewing gum while the clock kept running.) Afterward, one Duke player groused, "When you walk off the court you feel like you haven't even been in a game."

Against the Tar Heels, State again tried to keep it a low-scoring game and trailed by only 5 at the half. The All-American captain wasn't having that in his last ACC game, though, and did something unprecedented: He asked Coach Smith and the assistants to leave the dressing room so he could speak alone to the team. Ask Larry these days what he told the guys and he'll crack, "Probably where we were going drinking after the game." But Charles Scott, in the biggest game of his young career, recalls "I zone out everything when I'm playing, but I remember he kept saying, 'Act like we're 13 down all the time!' In the second half, Larry just took over and we went ahead, but we kept playing like we were down. He made us play desperate."

The Heels' desperation trampled State 56–24 after halftime alone, staining them with another dubious record: The 37-point margin of their loss remains the largest in ACC Tournament title game history. The slaughter was so obvious that Larry came out of the game with 4:59 still on the clock to a standing ovation. Coach Smith was the first to be lifted to clip the nets of his second-straight ACC Championship, and the second one hoisted was Miller. Then, reported the *Greensboro Daily News*, "Miller, a basketball net around his neck, trotted to the sideline, awaiting the awards presentation looking like Native Dancer after the Kentucky Derby." In the end he collected the team trophy as captain and the Everett Case Award as the tourney's MVP for the second straight year.

A few days later Larry also won the ACC Player of the Year award for the second straight year—and remains the only Carolina player ever to claim the award twice.

It was probably inevitable, then, that it would later be announced that Larry had won the 1968 Patterson Medal, the highest athletic award over all sports at North Carolina, becoming the first basketball player to win that distinction in eleven years.

Also selected First Team All-ACC in his first eligible year was Charles Scott: "I think it worked out well," Joe Brown says of Scott's groundbreaking season. "He and I roomed together on road trips, and I enjoyed rooming with Charlie. He went through things the rest of us were unaware of, but he didn't make a big deal of it so we didn't either. And he was a tremendous teammate. I know I'm glad he ended up where he did."

Remarkably, except for his sophomore year at UNC, the teams that Larry Miller played on had won a championship every year he ever played basketball, beginning in middle school at the Boys Club.

*

Five nights later, Larry got out of a late class and walked straight across campus to what could have been Memorial Hall, where Mitch Ryder and the Detroit Wheels were performing a concert. Seats had been saved for the basketball team in the front row, and all was cool until the singer announced a dance contest, inviting a challenger from the audience. It took only a nanosecond before the crowd started chanting, "Mil-ler! Mil-ler!" . . . and then they sent a girl up, too. Then Ryder picked a band member and another girl and the contest began. "Talk about coming off the bench cold, into a hot fire," Larry recalls. "They start playing 'Funky Broadway' or something, and we're dancing, and then I call out, 'Hey, Mitch! You got something with a little more life in it?' So then they play 'Devil with a Blue Dress' and we're dancing away . . . and then it's time to vote . . ."

First, Mitch held his hand above his equally famous bandmate and got a polite round of applause. Then he held his hand over Miller's head—and the crowd exploded with cheers that wouldn't stop. The singer of the #4 song in the country turned to stare for a long quizzical beat . . . "Who the hell *are* you??"

The captain of the #3 team in the country just smiled.

*

The team was now so beloved that the next day one third of the entire student body turned out for a pep rally behind South Building to send them off to Raleigh to defend their East Regional title. Dean Smith made a joke about Larry's dancing, and Larry was so confident his Heels would advance to the Final Four in California that he cracked, "I'm waxing up my surfboard, letting my hair grow long, and I'm planning to bleach it when we get to LA." Joe Brown was typically more tempered, but captured the moment saying, "Well, here we are, right in the middle of the big time."

*Right in the middle of the big time: UNC's student body
sends their East Regional champions off to what was
not yet known as the "Final Four."*

Carolina caught a break with the Regionals in Raleigh, making them the hometown favorites in normally enemy territory. Their first test was a big one, though, undefeated 23-0 St. Bonaventure with big Bob Lanier—6'11" and 265 pounds of Second Team All-American as a sophomore, and destined to be the #1 pick of the 1970 NBA draft. Rumor has it that Dean Smith got under Rusty Clark's skin by sympathizing that he should just do the best he could against Lanier—but Clark will tell you his coach said that before every game. Grubar still enjoys the memory: "Lanier was All-American, but Rusty just dominated him."

The story is in the box score: Lanier got his points and rebounds, but was held to 41% shooting by Clark, who shot 69%. And a 6'4" forward shouldn't be collecting 16 rebounds and 14 free throw attempts, even if he is Larry Miller, against a 6'11" future Hall of Fame shot blocker who finally fouled out of the game. The Bonnies had two 23-point scorers, and Miller and Scott were in the 20s, too, but Clark's 18 points were the Tar Heels' edge in the surprisingly comfortable 91–72 win.

The Regional final against Davidson was tougher. That game started dangerously for UNC, with Davidson blanketing Miller so well that he didn't take a shot for more than 10 minutes, leaving Carolina trailing 34–28 at the half. Scott scored his usual 18, though, playing strong defense in a team effort that held Davidson to 35% shooting. And then Rusty Clark stepped up to dominate with 22 points and 17 rebounds, making him the MVP of the entire East Regional and sending Carolina back to the Final Four.

Now, with the emergence of Scott and especially the assertive play of Rusty Clark, Miller was convinced that Carolina's combination of fine-ly-tuned speed and depth could run any team in the country ragged. Yes, even mighty UCLA whose Goliath would have to rest *sometime*. For the first time all year, his confidence matching his boundless energy, the Tar Heel captain was looking forward to an upset and was heard saying, "We can actually beat those guys."

*

By now, Miller, Scott, and Clark had been invited to try out for the U.S. Olympic team that would play in Mexico that summer of '68. Miller, however, had been playing basketball almost nonstop since the World Games in Tokyo, and once Carolina played in the Final Four he would have to head straight on to two weeks of Olympic trials. "I don't feel I could take it," he admitted for perhaps the first time in his life. "I'm beat. Charlie is going to try out, and that's ideal for him. But by going to the World Games in Tokyo my junior year, that was enough for me."

\*

Returning to the big time at the Los Angeles Sports Arena, the Tar Heels now knew better than to look past their Midwestern semifinal opponent as they had against Dayton. Ohio State was the Big Ten champ, and although not frightening at 21-8 they had edged Kentucky by a point to get here. So the Tar Heels stayed focused, playing a beautifully balanced game with all five starters scoring in double figures led by Larry's 20, a surprising 17 from Bill Bunting, and Rusty's 15, sinking 77%. With Scott adding 13 and Grubar 11, and all clamping down to hold yet another opponent to making only 35% of their shots, the 80–66 win was a model of efficiency.

The following day's National Championship game has been much debated, with some saying it was decided by strategic choices made before players even set foot on the court. Coach Smith had made the unusual move of letting his team watch the rematch between UCLA and the top-seeded Houston squad that in January had given the Bruins their only loss in two years. UCLA's revenge win was a 101–69 slaughter that had to be sobering if not daunting for the Tar Heels on deck.

And then there was the game plan: Recalls Charles Scott, "I remember distinctly Coach Smith asking the day before how we wanted to play, and Larry and I wanted to run. And we were disappointed when he went with the 4-Corners. But at that time you never, ever felt you had the right to question what a coach told you."

Coach Smith later noted that young men are not as realistic about their abilities as coaches, and perhaps UCLA had the talent to outrun the Heels no matter how they played. But in turning away from the fast-paced abandon that had gotten them here, the Heels' fast break pressure that made the Wolfpack buckle and had Carolina brimming with confidence coming out of Charlotte was left behind in the locker room on this night. Instead, North Carolina played with uncharacteristic caution that had many observers thinking they were playing to hang close, hoping to strike at the end, rather than to win . . . (in other words, like NC State).

It didn't work.

"The team went out mad at Dean's game strategy," Jim Heavner recounts. "I was there watching it. I remember in the first 2 or 3 minutes Rusty got the ball at the top of the key, and Alcindor just backed off, like 'Okay, you want that shot? Take it.' And Rusty was a really good player, but he shot the damnedest brick you've ever seen."

Larry's first shot attempt was a layup, which clanked off the back of the rim, and ever after he has wished that he dunked it—even though the dunk was banned that year. Later he told *Tar Heel Monthly*, "Even if it wouldn't have counted, I should have done it just to let them know I wasn't scared." For that, and to fire up his team for the fight, because basketball without the dunk was like tennis without the overhead slam—a sport without its exclamation point—and that night the Tar Heels were sorely missing their psych.

The nature of the 1968 National Championship game is all too easy to explain: Lew Alcindor. (It was not until later that summer that he converted to Islam, and three years more until he publicly used his Arabic name, Kareem Abdul-Jabbar.) He dominated the action with 34 points, shooting 71%, with 16 rebounds while playing a robust 37 minutes. And he defended the basket so well, batting away at least 7 blocks without fouling out, that this time it was Carolina on the wrong end of shooting only 35%. Miller and Scott were actually the second and third highest scorers of the contest (with 14 and 12), but Clark only managed 9 on four made baskets, and *Sports Illustrated* accused the rest of the Heels of being reluctant to shoot at all. Aside from Lucius Allen's 11, all the other Bruins scored in single digits, too, but that was enough when passing the ball around until they could lob it to Lew. "We played like we were intimidated," admits Heavner, "and UCLA played with a happy arrogance." In other words, on this night UCLA stole North Carolina's soul.

After the 78–55 verdict, three other Bruins joined Alcindor on the All Final Four team, chiefly for their work against Houston. The only player named to the All Final Four team not wearing UCLA's colors was Larry Miller. Carolina had lost their psych at the very last moment, but at least they'd lost by less than Houston. And if it was any consolation, the gifted Tar Heels had accomplished the only realistic goal at the start of the season: They weren't the greatest team in college basketball history, but they were champions of all the rest.

*

Returning to Chapel Hill, Larry was as close to gratified as any player in America not wearing UCLA colors could be. The frustration of the losing game plan would fade after the Heels gathered one last time for the team banquet—"That's one I did make"—to digest what they had accomplished:

Charles Scott, only a sophomore, had joined Larry on the All-ACC team, auguring good years to come.

Larry not only won the Patterson medal as UNC's best athlete in any sport, he also won the Atlantic Coast Conference's Athlete of the Year award for the entire conference in all sports.

Said Bones McKinney, who had recently coached Wake Forest to the Final Four and was known as a colorful, if grudging, commentator, "Larry Miller may be the best player ever to compete in the ACC."

*

As the team disbanded, Coach Smith stood ready to work on Larry's future, but first Larry had something else in mind—freedom. If Dean's offer was essentially "You work hard for us and I'll work hard for you," Larry's counter was more like "Wait a minute, you left out the fun part! If I worked hard for the team, now I get to play hard."

Conceding his lapses bouncing for Martha and the Vandellas and keg parties with the Pagans, Larry says, "Dean didn't like the way I ran my off-season. That's where we didn't see eye-to-eye. I'd listen to his advice, but then say 'I'm going to do exactly what I want to do.' That's when we'd get into religion and drinking and partying and . . . I'd say, 'Hey, this is the way I am. You got *me*.' "

Now released from team obligations, Larry let his sideburns grow and drank beers on "Avery Beach" (right outside the dorm's door), where the team held court by invitation only, Rolling Rock required for admission. "The football players had to walk by on their way to spring training," he recalls, "and they'd boo us because our season was over." Catching up to the counterculture, he listened to a lot of "mind music" with his friend Monty, and watched performers like Joe Cocker while sitting on the football field in Kenan Stadium. "In my head I was in Woodstock the whole rest of the year."

*

An item from BarefootButcher on the Carolina message boards: "My best friend and I used to go up on campus and knock on the athletes' doors to see if we could get any stuff from them. When we knocked on Larry's door . . . Dick gave us his sweatbands. Larry gave us a can opener."

*

One day, Larry mentioned to Bo Wood that he was looking for an off campus apartment to escape the constraints of Avery, and Bo's wife Suzi piped up, "Hey, what about the one right across the hall from us? It's open." In short order, Larry moved into University Garden Apartments, was soon joined by his music and film buddy Monty, who also needed a place to live, and there they established a '60s prequel to the TV sitcom "Friends."

"It was four of the most different people you can imagine," Suzi recalls. "Monty was very wealthy, from Bethesda, his father a big power attorney for D.C. people, and Jewish. Then Larry, from a blue-collar town, a Catholic. Bo was Protestant and kind of in-between, and then 'nice Suzi' from this little maple leaf town. But it all just worked . . . and they enjoyed their pranks. One night someone passed out on the sofa and we couldn't wake him up—but Larry knew how to fix it. Bo picked up one end of the sofa and Larry got the other, and they carried the thing out to the front yard, so the guy would wake up outside in the morning."

As a happily married woman, Suzi had a ringside seat on Larry's love life that spring. The apartment house had its own pool where they'd hang out, and she still recalls how Larry toasted himself. "He's got that skin that tans, but he would also use olive oil mixed with iodine. He certainly had a string of girls there. It was constant. But he never had to go hunting for attention; they kind of strolled right by him." (Including some who forgot they were committed elsewhere and wanted to follow him anywhere.) After the Silver Bullet, Suzi best remembers a Duke student who apparently made the rounds. "I think she broke up someone's marriage over there. Larry said, 'She was a busy, busy girl.' She was a pretty girl, too, I have to say—but he didn't get attached." (Thank goodness, as we shall see . . .)

*

Larry still had classes to wrap up his degree, but with empty pockets to fill after not working at Buff's last summer, he was eager to make money—and now no longer an amateur, he could do it playing basketball. Accustomed to barnstorming around the Lehigh Valley in the off-season, he banded together with the best of his ACC opponents—Duke's Mike Lewis, State's Eddie Biedenbach, South Carolina's Skip Harlicka—who became known as the Miller All-Stars, and began playing exhibitions against other semipro teams in towns around the south. It was showtime, Larry averaging 50–55 points a game (at least one in the 70s) as the fans treated them like rock stars, especially in the North Carolina towns. "It got so hectic, for one of the games I pre-signed some autographs and just threw them into the crowd." Making a sweet couple of hundred bucks a night off his star power, it wasn't long before Miller stockpiled a nice wad of cash to tide him over until the pro league drafts came calling with his future.

*

In 1968 the National Basketball Association was facing an existential crisis. For a generation the only pro league in the country with a national reach— still always featuring the Celtics who'd won nine of its last ten champion- ships—the NBA was suddenly being challenged by an upstart league using funny, multicolored balls, exciting new rules like the 3-point shot, and out- right showmanship. Worst of all the inexperienced owners of the fledgling American Basketball Association teams were businessmen with money to spend. Earlier in the decade, an upstart football league called the AFL had bushwhacked the NFL by signing 75% of the established league's first-round draft picks, including the Heisman Trophy winner. Mindful of this, the NBA had a problem: With the league finals not ending until early May, and their college draft slated to begin May 8, how could they prevent the new league from scooping up the best college talent before it was their turn? The solu- tion: On April 3, a month before their season ended, the NBA drafted its first round only, laying claim to the best of the best.

With Lew Alcindor and Pete Maravich still underclassmen, only three consensus First Team All-Americans were available. Unsurprisingly Elvin Hayes was chosen first (and instantly became the NBA's top scorer the next year). Wes Unseld was picked second (and even as a rookie became the league MVP). That left Larry Miller . . . who was still left after the first eight play- ers taken were centers, reflecting the league's obsession with height. Then left behind again, even when less honored forwards and guards were chosen. (Some genius from the Atlanta Hawks actually skipped over the two-time ACC Player of the Year in favor of South Carolina guard Skip Harlicka whose senior stats were good but who washed out of pro basketball his first year with a 4 ppg average.) By the end of the day, Larry Miller had not been chosen for perhaps the first time in his life.

People who had seen Larry play found this mind-boggling, but there were explanations. Billy Cunningham relates, "I would guess he was seen as a 'tweener.' Everybody in those days would look for a certain size to put you in a cookie-cutter position. To be a small forward, you've got to be 6'6". If he's a 2-guard, did he have the range to be consistent outside?" Billy concedes that scouting was haphazard in those days, and Scott Beeten thinks it's possible the league failed to evaluate a player whose heart played beyond his height.

Roommate Suzi was there for Larry's reaction: "He was never a whiner. He may have made a statement like, 'Hey, boy, guess I'm getting humbled here.' It was a rude awakening. But whether he was losing sleep about it, I don't really know." What he was certainly losing was respect for the NBA's common sense, its underwhelming contracts and, yeah, "It was a personal affront to me. After that, I kind of soured on the NBA."

Meanwhile, the ABA, hungry for legitimacy, recognized the plum left sitting on the table. Specifically, the owner of the Los Angeles Stars—who had witnessed Larry's play in the Final Four up close, and had also noticed the looks Larry drew in Hollywood and saw promotional opportunities for this cover boy of 1968's *NCAA Collegiate Basketball Guide*—quickly made Larry the Stars first-round pick. At that point, as far as Larry was concerned, "If I got a fair offer from the Stars, I was going to take it—because I was pissed."

\*

One of the sportswriters covering the ACC that year was Leonard Laye of the *Charlotte News*, at first a familiar face in the locker rooms and then a friend. "We all wound up hanging out, and Larry's personality was so outgoing, he could adapt to anybody," says Laye who also covered NASCAR. One day after basketball season he invited Catty's amateur drag racer to come along to Rockingham Speedway, then a three-year-old flat oval track in the sandhills below Pinehurst. NASCAR was much more informal back then, and Larry got a celebrity seat for the ride of his life when Leonard told him that, next time there was a caution flag, he wanted Larry to come down to the pits with him.

"So next time there was a yellow flag—this is actually *during* the race— Leonard and I jumped into the pace car, hunkered down in the back seat behind the driver, and he heads out on the track saying, 'Don't put your head up until I tell you to look.' So we're driving around the track, and suddenly he says 'Look!' I look up and all these cars behind us are going 90 or 120 mph down the straightaway right at us . . . and then we veer into the pits, and they wave the flag, and these guys are off! So I really got hooked on it after that." And that was just a taste of the extreme fun waiting on Larry two more years down the road.

Larry's own wheels, however, went out of commission that spring after the beautiful GS400's driver once again had trouble getting it home one night. "That one bit the dust when I gunned it up the hill to University Gardens. The street was dark and someone had parked his car hanging out in the road, and I smacked right into it. So my car was totaled."

*

In an era when pro teams refused to talk with an agent, Carolina players often put their trust in Coach Smith. Following through on his pledge to be the servant of every player in the off-season, determined to help Larry be successful, Smith consulted people about the state of play in the pros and bided his time. Then the LA Stars invested in a Hall of Fame coach, the former Boston Celtic Bill Sharman, on April 29. At that point, with the rest of the NBA draft set to resume in a week, the leverage was with Smith and the only remaining All-American: Did the Stars want to wait, roll the dice on which NBA team finally offered Miller, and risk a bidding war? Or were they ready to make their best offer for the stud matinee idol before the NBA got back in the game?

Two days after joining the Stars, Bill Sharman was in Chapel Hill.

Still stung that no one from the NBA had even talked to him prior to their first round, Larry was in no mood to wait for a league whose opinion of him was still uncertain and, instead, looked to where the love was, telling the *Greensboro Daily News,* "I saw what happened to Bob Lewis. He signed with San Francisco and didn't get anywhere last year. At least with Los Angeles I'll be starting."

Suzi Mutascio recalls, "We were actually there when the pro teams were courting Larry. I remember the day he came in and said, 'This is it, I'm going to talk to the reps from the LA Stars today. Keep your fingers crossed for me, and I'll be back later.' He was nervous, I can tell you that. And when he walked back in our open door, he kind of just floated in saying, 'I did sign, I hope I made the right decision. It was six figures, so I hope that's what I should have done.' He's kind of bouncing this off us, and I didn't know much, but I said, 'Sounds good, Larry.' "

In fact, it was a terrific deal. The ACC players taken ahead of Larry in the NBA's first round got offers of $17,500 for their first year—and if you don't like our draft, Uncle Sam has one for you. The Stars offered $25,000, and by the time Coach Smith had Carolina's legal people look over the contract, Dean had talked them up to $35,000 a year . . . for three years . . . guaranteed . . . *and* a $5,000 signing bonus. "That was a monster contract back then," Larry explains. "And Dean got the money put into escrow, so no matter what happened to the league I would be paid. So I was happy with that—and you only worked half a year, so you could make more on the side if you wanted to."

"Dean pulled all the strings for those kinds of things," says Monty Diamond, who came to know a lot of players. "They left it up to him to handle, and he did. He got the best deals for all those guys."

(Jim Heavner recalls that a decade later, when Phil Ford was drafted #2 overall, Smith didn't like the Kings' offer and bluffed that Ford had a better offer from Spain—and would return in a few years when he could be a free agent. "Dean had Phil on the way to the airport—he'd actually bought him a ticket—when the Kings caved and he got him a much better contract. I mean, Dean could play poker.")

*

Now, between the wad of cash he'd pocketed barnstorming the south, the insurance settlement from the wrecked GS400, and the contract from the Stars, Larry finally had himself a spanking new white Corvette convertible— not the one Mama Leone's tried to bribe him with . . . not the one he borrowed from Reggie to drive through the dark four springs earlier—this was all his, and he had earned every penny of it. The man and machine were clearly made for each other, as Larry cruised through the village in bloom with the top down, bare chested, sunglasses on, music booming, and coeds flocking to stare in his wake.

"I remember *that*—I rode in it!" laughs Charles Scott. "At that time Larry's Corvette was the biggest thing on campus!" The Heels' two All-ACC spark plugs could hang together in Chapel Hill, but moving on in almost any direction meant traveling separate paths. Vacationing after the season, for instance . . . "You've got to understand the south in the '60s—blacks and whites did not coexist—so at times there was no way we could hang out together. If they went to Myrtle Beach, there was no way I could go—because no black kids were allowed on the beach! Or going down to The Masters, there's no *way* I could go." Professionally, too, Charles notes, "After the season I had to go to the Olympic trials, came back in April to finish school and then I was gone up to West Point. And then I didn't see Larry again, because he was playing out in LA."

Meanwhile, Larry was being courted again, now by several NFL teams like the Dallas Cowboys who sent a letter inviting him to try out as a free agent tight end. He was flattered, of course, but already had a better deal in LA. Instead, he kept playing All-Star games in places like Greensboro, where the *Daily News* reported: "Miller was delayed in entering the Grimsley Gym because of a blonde in a miniskirt. She followed him from a stop light and parked beside his Corvette." But the only female to win his heart that year was a real dog . . . a puppy named Timi.

That story begins with Larry and "just some girl that I met one night" (whose name he can't remember), and the girl had a dog named Schatzi (apparently more memorable). "She was a beautiful German Shepherd puppy, but would poop and pee all over her living room because the girl wasn't taking care of the dog—and she asked if I would want it. And of course being the dog lover I am I readily agreed." (Recalls a wry Suzi Mutascio, "I think the girl only lasted two more days after he got the dog.") "Then there were various times when my roommate Monty and I were imbibing, and there was a James Brown song where James shouted out 'Tim!'—so we came up with

Timi as the name for the dog." Over the next years, Timi would share more of Larry's adventures than any other living creature . . . until it was her time to go.

\*

It was May, and Larry was finishing up his academic credits, when a romantic liaison boomeranged, threatening everything he'd worked for at North Carolina. No, Larry hadn't done somebody wrong—the young lady had—and he was about to pay the price. The busy, busy girl who Larry (among others) was dating had been writing papers for Duke football players, a violation of the nearby university's Honor Code, a scandal that caused at least one player to be kicked off the Duke team.

"Then rumor had it they thought I had something to do with that, and they were going to get back at me by setting me up. They might plant some drugs on me, or cause me some other problems." Realizing he could be ambushed at any time with charges that could void his ABA contract and stain his own and his school's reputations, Larry saw only one option: "We skedaddled fast out of Chapel Hill and up to Pennsylvania to stay with my parents for the summer." (Let the record show that "we" includes Timi, not the girl.)

The hasty departure came at a cost, though. Trying to do it all that spring, Larry had sometimes missed classes while barnstorming out of town where he had to stay overnight and he'd fallen behind. So after he called Tommy Lloyd to say he was taking off abruptly—still one credit short of his degree—Larry's academic stat line ironically reflected the antithesis of his career at UNC: "Incomplete."

\*

Even as Larry set off from Chapel Hill, he left North Carolina with one more critical "recruit" that he and the world were as yet unaware of. Up in the mountain town of Asheville, a high school coach had been raving about UNC's program and especially Larry Miller ever since witnessing "The Shot"

*A 1968 full-page ad in the Wall Street Journal, heralding
the emerging glamour of North Carolina's winning basketball programs
to tout the state as a land of opportunity.*

at Wake Forest. That spring, one of his players turned down a full scholarship to Georgia Tech toward a career in Engineering, hoping to follow in his coach's footsteps by working his way through UNC instead. The boy's name was Roy Williams.

Decades later, now a Hall of Fame coach with three NCAA championship banners hanging in the Smith Center rafters, Coach Williams recalls, "Larry Miller was one of those mythical figures to me, seeing him play on TV—he was one of my heroes. There's no doubt in my mind that the success that Coach Smith had in those three years, in which Larry was certainly a dominant figure, is the reason that I chose to come to North Carolina. That laid the road I was going to travel."

\*

The following year, Charles Scott would fill Miller's star slot and, along with the class of '69, win Coach Smith's third-straight regular season title, third straight ACC Tournament championship, and UNC's third straight Final Four appearance for an unprecedented "three-peat" that's never been matched by any ACC school to this day. Charles would ultimately pass Larry as UNC's second all-time scorer, become a two-time All-American and three-time All-ACC player, himself, and go on to be a five-time pro All-Star and NBA champion with the Boston Celtics. And yet, four decades later, when the *Durham Herald-Sun* chose the Top 50 College players in the history of the esteemed ACC, Larry Miller—still the only UNC player ever twice-named ACC Player of the Year and ACC Tournament MVP—led the entire UNC cavalcade of stars at #5, followed by Scott at #7 and Phil Ford at #8 (Michael Jordan was picked #11) illustrating that, for those in the know, Miller's significance to the Tar Heel program and the glamour of the ACC was about more than statistics.

Charles Scott, for one, has never doubted who the keystone was of modern North Carolina basketball. "People need to understand, Larry was the winner who made Coach Smith a winner. Like Bill Russell started the Boston Celtics tradition, Larry Miller *is* the tradition that Carolina talks about. Everything starts with him."

# CHAPTER 8

# LA STARS & BOOGIE NIGHTS

Larry's white Corvette was the coolest car that ever pulled into the driveway on Wood Street, but arriving home unexpectedly he discovered his parents were away in the mountains. They already knew about the Stars contract, though, and that their grateful son was transferring $5,000 a year to them as a gift. "They didn't need or want that, but I wanted to do that for them."

Once Larry unloaded the car and settled Timi, there remained one last mission to cap his college playing career: He retrieved the letter his mom had saved for four years, and finally read Vic Bubas' best wishes for a college experience that was now already in the record books. "After the last game against Duke I told Coach Bubas I hadn't read it yet because I'd been too torn up about my decision. He just wished me good luck and was nothing but a gentleman." Now, Larry was relieved to find the letter was incredibly gracious and classy. "It was a great letter. I really respected him."

Then Larry wheeled the white 'Vette around Catty, introducing it to all his old haunts and old classmates like the Rough Rider's team manager. Recalls Doug Miller, "I was walking home from the playground basketball court when a new Corvette pulled up beside me. Then the window buzzed down and the driver called out, 'Herr D, hop in!' So Larry gave me a lift up the hill to my house. He told me he had just signed his pro contract with the LA Stars and that he had an upcoming TV appearance on The Dating Game."

Larry stopped by Buff's garage, of course, but for the first summer in recent memory—with a dream job waiting for him a continent away and more than enough money to have too much fun on—he didn't need work at the gas station. Instead, Larry's instincts told him this could be his last chance to play hard, and if there was fun to be had, he'd earned the right to grab all he could.

It had been two years since running wild with the Pagans gave way to the rigor of Coach Smith's first ACC championship and Final Four campaign. Following that, Larry got barely a whiff of the Summer of Love on his way to play for his country overseas, and then he'd plunged into another relentless run all the way to the final game of his last college season. Add to this the 30-game barnstorming tour that spring—virtually another full season, making essentially two seasons in one—and it's no surprise that Larry was physically and mentally drained. All he wanted now was a summer off, perhaps to explore that strange new trip the rest of his generation were on.

The upstanding Miller home was no place for what Larry had in mind, though, so he did what Lehigh Valley boys have always done chasing hedonism away from prying eyes—he went "down the shore" to Atlantic City. There he met a good guy named George Sutor who played at LaSalle and was tending bar at a place called Maloney's. The bars at Somers Point would open at 2:00 in the morning, so you could stay up all night if you wanted to be crazy, the beers at Maloney's were seven for $1 and, with birth control pills now widely used, the love was free. Sutor soon fixed Larry up with a share in a party house in Margate for $150, and there he spent most of his summer immersed in the indiscriminate pleasures of the '60s counterculture.

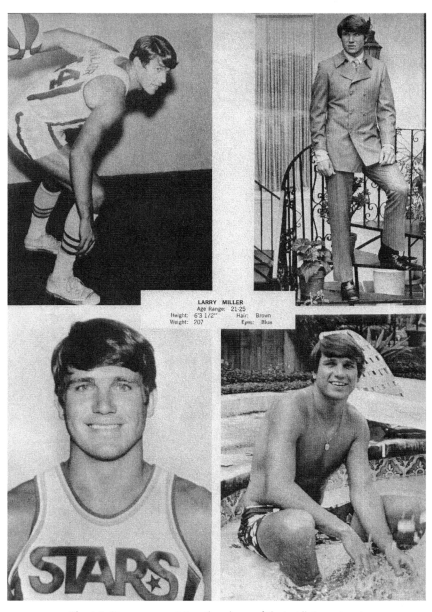

LARRY MILLER
Age Range: 21-25
Height: 6'3 1/2"  Hair: Brown
Weight: 207  Eyes: Blue

*The LA Stars, recognizing the draw of their All-American's good looks, encouraged his flirtation with acting. The Edwardian suit in this talent agency headshot was only the beginning of Larry's sartorial adventures in the 1970s.*

Larry was on the move all summer long, making sure that whatever was being passed around, he would be in on it: "I was on speed dial back then. 'Who needs me now?' Somebody calls me up, 'Okay, I'll be right there.' I didn't want to miss anything! Just keep going. I worked out a little on the beach . . . but I was driving a Corvette, not thinking about basketball."

*

One adventure that freewheeling spring was a rendezvous with Monty at his grandparents' place on Fifth Avenue at 87th Street in New York. ("That place was big-time, overlooking Central Park.") From there, the college boys did the town, seeing bands at the Fillmore East, and networking with the city's Carolina mafia, including the legendary beauty, Zacki Murphy. "She'd been a model for a year, although she was short for a model," Monty recalls. "And she treated us like country cousins, because she'd already arrived and thought of us as Chapel Hill people." That didn't bother Larry at all: "Of course she was full of herself, she was supposed to be—she was a hottie. But that was just a short visit, because I was moving around so fast . . ."

It wasn't long, though, before Larry realized he was hooked on a female so close to his heart that he would chase her for years. Yes, we mean Timi. Larry had gotten his mother a cute stuffed monkey doll which Timi paid too much attention to while no one was looking . . . until Larry came home and found she'd torn it to pieces. "And of course I got mad at her and sent her out to the yard. But the gates of the driveway were unlocked, so when I went out again she wasn't there anymore. I assumed she'd gone and left me, so I drove my Corvette all over town, looking for her everywhere, until I finally gave up and came home feeling awful. And as I got out, I glanced in the back seat and there she was . . . just staring at me. She'd been there the whole time."

As the summer unfurled, with Larry commuting between Catty, the Jersey shore, and Los Angeles, Timi was often left in his parents' care. "But she went down to the shore with me a couple times, and everybody loved her," he remembers proudly. "And my parents would take her up to the cabin on weekends if I wasn't there."

\*

Larry had outplayed the NBA's rebuff to score a monster contract, and then dodged the vengeful Blue Devils, but suddenly his happily-ever-after was bushwhacked by an even tougher threat right there in his own back yard: His local draft board, noting his college deferment had expired, summoned Larry to a pre-draft physical. "Getting drafted to Vietnam wasn't imminent," he recalls, "but I was still among the hunted." So was his grade school buddy, Tim Fisher, and one morning they met up at the Salvation Army in Allentown at 5:00 AM for an uneasy bus ride together to the Army hospital in Wilkes-Barre. It was there, after being measured, poked and prodded, that Larry got one of the biggest surprises of his young life.

Unable to bend over fully because of a knee he'd torn in a high school football huddle, the two-time ACC Player of the Year was declared 4-F and disqualified from military service. Larry—who'd been ready to take what-ever was coming—knew better than to dally when good luck whistled, and scrammed out of there. "I was so excited I didn't wait for the bus. I hitchhiked all the way home way before anybody else was done." Relieved and elated as he waved a thumbs-up to the world, Larry was still too young to know that not all good luck goes unpunished . . .

\*

Larry rode his good fortune all the way to Los Angeles to meet with the Stars, who put him up near the same MacArthur Park that was the subject of a romantic radio epic about someone leaving a cake out in the rain. Living virtually in the soundtrack of 1968's biggest hit, he thought, "Am I living in a dream here or what?"

The Stars, assuming they had the answer to every rookie's prayer to avoid Vietnam, had already made arrangements for Larry to join the Long Beach Reserve. The deal meant he'd have to sign up right away, spend the summer going through Basic Training, and then he'd be out just in time for the basketball season. To a spirited twenty-two-year-old kid already ground down by the pace of success, though, the offer felt like an ambush—one more straightjacket of rules and regulations feeding him relentlessly into yet another long season of schedules and following orders with nary a break. "So I told the Stars 'I'm 4-F, I don't think we have anything to worry about.' Also I don't know if the Guard would have accepted me at 4-F. So I chose a summer of sin and debauchery over common sense."

Larry first arranged to crash in Manhattan Beach with a group of guys including new teammate Steve Chubin, just paying them something whenever he stayed there while getting his new life squared away. "It was La-La Land and I was right in the middle of it. It's tough to recall where I was when, because that whole summer was such a haze . . . like, 'I'm in a daze.'"

Life was less glamorous back in Pennsylvania, and it was about this time that Larry got a call from his mom. "She told me Timi had been in such pain that she had to let her out in the yard. And finally she pulled a tapeworm out of Timi's mouth—something like twenty to thirty feet long—and she saved the dog's life. I don't know if I could have done that.

"But I had such a good time that summer—I was everywhere. One weekend I decided I'm catching a plane back to the East Coast. So I got a ride from Manhattan Beach to LAX, flew to Philadelphia, and someone took me down to Margate—so I was on the beach of both oceans the same day. And it was nonstop parties . . ."

To this day, Larry sounds like an anthropologist amazed by what he found. "Down there we had five bedrooms, but nobody had their own room. One time I was taking a shower and a girl came in and took a shower with me. I have no idea where she came from. Another night, there were so many people there I slept in a closet with this girl, and I had to put my feet up in the air. Then another night I was asleep with a woman I had just met, and George knocks on the door. He says, 'Mills, I got you another one.' So the girl I was with got up and left, and the other one came in. That was obliging of both of them. And I never even knew either one of them! I'd be thinking, 'Why would I want to go to LA right now? Because look at this!' George told me that one day he was with six different women. But I wasn't even close, I was just enjoying myself. Talk about a Summer of Love.

"In hindsight, not going into the Reserve was probably the biggest mistake of my life," Larry reflects. "I would have been in great shape that fall, and gone in every summer after that, and eventually become an officer and had a second career in my life. But I needed a rest, and having fun every day sounded great to me at the time."

*

However reluctantly, Larry recognized that all summers come to an end, and following his routine of previous years he started running on the beach in late July. That's when George Sutor suggested they go up to Philadelphia to stay with his family and play a game or two with the Baker League. The Baker League was informal but dead serious, like Catasauqua's summer league on steroids, more similar to the Rucker Park games in Harlem where Charles Scott and other legends made their names.

This was the year that Martin Luther King was killed in April (on Larry's birthday) and Bobby Kennedy had been shot that June. "This was where the riots were, and I'm this white guy pulling in with my white '68 Corvette with racing slicks—and I hit a pothole that busted my oil pan. They said, 'If you leave your car here overnight, it'll be up on blocks and taken apart by morning.' Fortunately, the sponsor of our team had a gas station and he had it towed right away and fixed by the next morning, ready to go."

The local players' main impression of Larry was that he was . . . very tan. "One of the guys on the team looked at me and said, 'Damn, you're so dark, if a riot breaks out and the cops come after you, just pull your pants down and show your white ass and they'll let you go.' "

This competition was a reality check for Larry as he began playing himself into shape. "I tried to play, but I wasn't a regular and I'd been enjoying myself too much to impress anyone with my basketball skills." And that was before 1968's NBA Rookie of the Year, Earl ("The Pearl") Monroe, showed up at halftime and really sharpened Larry's attention.

"The crowd is chanting 'Pearl . . . Pearl . . . Pearl . . .' and he had 49 points in the second half. And I was my fat self, but he gave me the ball some and I had 20 or 30 points—not bad, but I was kind of embarrassed I didn't look anything like him. Watching him when the crowd went nuts, you were watching magic . . . magic. That's what it's all about—the neighborhood— you had to be there. Later on, one of the All-Pros said, 'God couldn't guard him.' "

Sobered that he had serious work to do, Larry realized it was time to get off the beach and head to LA. "It was good timing, because if I'd stayed there in Margate my demise would have been imminent. Taking the summer off turned out to be a mistake, because normally you like to go into your first year in impressive shape, and I wasn't established. I know I was really bad, but by the time the season started, I couldn't have been that far off."

*

Larry was now so flush that he could hire someone else to drive the white Corvette out to California for him, while he flew in for good with Timi on board. He would still be living on the beach, but life on this ocean was seething with ambition and endless possibilities a world away from the Lehigh Valley.

Almost as soon as Larry arrived, he was contacted through the Stars' office by a legendary talent agent who'd watched him play in the Final Four. Vincent Chase (his name would later be borrowed for the lead character of the HBO hit "Entourage") set Larry up with acting lessons at Universal Studios, so the rookie could double down on Hollywood stardom.

"I used to be able to drive into the Universal campus—I had a pass— and the tour buses would go by with people staring, thinking I was some sort of actor. One of my study partners was Fredricka Myers, and one day Robert Conrad, the star of 'The Wild, Wild West' show—he was only 5'8"—came up to me and asked me to introduce them. It turned out they dated for a while, and he actually got her a starring role in a TV movie called 'D.A.: Murder One,' but then they parted ways. I guess that's how Hollywood works. Back then everybody was surging to be in the spotlight, trying to get connections, and I was involved in all of that—not only because I wanted to be part of it, but because, being on the Stars, I already *was* part of it. I could get all those promotional gigs, because being a basketball player I had something else to talk about as an actor. So when I started to study acting, they accepted me."

*

Meanwhile, the ABA was still auditioning, too. When Bobby Lewis graduated a year ahead of Larry, there were so many problems with teams and players not getting paid that Bobby relates, "What Coach did for Larry, negotiating with the ABA, he couldn't do for me because the league was not established enough that you could deal with anybody." (Instead, Lewis took the take-it-or-leave-it offer from the NBA's San Francisco Warriors, including a seven-year stint in the National Guard.)

The new teams had a plan though—add showmanship like oddball cheerleaders and halftime dunking contests—and by the second year it seemed to be working. Ticket sales were up in most cities, seven of the eleven teams now had TV contracts, and the Anaheim Amigos, rechristened the Stars, would now play in the downtown LA Sports Arena.

This was a lure to the future Hall of Fame coach of the NBA Warriors, Bill Sharman, who'd gone to Southern Cal and considered the Stars' new home one of the three or four best basketball arenas in the nation. The Stars threw money at him, of course, but Sharman was also intrigued by pioneering a new league. Known for bringing out the best in younger players, and convinced the Stars' owners had deep enough pockets to sustain losses for several years, Sharman saw potential in the overlooked All-American Miller and—mindful that the ABA favored teams signing local stars—openly hoped to add hometown hero Alcindor in the following year's draft.

Larry Miller's mission on joining the Stars was simpler: Find his best role in a whole new game, silence the skeptics, and prove he belonged. In high school and college, Larry's broad array of skills was a gift to Coaches Mushrush and Smith who could deploy him wherever they needed dominance. For many in the pro game, though, Larry was not both a forward and a guard—he was neither. As early as the ACC Tournament in Charlotte, scouts warned that desire, toughness and being a complete player would not be enough for a "tweener" who didn't fit the regimented way the pro game was played.

Introducing local fans to the Stars' new catch that summer, *The Los Angeles Times* had dutifully described Larry as the top athlete from one of the country's toughest conferences. It paid homage to his All-American frame and looks. And then the paper went on to warn that he was essentially a cripple: "He has a collapsed cartilage in his left knee. The first knuckle on his left, shooting, hand is about half the size of a ping-pong ball because of traumatic rheumatism. The abductor tendons in both his upper legs are torn. And last week, after initial workouts with the Stars, he was suffering from foot infections in four separate places." Ouch.

These conditions were not widely known in ACC country, where Coach Bubas referred to the indestructible Player of the Year as "Superman." Larry, himself, shrugged the injuries off. "The only things that really bother me are the torn leg tendons," he told *The Times*. "I hurt them in practice before the World Games. I was supposed to take three months' rest, but I just got some shots and played anyway. Maybe because of that, the legs bothered me all of last year, so I was really hampered."

Preseason camp ran through September, and Larry set out to prove that he could still be a forward, even at 6'4" and not yet in top shape. And Sharman liked his rookie's attitude, comparing him to Rick Barry who treated everything like a war. Having laid out enough money to keep the All-American away from the NBA, Sharman planned to get his money's worth by using Larry as a swingman, comparing him to Elgin Baylor: "I think he drives for the basket as hard as any college player I've ever seen."

*

It was during training camp that Larry realized the scale of Los Angeles was also a drawback. With Sharman running two practices a day in North LA—spread out from 10:00 AM–1:00 PM and then 5:00 PM–7:30 PM, there was hardly time to drive up and back from his beach digs twice, so Larry simply hung out between practices with his black teammates—Eldridge Webb,

Warren Davis, and Merv Jackson. "We'd get some wine and tell stories and became really good friends. That's how I got through that first year. It could have been good, but we had no leaders. We were all rookies or veterans who didn't show any leadership.

"I used to go down to Watts with those guys to party at the clubs with them—I was in Watts after the riots—and I did just fine, probably because I'd been to so many all-black clubs where I was the only white person in there. One night in Watts with my buddies—they knew I drove a Corvette—Eldridge Webb wanted me to take him to the store, and on the way back we turned a corner and I spun the thing out, lost control of it, we were heading right for a tree . . . and all of a sudden it made a U-turn and flipped right into a perfect parking spot. His eyes got so big—'Motherf—how did you do that?!' I acted like I knew what I was doing, but I had no idea.

"But then, on the road, we'd go into a place in Houston and my black friends couldn't get into the clubs there. They said my buddies weren't dressed properly. I just said, 'Let's get the hell out of here.' It was a strange time."

One thing Larry appreciated most definitely about being a pro was the freedom to operate without Coach Smith's spies tracking his behavior. He could go off and do almost anything—which he did—still burning the candle at both ends. Late one night back in Charlotte, the phone rang in Leonard Laye's house and it was Larry on the line. "He said, 'You're never going to believe this—it's expensive out here! I'm spending fifty bucks a night when I go out.' Because back in those days we were used to going home after a game and drinking beers or whatever. Or if we went out, ten dollars later you were good. So I was like, 'Fifty dollars?!' I was blown away."

✳

The new team was fighting for fans against the established Lakers, featuring stars like Jerry West and Wilt Chamberlain, so they had to pull out all the stops. The Stars promoted the ABA with raffish team photos, and Larry remembers TV appearances playing ball with little kids ("Truth or Consequences, maybe?"), and almost getting onto "The Joey Bishop Show."

"He wanted me and the coach to come on, but Coach kept us in practice too long, so when we got to the studio it was too late and we just sat in the audience and watched it."

The highlight of Larry's guest slots was his appearance on "The Dating Game," in which Larry, teammate Bobby Warren, and a third guy competed for the favors of an aspiring actress who couldn't see them. It didn't go exactly as planned. "My first mistake was saying I was from Allentown—which is where I was born—which got all the people from Catty ticked off. But then I won the girl, I think because her agent deemed that I was the best fit for her." Suzi Wood, who was watching back East, remembers how he did it. "The girl asked, very earnestly, 'Will I fall in love with you?' And you know how confident Larry is—he says, 'Eventually.' And we were all just cracking up!"

The prize was an overnight trip to Las Vegas for the instant couple, but there was a hitch—the Stars had a game scheduled that night—so Larry gallantly gave away the trip to the girl and her boyfriend. (Of course the girl had a boyfriend; TV dating was simply career PR.) "And I thought that was it . . . until a couple weeks later her agent calls me up and asks me out. It turns out he was gay and he thought I was, too, because I didn't go away with the girl. So I went on 'The Dating Game'—and I won a guy! That's gotta be a first."

*

It only took Larry a couple of weeks to get in shape because, even when he was living on beer, he'd been running every day. He'd finally played his way into condition and life looked pretty good until, right as the season started, the Stars played an opening game against New Orleans that set the tone of his entire pro career.

"I started, and I'm having a decent game [high scorer, actually], shooting about 20, maybe 13 rebounds. The game is on the line, coming down to the wire—I think we were tied with about a minute to go—and Coach Sharman pulls me out of the game. Okay, I figure it's a breather and he'll put me back in . . . but he never does, and we lose. And I'm just dumbfounded.

This is *me*, my whole career is about the end of the game—that's where I belong!"

Anyone with a passing knowledge of Miller's rep should have known he was a crunch time winner—the kind of player who, in later decades, would be nicknamed "Money." Even with very little television exposure in 1968, how Sharman could have missed this essential quality of his prize rookie was a head-scratcher, since leaving this guy on the bench as a game expired was like stepping over a hundred dollar bill on the sidewalk. But as baffled as Larry was, it never occurred to him to ask for an explanation—and Sharman never offered one. "You just didn't do that in those days," Scott Beeten says. "It wasn't respectful."

"So that was the harbinger of things to come," says Miller, reliving the echo of his old summer league lesson that you're not always in control of your own destiny. "And it would happen again and again. At first you don't know what's what. Sharman was an astute basketball guy, and I guess a lot of that was my fault, because when I first got there I was still not in the best shape—though I got in shape pretty fast. I guess he just wanted somebody better in. But apparently he didn't know anything about me."

*

Later that fall, Larry ran into a couple of guys who had a place down the coast on Hermosa Beach and were looking for another roommate. There, in the spacious house at 52B Strand, Larry and Timi finally settled down (if you can call it that) right on the water. There were four other roommates, seven surfboards in the garage that belonged to everybody, and as he told a local scribe, "We've got something going on here all the time—and the place looks it."

"The boardwalk was right there, it was just a great location. We'd open the doors at night—this was before the Manson killings, so people still left their doors open—and Timi would walk out to the beach and spend hours walking along the water. No one was out there at night, so she was safe to come and go as she pleased and loved to roam. And when she got back, then we'd close up. You couldn't do that these days."

When Larry first moved in he got one of the downstairs bedrooms where he played hard and happily with only the willing, with no harm and no fouls called. The beach pad was catnip to Larry's young and restless queens-for-a-day, like the stewardess who sent him precise Arrival and Departure schedules of her LAX layovers (= sleepovers). And then there was the playmate from the next town down the beach, forever known as "Wanda from Redonda."

Living in the manner of twenty-two-year-olds with a casual sense of privacy, Larry had two mattresses on the floor of his downstairs bedroom, one of which was sometimes crashed on by his teammate Steve Chubin. "He knew Wanda was coming by, but he wanted to abstain from sex to hype his game up, and he said he'd just sleep and not say a word. So she and I started fooling around in the dark, and about the time she's getting ready you can hear it and her legs are around my head—and all of a sudden we hear this voice in the dark like a PA announcer: '*Substitution . . . Chubin for Miller!*' And she froze so hard her legs almost broke my neck. So we jumped up, both of us covered in sheets, and ran right out to the ocean and finished our business on the sand."

Of more concern to Larry was the welfare of his main squeeze, Timi. Larry's roommates liked the pup so much that when he traveled away with the team they wouldn't let her out. Instead they'd sit around the big room upstairs eating on the floor and let the dog poop all over the place. And they lived with it until Larry returned home and had to clean it up. And those were the good times.

"One time, when I was on the road, they told me she didn't come home for three or four days. There used to be a dogcatcher on the beach, but he never could catch Timi, so they called around looking for her and finally went to the ASPCA. It turns out she was in a shelter because she'd fallen into the water and gotten caught up with some logs, and somebody had rescued her. So they hauled her back after being gone almost five days—and she made it through LA."

*

The white Corvette's days were numbered, though, and it would not live to see 1969. It met its demise on the 405 expressway when Larry, with a 52B Strand roommate, skidded into a concrete barrier going about 80 mph. Fortunately, they hit it on a glance, causing the car's fiberglass body to disintegrate around them while leaving the guys untouched. The four cops who immediately arrived at the scene found them still strapped into their bucket seats in the frame, laughing hysterically. "The cops asked us, 'Is everybody alright?' and we said, 'Yeah, fine' . . . and they left us alone." One more time, Larry had faked out Death behind the wheel of a car, like a matador tucked behind his red cape as tragedy hurtled by, missing him by a whisker.

More reflective now, Larry says, "When I got a little older I started slowing down. But out there that first year I could have killed myself. Being young, having all that money, and with my free spirit—especially in those times—there were so many ways to go . . ."

*

Playing forward early in the season, Larry learned the hard way that he was, after all, simply not tall enough to have the impact he wanted there (in part because the ABA's heavy contact seldom resulted in foul calls for his customary 3-point play). His tenacious defense kept him on the court, though, and by December Sharman was starting him at guard, overcoming a slow start to average about 15 points a game. "At guard, I've got a better chance to take my man inside and work on him," he told the press. "I'm driving more than I ever did at Carolina." He wasn't yet playing his typical Miller game, though, not shooting as much from outside, but he knew he needed to start. Most important, although his playing time ranged from the full 48 minutes to less than 24 minutes a game, he was getting far more court time than his NBA brethren, just as he'd expected. As he told *The Charlotte Observer*, "I talked to Bobby Lewis the other day . . . and until some people get hurt he isn't getting a chance to play. No matter how good you are, you can't make it sitting on the bench."

Larry got a taste of the musical chairs nature of the unsteady ABA watching his voyeur roommate, Steve Chubin, bounce through three different teams in December alone. "He got traded away to Minnesota, and their first game back in LA I went up to his room to say Hi. And the door was wide open, Steve was there naked, a car dealer there was naked, and a lady in bed was naked but covered up. Now, that team had a badass coach, really into discipline and doing bed checks, but they had the door open, not caring about anything. And after smoking some cigars, I said I had to go hit curfew and headed off to the elevator . . . and when the door opened the coach got off. So as I'm going down I knew this wasn't going to be good—and Steve was traded and on a plane to somewhere else the next day. But obviously he didn't care."

\*

The big promotion in early December was the Stars hiring the belly dancer, Little Egypt (granddaughter of the original Little Egypt, whose performance at the 1893 Chicago World's Fair allegedly gave Mark Twain a near-fatal heart attack), and her job was to, um . . . teach the players how to exercise their pelvises? Yeah, that's it. And, by the way, what a swell photo op she provided by putting the mop-topped Miller through her erotic poses. "It was a gas," Larry told a reporter. "She taught us some exercises Dean Smith never did. The one I liked best was the one where you cup your hands behind your head and roll your belly. It really builds up the solar plexus." Sure, pal.

*Larry studies Little Egypt's belly dancer moves in an item that appeared in Sports Illustrated.*

By the turn of the year, Larry was seeing time at both guard and forward, and if not dominating as he had in school and college, he was firmly established as a starter now leading the team in scoring, often hitting in the mid-20s. He was also an unabashed booster of his new league, pitching that ABA games were as well played and entertaining as any in the NBA, and that the older league's players were coming to envy the better-paid insurgents. "Whenever an NBA player knocks our league, you know it's really the NBA owners talking," he told *The Los Angeles Times*. "The owners have told them to say those things. But I've talked to NBA players, and they can't believe the salaries we're making. I played with Earl Monroe in the Charles Baker League in Philadelphia, and he said he was sorry he didn't sign with Pittsburgh in our league. He was thinking about pride when he signed with the Baltimore Bullets [NBA]. But there's a time when you say the hell with pride. You've got to make a living."

*

That February of 1969, the constant morphing of ABA rosters broke in the Stars' favor with the arrival of an NBA talent named George Lehmann. Four years older than Larry, a deadly shooter, and a cannier student of the game than many coaches, Lehmann would one day become Larry's favorite teammate in the pros . . . but not with the LA Stars.

As a high school senior, young George was allowed to play with a junior college team, and at Campbell led the entire nation's junior colleges in scoring. There, he was spotted in a game against UNC's JV by Assistant Coach Smith and offered a Tar Heel scholarship by Frank McGuire—but Wake Forest coach Bones McKinney swiped him by promising his mother he'd personally take the boy to church every Sunday. That didn't work out, though, and leaving college behind Lehmann had to tread water for several years in the Eastern League, by rule waiting until his class graduated to receive an NBA bid. The silver lining was that the Eastern League shot the 3-pointer, and soon George was the best long-range shooter in the game. He was finally playing in the old-school NBA when word got around that the fledgling ABA shot the 3-pointer *and* was paying more money. The math on that was pretty obvious: GL x 3 = \$\$\$. So when Lehmann ran into Coach Sharman in an airport one day and fell into discussion, it was fated he would soon be suiting up for the Stars.

"When I got there and met Larry, he was their best player," says Lehmann, who saw Miller score 33 in their first game together. "To me, he was extremely gifted in certain areas of the game, and the game was starting to change. Bill Sharman was already saying the 3-pointer was going to change the game which, as you know, it has. So I was there and Larry was a proficient 3-point shooter, left-handed, extremely strong, and Larry was the best in the league at going backdoor [cutting to the basket behind the backs of the defense]. I always used to say, 'Larry could go backdoor on God.' "

Lehmann, who was married with kids and not running with the Hermosa Beach crowd, also remembers, "Larry was one of the best looking guys in the league, and after the games there'd be girls all over the place looking for him. I used to joke in the locker room to the rest of the team, 'You guys are all hanging around with Larry just because you're trying to get his leftovers.' And basically that was the truth."

*

At this point, Larry's life was on such a roll that it seemed the only way he could lose a girl was by pretending. Still taking acting classes at Universal, he practiced a scene from the show "Ask Any Girl," in which he lures a young lady up to his aunt's empty house and tries to take advantage of her—but the girl fights him off and finally leaves by herself. "I like the scene," Larry cracked to *The Charlotte Observer*, "but I don't much care for the way it ends."

In real life, the blue-collar kid from the Lehigh Valley still preferred playing the hero to becoming a featured creep in Hollywood stories. In fact, one of his favorite nights with a woman that year involved his new ride—one of the classic sports cars of all time, a 1969 British racing green Jaguar XKE—and a damsel in distress who he gallantly never laid a finger on. "I was driving the Jag home one night when I saw a girl about my age hitching, so I stopped and asked where she was going, and she said Newport Beach. Now that was pretty far, and I'd been drinking and it was night . . . so I said I'd take her as far as I was going. Then it started to rain. So I said, 'Don't take this the wrong way, but it's almost midnight, raining, and I don't feel good about you hitching. And I've got a big place on the ocean, I can give you your own place to sleep, and put you back on the highway in the morning.' So she agreed. I cooked her a midnight breakfast, put her to bed in the great room—alone— and the next day took her out to the highway. See, this was still the spring before Manson . . . when people had an open door policy."

*

The Stars ended the season a disappointing fifth in their division, but Larry had more than succeeded in proving he belonged. Recovering from a slow start, he'd finished strong with a 17 ppg average, not only making the ABA's All-Rookie team, but also runner-up as the league's Rookie of the Year. When Coach Sharman told UPI, "Larry is a nugget," his future success as a pro seemed assured . . . one would think.

Life at the beach was satisfying, too, as Larry had graduated to the big room on the top floor, with a roof deck and a wall of glass looking out over the ocean. There was just one hitch in the upgrade . . . the dogcatcher. "The guy never saw me with Timi, but month after month he went up and down the beach looking for her. Unfortunately, when we got that big glass-enclosed second floor, one day he saw the dog looking out the window and he assumed that was the same dog he'd been chasing and gave me a ticket. But he never did ID the dog on the beach, or catch me with her. That's why I didn't take it seriously."

Perhaps he should have.

*

Freed of team obligations by May, Larry found time to drop into Chapel Hill where he sat down with a familiar face, Art Chansky of *The Daily Tar Heel*. "I've been wanting to come back for a long time," he said, before relating that, in addition to hanging out with his idol Jerry West, and Billy Cunningham when the 76ers were in LA, he'd also been exploring business opportunities. In fact, Larry was doing so well financially that, at the encouragement of Tar Heel pros Doug Moe and Larry Brown, he'd signed with a business manager, Jim Hand, who also handled investments for Rick Barry and glamorous football stars like Lance Alworth and Deacon Jones from the Rams. Together they were talking about investing in a national restaurant chain, dividing up the country so that each player's name would banner the eateries in his own home region—and Larry was getting North Carolina and Pennsylvania.

Larry also talked about his acting career—he had a big screen test scheduled when he returned to the West Coast—and dropped the tidbit that Vincent Chase kept encouraging him to bring Dick Grubar out to Hollywood for a screen test as well. But Larry remained noncommittal about moving on from pro ball, saying "Right now I have a lot of security in the game" . . . despite still grappling with the brash league's style of hand-to-hand combat—literally.

"More things go on in the pros than I ever thought possible on the court," he told Art. "I've had more things happen to me on drives and layups than you would ever believe. It was only toward the end of the season that I learned to defend myself." (Decades later, Larry still recalls Warren Jabali's sneaky trick of pushing down on a shooter's shoulder to boost himself up for a block, while lenient refs daydreamed nearby.) For all the preseason warnings of his battered condition, though, Larry still had an enviable record of never missing a game due to injury.

"I've missed Chapel Hill," Larry concluded. "I'll always want to come back here." Curiously, the recent development that the ABA's Houston team was relocating to play the following season as the Carolina Cougars—and that Larry was back to play ABA exhibition games in Charlotte and Raleigh, where "Mod Man Larry Miller" drew the loudest cheers—was never mentioned.

*

A year after skedaddling from the sore losers in Durham, Larry should have been safe in Chapel Hill. But when trouble got lonely, it often came looking for Larry. One day, he ran into a friend named Raymond Williams who had a convenience store on Franklin Street where Sunrise Biscuits now stands. Williams loved racing cars, had a pal flying up from Fayetteville to pick him up for a private flight to the Indianapolis 500 over Memorial Day, and he promptly invited Larry to come along. "It was a small plane, and I didn't know the pilot, so I asked if he was reliable and I was assured the guy was. So then I guess we're up over Asheville when this pilot says, 'I think I need a drink to get over these here moun-teens'—and he opens a flask. And now of course I'm thinking I may be doomed. By the time we get outside Indianapolis, he's looking down at roads for a marker, and I realize he's just winging it. There's no flight plan filed, no map. The guy was nuts, just flying by the seat of his pants.

"We finally made it in, and saw Mario Andretti win that race. But later the pilot picked up a couple of deaf and dumb girls—really, they were talking in sign language—and the story I got is he brought them back to his room that night. So I was happy I had to go straight on to LA from there, for that screen test scheduled at Universal, instead of going back to Chapel Hill with them. On their way home those guys ran into a mountain storm that forced them down somewhere—so that three-hour flight took them twenty-one hours going back. But I sure seem to attract 'em . . ."

\*

Larry never did sign a contract with Universal—although he could have. At the end of acting school that first year, all prospects had to perform a skit for the staff to see who would be offered a deal. "And I had a tooth pulled right before that, so I was on medication when I went up and did it. But it was good enough that they tendered me an offer—the typical seven-year deal back then, where you were owned by the studio and they put you up for different parts. Shelly Novack, a buddy of mine who was with the San Diego Chargers [and also discovered by Vincent Chase], guest starred on a lot of westerns and cops shows, and if I had stuck it out you could be watching me on reruns now. But I'd only get $700 a month, and they wanted me to quit basketball [$3,000 a month]—and at that point I wasn't ready, and said 'No.' "

*

That spring, Lew Alcindor graduated from UCLA and turned down the ABA and the Harlem Globetrotters to accept $1.4 million from the NBA's Milwaukee Bucks. Before he left, however, he played in a couple of pickup games where Larry finally got to know his National Championship nemesis. "But he was a really introspective, quiet guy. I don't think even the other black guys I played with really knew him. It's not that he didn't get along with anyone. He just didn't go out of his way to speak to people."

A more brutal pickup contest caught Larry by surprise one day when one LA party led to another. He was at a gathering in Hollywood, talking with the Philadelphia Eagles' Tim Brown when the running back ("a really nice guy") told Larry he was heading off to Jim Brown's house—Did he want to come? This was an invitation to athletic Valhalla. Considered by many the greatest football player of all time, Jim Brown was an athletic marvel who had also averaged 38 ppg for his high school basketball team, been a First Team All-American in lacrosse at Syracuse, and finished fifth in the national decathlon championship. At age thirty-three, he was now having success as an actor but was still tough as nails. Oh, and he had a reputation for being ornery.

"So we go up to Jim's house and Tim Brown says, 'Jim heard you're a basketball player, he wants to play you one-on-one.' Now, apparently Cookie Gilchrist, a 260-pound fullback for the Buffalo Bills, was rooming with him, and the story is they were tussling on the basketball court and got into a fight and Jim tossed Cookie off the side of the mountain. So I was a little wary of getting his ire up because Jim is a big man. And I've been drinking all day at this point, but okay, I say I will . . . and he just beat the hell out of me physically, and I didn't want to embarrass him first game so I took it. But then, after he was whipping on me, he asks do I want to play one more? And the second game I got serious and I blew him out.

"So then we went into his house, a beautiful house, and he says, '*Mi casa, su casa.*' And there on the hillside overlooking all of LA was a pool with four naked Swedish women in it. And the girls served dinner totally naked—they'd put a towel around, but when they sat you could see everything. So that was dinner: eating steaks and looking at their butts. And I'm like, 'Whoa . . . this is insane.' I didn't mess with any of them because I had a date later, but that was a once in a lifetime experience for me.

"I was only twenty-three that year, and it was a lot to digest out there. There were no drugs involved, but at that point there was no relationship deal in my life—LA is so spread out—and it was just one after another . . ."

*

More typical for Larry were lighthearted gatherings like The Naked Roof Party. (Some people nickname their houses or cars; Miller names his parties.) It began up in the Hollywood Hills after he picked up a girl and spent the night at her place in Topanga Canyon—"It's all gullies, you don't know where you're at"—and then woke up realizing he was late for a 6:00 AM practice. "So then I invited her to my place at Hermosa Beach, and somehow we got other people out on my rooftop deck—I spent that whole summer out there, looking right onto the beach—and everybody got naked. Suddenly there are people hanging out of balconies with cameras, and helicopters overhead . . . I think we were on the news at that point. If there had been cell phones back then, I wouldn't still be around after the stuff I pulled. And then I never saw that girl again. It happened a lot like that: You meet somebody . . . and then they're gone."

*

So much was available to Larry that he could never be sure how a night would end. One day began sensibly enough, working the LA Auto Show for a couple of hundred bucks along with UCLA coach Wooden and a few television actors. In the course of meeting some of the women displaying automobiles, he introduced himself to one lovely and mentioned he was a basketball player.

"And she says, 'Oh, I have a date tonight with a player—Wilt Chamberlain.' Then I leave and go up to this bar in North Hollywood and I see Wilt, who I knew, at the bar. I say, 'Hey, I just met the girl you have a date with tonight,' and he looks puzzled . . . and then it clicks: 'You're right, Larry, I forgot all about her. You want her?' That's how he treated them, just giving them out like they were extras. I said, 'Wilt, I can handle my own business, but thanks for the offer.' "

Larry surpassed Wilt's high school scoring record, but he never came close to the seven-footer's most famous record—a claim of scoring with 20,000 women. On the other hand, maybe that record should come with an asterisk: "He told me that most of them he didn't have sex with, just fooled around with them. And later on, a guy who played with Wilt told me that sometimes he turned his Great Danes loose with them instead . . . whatever that was. And these were beautiful girls! But I guess they wanted to be on that list of 20,000."

\*

The worst of LA's perversions, of course, were the creepy-crawly Manson gang killings that August—and only later would Larry realize how close he came to being in their path. The party at the house of a guy named Harold True was just another big Hollywood bash, none of the guests, including Larry, aware the little known Manson had asked their host to let his pack of women live there. True refused, so a week after that party—with Sharon Tate's slaughter suddenly screaming from the headlines—Manson's crew came skulking in the night to kill him, too. True wasn't home, though, so the frustrated hit squad randomly turned their bloodlust on the unfortunate LaBiancas sleeping in the house next door. Larry knew he was never in any real danger—"That was a big party and they wouldn't have tried anything with all those people there." What gnawed at him was recognizing the cult leader's mania as only the most extreme outbreak in an epidemic of desperation for fame that was infecting the Golden State's soul and making it sick.

\*

The Stars approached Larry's second pro season with guarded hopes, tamped down after the prayer for Lew Alcindor went unanswered. But with three All-Rookie players now a year older, some newly drafted height, and experience from sharpshooting vet George Lehmann, Sharman gamely predicted, "We'll be a contender this season." Larry was upbeat, too, even keeping a diary during a preseason tour of the league: "Love the trips, can dress up, meet new people, see old friends. This one is real good because we go back to PA and NC where I played high school and college ball. Good trip so far—champagne, good food, nice hostesses . . ."

Someone was generous enough to schedule an early October exhibition against the Pittsburgh Pipers at Allentown's Rockne Hall as a "Welcome Home" night for Larry where he'd played against Central Catholic (and where Lehmann had once scored 45 points as an Allentown Jet). The Stars won and Sharman praised Larry's "sheer aggressiveness," while noting his outside shooting was still not sharp. "But this is something that will come . . . He's got a lot of great years in front of him."

But this was not to be one of them. By mid-October Larry's entries included "Got lost. Were late. Made us run. Fought in scrimmage" . . . and "(12 o'clock curfew) Missed 1:00. $50 fine." His entry for the October 17 season opener against the New Jersey Nets is a portrait of frustration: "Nets place had new paint, bad odors, cold showers, etc. Won game easily. Had good game what little I played. Went back on D and Bill screamed to help press. I screamed back I was trying to help. Pulled me (start of second half) would not have gotten back in if Stone hadn't got in foul trouble. Believe this is end w/ LA." This was for a game in which Larry scored a team-high 19 points with a Catty contingent cheering in the stands.

Still, Lehmann and Miller (there are those initials again) made an effective duo for a while, as on Halloween when they poured in 26 and 21 points for a win. But the season hit a pothole in the first week of November when the Stars lost their new scoring ace as the result of a fluke accident. Recalls Lehmann, "I played the last quarter of a season for the Stars, but when I was driving my family out for that next season's training camp my wife got run

**LARRY MILLER**

SATURDAY, OCTOBER 4, 1969 / 8:15 P.M. / ROCKNE HALL

# PITTSBURGH PIPERS
# VS
# LOS ANGELES STARS

OFFICIAL PROGRAM   25¢

*The flyer advertising local hero Miller's "homecoming"*
*ABA game at Allentown's Rockne Hall.*

over by a car in Scottsdale, and she had to go to the hospital with a fractured head. When we got to LA she wasn't healing well, and eventually the doctors suggested I return her east to her mother and father. So I tried to get traded back east, and finally I went to the New Jersey Nets.

"Sharman was a unique individual. If you said you wanted to play somewhere else, he'd send you there. I had set the ABA record with 27 points in one quarter, I was the best shooter on the team, but when I asked to go back east that's what he did for me." It was a lesson that Larry would remember—and sooner than he expected.

With Lehmann gone, defenses focused on Miller and his point production dropped. Things got rougher on the court in other ways, too. "Jimmy Jarvis stole the ball from Warren Jabali—the guy who beat me out for Rookie of the Year—and Jimmy was driving down the floor when Warren, who was a real militant guy, knocked him down. And as Jarvis was rolling on the floor, Jabali jumped up in the air and stomped Jarvis's head into the court. His face and eyes were a mess. And I was the closest guy, so I went and knocked Jabali over—otherwise he probably would have stomped his head some more. Today they might have suspended a guy for the season for doing that, but being the ABA and he was a star, they just threw him out of the game and that was that. He didn't even get a suspension."

Life was getting hinky off the court, too. "One night I was driving the green Jaguar and passed these cops going the other way. They didn't clock me, but they turned around and stopped me saying it *looked* like I was going too fast. I knew it was just a harassment stop, and I got cocky, giving them crap. But that was a time when things were getting nasty with the cops. The hippies were going crazy, and I had long hair . . . Then their commander came by and heard the story and told them, 'If he says another word, take the nightstick to him.' So I shut up. Then they checked my warrants and I had that citation for having my dog out on the beach—and obviously I hadn't paid the ticket for that. So they took me to jail for having a dog on the beach! I was there a couple hours until I found some girl to bail me out."

Even more souring of LA's mellow vibe was the discovery that Jim Hand, the trusted business manager and mastermind of Larry's future restaurant chain with other athletes, was in fact nothing but a crook—and the restaurants were all just a scam. "He never got me any appearances or negotiated for me. He just changed my contract so he was collecting my money, and he got me into some land in Simi Valley that was worthless—desert, basically. I guess he got kickbacks. So we lost some money there before I got out of that."

*

It was around this disenchanting time that Miller ran into a woman he now feels influenced him more than anyone in the world, other than his parents. And he can't even recall her name.

"I'd met this girl before on the beach, and she was beautiful, going to acting school same as me, typically wanting to be famous. Then I ran into her six months or a year later, and she looked so much healthier, more natural—totally changed. She'd been living off the land in Hawaii, and changed her lifestyle, becoming vegetarian. So we went to my place and I made her a bowl of fruit—we never even kissed but we talked for hours—and that's the last time I ever saw her. But I quit eating meat that day in 1969—that's all it took was a girl. And before long I decided to leave LA.

"Actually it was all a bit much for me. I was wearing so many hats there, and I was pulled in every different direction. And I realized I just didn't want to do what that whole Hollywood thing was about. I'd had a taste of fame with basketball, but that was different—fame that you earned—not this 'Get your face filmed and you're famous' stuff. I didn't want any part of that. And today, people would still walk on hot coals to go out there and be famous. But all the outside stuff that was going on was actually bad for me, because I knew my appetites and there was just too much on the plate out there. So I asked to get traded back to Carolina.

"I only met that girl twice, but she's like Mother Theresa for me. She probably saved my life. I'm sure she doesn't know it, but God bless her."

\*

Larry had an ally in his Charlotte newspaper buddy, Leonard Laye, who began teasing the Carolina public with articles like the unsubtly titled, "Miller Would Like To Be A Cougar." Describing his frustration with limited playing time on a team using ten interchangeable players, Larry was careful not to criticize Sharman, only saying that "I never know when I might be coming out of a game, so I find myself pressing a lot and I'm missing some shots I might ordinarily be hitting." Then Larry nudged the Stars to at least get something of value for him by adding, "I will probably quit playing next year to concentrate on acting unless things change with the Stars or unless I'm traded to Carolina."

Meanwhile, Laye pointed out that in two Stars vs. Cougars exhibition games, Larry had drawn more crowd response than any of the first-year Cougars, and he got the Cougar General Manager Don DeJardin to admit, "Everyone knows there have been discussions between us and Los Angeles in the past. We have been laboring under the impression that Larry Miller was an 'untouchable.' The comments that have recently been made (by Miller) open this up." Sharman—still smart enough not to hold a discontented player captive—conceded, "If the deal is right we'll trade anyone. But I'd have to get an awful good player—or two players—for him."

The month of November, 1969 is charted by erratic box scores, indicating a team and a game with no consistent rhythm in which Larry could play with his customary abandon. There was single digit scoring . . . then 18 points . . . followed by games in which Larry took only one or two shots . . . or didn't play at all. The DNP was his own fault, though: "I missed a promotion up in the Valley after they'd advertised me, and they didn't play me the next game. So it was very apparent that what you did off the floor was going to reflect on you *on* the floor—which hadn't normally been the case for me, but it was this time."

That slackness was followed by a late November game in Raleigh, with Larry pouring in 26 points against the Cougars in what had to be an audition that boosted attendance by 33% for that game alone. Little more than a week later, the trade was made and Larry was a Star no more. By early December, when the Altamont Festival in San Francisco exploded into Hell's Angels violence, putting a nail in the coffin of West Coast flower power, Larry was already a continent away.

Many years later, he conceded "I would have liked to stay with Sharman, who was a very nice person and a very good coach. I wouldn't have asked to be traded if there wasn't a basketball reason as well as the life out there. But I could see some of the personnel moves Sharman was making. He was bringing in people like Zelmo Beatty [6'9"], and it was looking like they were changing over and I didn't fit in. I could see the writing on the wall. I knew I could play guard, because I did it well, but I guess I was still fighting the stereotype.

"Plus I figured, Carolina . . . it was such a good ride the first time around, what could possibly go wrong? Little did I know what I was walking into with Bones McKinney . . ."

CHAPTER 9

# BONERS

Horace (Bones) McKinney—called by Life Magazine "a dead-ringer for Ichabod Crane"—had been a Carolina character for years. After a fine playing career, he'd coached Wake Forest to third in the nation in 1962 before retiring to work for the NC Department of Corrections, but he retained a sideline as color commentator for Saturday's ACC Game of the Week telecasts. He reveled in the spotlight, proudly noting his initials were H.A.M., hamming it up as a coach with sideline antics like strapping himself to the bench with a seat belt to contain his gesticulations. Now, touted by the Cougars as the "Barrymore of the Bench," he was beloved by the media for his storytelling and quotes . . . but less so by players like George Lehmann:

"When I was at Wake Forest, half the time he wasn't even at practice— he was out at luncheons giving speeches, being an ambassador for the school, and himself. Bones was not a great coach, but he was a great salesman and energized people. And players, when they met him, wanted to be around him . . . but after a while, you didn't want to be around him."

A complex man, McKinney was an ordained Baptist minister who, scuttlebutt holds, Wake Forest didn't want around when he did that which he ought not to have done. As blogger RamFanatic notes, "Keep in mind the '50s–'60s were another time altogether from the norms we have today. Wake Forest was not exactly the place for a free spirit back then. They had just had a big controversy over whether dancing would be allowed on campus or not."

This was the showboat whose turf Larry was unwittingly invading. "At that time the whole Triangle situation was out of hand," recalls Lehmann. "I was amazed when I heard Larry was going there because Larry was a Carolina guy, and Bones went to Carolina but he really hated the Carolina syndrome. [Bones had also played for NC State.] When I was brought in a few months later, the GM Carl Scheer was making the moves, but Bones signed off on it . . . and I was surprised that he would bring Larry." (More likely the owner who traded for Miller, Don DeJardin, already knew what he wanted.)

In fact, Miller soon learned that his new coach had announced the trade by telling his future teammates sardonically, "Our savior is coming" . . . dinging Larry before he even walked in the door. This was the first time Larry tried playing for a coach who bore his own player ill will, and the twenty-three-year-old found it perplexing. "I guess he didn't really like me for some reason, but I didn't know what I did wrong. I didn't party in front of them or come in drunk. I didn't show that side of me to anybody on the coaching side. And he was a minister but a drinker, too. I got there after the season had started, and never fit in with them. I never really got a chance."

It wasn't as though Miller couldn't perform. In his first game as a Cougar that December he barely got his feet wet with 3 points, but two nights later he exploded for 36 points. That was followed by 29 points in Raleigh and 21 in Charlotte. Clearly Cougar management was getting the star power they'd been looking for . . . when the star could get in the game.

Later Larry would tell *The Morning Call*, "After the trade I started a couple of games and was scoring well and getting my share of rebounds. And then, I don't know what happened, but all of a sudden I didn't play. All I know is I didn't like it. I'd still like to know what happened."

Don Canzano (admittedly a Miller homer, but one who has seen a lot) notes, "That happened to tons of ballplayers, and I think it gets down to ego and jealousy. It happened to Rick Mount, the Indiana legend from Purdue, who was the Larry Miller of Indiana. His coach when he turned pro with the Pacers was a previous Indiana legend—and he experienced the same junk Larry did. It's like these guys don't want you to steal their thunder. And Larry's not like that. He realizes that there are guys who are going to come after him, that I'm going to be eventually forgotten—which we all are. Different personality. But I think it's just human ego."

*

The Cougars had an innovative business model (proposed by Frank Deford), serving the entire state by rotating home games through Charlotte, Greensboro, and Raleigh rather than playing in one arena only. By early 1970 they were already outdrawing every ABA team except Indiana—and some NBA teams, too. Arriving in mid-season, Larry quickly rented a three-bedroom house in the middle of the state outside Greensboro where, down a half-mile dirt road, Timi could run wild in a beautiful setting on twelve acres with a six-acre lake.

Almost immediately, Timi delivered a litter of pups, and Larry kept one of them, dubbed TJ. The dogs had the run of the place, and Larry cut a hole in the garage door so they could get in and out as they liked. That way, when Larry went on the road, they had shelter and freedom, and the little neighbor girl would come by twice a day to feed them.

"One time that my parents visited, we drove out to the main road and I could see the dogs were following, so I had to pull over. And then I saw that Timi was under the front of a bus getting ready to pull out. I had to stop the driver from moving, and take her back and lock her in the house so she wouldn't follow us. So there's another time she dodged a bullet. It's amazing she got through those things."

Meanwhile, the Joe Namath of the ABA ran a little wild, himself, living as he wanted outside the bull's-eye of fame. Before long, his Greensboro pad was the envy of all, like visiting writer Ronald Green who would admire "the throbbing music pouring and oozing and zapping out of $3,000 worth of stereo equipment filling one wall of the den . . . Led Zeppelin, Blood, Sweat and Tears, Vanilla Fudge, and Creedence Clearwater Revival." In a nod to fond memories of Avery dorm at UNC, Larry still had the oversized photo of Ursula Andress in an advanced stage of undress—so sentimental—but Larry's own wardrobe was now rock star mod, including a chocolate-brown body shirt, laced up the front, with a big fold-over collar and bell sleeves, atop red-blue-green-brown striped bell-bottoms. Or, if he felt like going the full Tom Jones, aqua colored velvet bell-bottoms and a flowing white satin shirt with lace at the collar and cuffs. But the pad's *pièce de résistance* (meeting very little resistance, apparently) was a big round bed with satin sheets and a fur cover that he bought over in High Point (known locally as the furniture capital of the world). Larry's rationale for the designer chick magnet had a logic right out of *Spinal Tap*: "A round bed was great because you could never fall off one end of it."

Ron Green Jr. got to sit on the end line at games in Charlotte thanks to his dad's free newspaper tickets. He also got to hang out after the games, talking with Larry and scoping what the coolest dude in town was wearing: "That was at the height of really bad fashion, and I remember asking my parents for a full-length leather trench coat. They said, 'I don't think so.' I was such a huge fan of the Cougars and Larry that I wished I was a left-handed shooter."

\*

Meanwhile, Larry's off-court maneuvers hadn't lost a step, as observed by Leonard Laye, traveling with the team on Miller's first road trip back to Los Angeles: "We arrived at the airport a couple of days before the game, and this wonderful looking blonde was waiting for Larry at the baggage claim in an outfit that had holes all through it. I don't know what you call those, but it sure got everyone's attention. Then she and Larry disappeared and I didn't see him again until game day. And after the game we all went over to her place—keep in mind I was closer in age to the players than I was to the coaches—and that night went on till the wee hours . . . the wee *wee* hours. They stayed in touch for a while, but later she married a Los Angeles County sheriff's deputy."

*

Later that winter, Larry lost his suitcase during a road trip to play against the Pacers. Soon afterward, a classified ad appeared in the *Indianapolis Star*: "Lost: Aluminum team suitcase containing a basketball uniform and personal property. Keep the suitcase! Keep the uniform! But please return the little black phone book to Larry Miller, Carolina Cougars, Greensboro Coliseum, Greensboro, NC." Sadly, he never got it back, lamenting "There were at least a hundred numbers in Los Angeles alone . . ."

*

Miller's initial scoring burst faded to a mild 10.9 average for the season while the team finished third in their division. Playing time is not recorded in box scores from those days, but he was disappointed and—realizing he was at a crossroads with a coach who had the upper hand—he saw only one path forward: "I decided I could look at why I didn't play that first year a lot of different ways: It was his fault for not liking me. It was my fault for not doing the right thing. It was somewhere in the middle. So I decided to take all the blame that whatever happened was totally my fault. And I went into the off-season with the outlook that I'm going to dedicate myself to showing them that I could play: I'll improve my defense, come back with an open book attitude, be in the best shape of anybody. I'll do anything you want to make it work."

*

That spring, still with scant TV coverage, the Cougars drummed up support by traveling around the state in a van, setting up temporary baskets to put on clinics for neighborhood kids and exhibition games for charities. They even played in prisons against lifers and men on Death Row, who Larry recalls were "nice guys."

Even before summer began, Larry also spread the Cougar message by announcing basketball day camps in Charlotte, organized with Leonard Laye: two weeks in late June for middle and high school boys and—a late addition—a week in mid-July for girls nine and over that would feature heartthrob Dick Grubar. Larry even sat for a *Gastonia Gazette* interview with one writer's preteen daughters, promising their session would also include swimming, picture taking, possibly a fashion show, and his personal record collection. (So he was also coaching them to be coeds?)

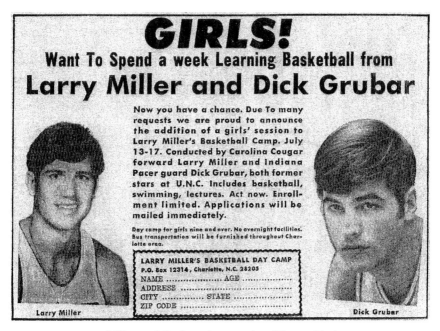

Miller and Grubar pioneered a different kind
of summer basketball camp.

Ron Green Jr.—still a schoolboy, himself—helped out at the boys camp, and best recalls the time he got a ride home with Larry in that dark green Jaguar XKE. "It fit him perfectly. And he had a girlfriend with him, and somehow the three of us got into that two-seat Jaguar. I remember sitting at a stoplight, and Three Dog Night's 'Mama Told Me Not To Come' was on and we were all singing along . . ." Young Ron never got the leather coat, but that afternoon he got to try on the life of a star.

Larry's cars always lived hard, though—even when parked—and Leonard ruefully remembers the morning his wife Shirley christened the XKE. "The house we were in then had a single lane driveway. And Larry and I had been out somewhere when Shirley went to bed. At the time, she had a 1963 Ford, and it was parked behind my car, but there was room for Larry to pull in behind her that night, which we did. Well, she had to go to work the next morning, so she gets in her car, looks in the rearview mirror and doesn't see anything because that car was set so high and the Jag was so low—she had no way of seeing it. So she starts backing up and runs right up on the hood of the Jaguar. Larry was asleep on the couch, and it startled . . . well, I think it startled me more than it did him. There wasn't that much damage, but there was a little, and Shirley was so alarmed."

Larry had better automotive luck going to Charlotte Motor Speedway with Leonard on a regular basis now, and becoming friends with the General Manager, Richard Howard. "I think Richard was in the furniture business, but he was a great promoter. At that time NASCAR races were just starting to get big-time—they weren't televised nationally—so he would bring writers down from Chicago and St. Louis to promote the sport with hospitality rooms all over town. The night before a race, one thing we did was make sure everybody was having a good time—enough drinks, enough companions— to party all night into the wee hours. Then we'd drive around the track at 2:00 or 3:00 in the morning and watch these people running around drunk and crazy in the pits.

"I knew a lot of the drivers, and some of them came to games when I was with the Cougars—Bobby Isaacs I believe was a regular. It definitely broke up some of my relationships with some women, though, because they didn't understand why I couldn't invite them. But I couldn't have a girl hanging around with me and watching some of the stuff we did.

"One time I actually drove the pace car in Charlotte with the queen sitting on the back, waving. I had the Clydesdales right behind me, and you've got to go only 10 mph so the horses won't get spooked. You set the tone for the whole race. But they didn't warn me, when we got to the first curve the bank is like 60-degrees—you can't see anything in the rearview mirror but asphalt—and it felt like we were sliding down and could roll over, and I'm telling the girl 'Hang on!' Can you imagine the car flipping over and I lose the queen in front of 90,000 people? So I sped up a little, and after that—same race—I was able to give the command: 'Gentlemen, start your engines!' That was a big thrill for me.

"Richard was a doozy. A lot of the drivers didn't have big sponsors back then—the lower echelons were doing it on a wing and a prayer—and he used to help a lot of them out. He had me sit in on some meetings with him in his office at the track—they were lined up outside his door—and they'd tell him a story about this and that problem. He'd say, 'How much do you need?' and dole out $600, $1,000, $2,000 . . . and he never took a note. This went on for a long time, that's how generous he was."

Larry wasn't just a spectator, though—he and Leonard were always on the lookout for business—and by the middle of June, Richard Petty, president of the year-old Professional Drivers Association, announced that the Charlotte firm of LM Enterprises (again those lucky initials) had been retained to handle all promotional activities. Yes, the company was essentially Laye and Miller who knew both sides of the star-making business. Joined by drivers Bobby Allison and David Pearson, Petty announced, "We are at an important stage in the progress of the PDA . . . It is neither practical nor possible for a driver or any small group of drivers to devote enough time to the many functions of the association."

*Miller and Leonard Laye flank Richard Petty in 1970,*
*his arm in a sling for a broken shoulder after*
*surviving the first major NASCAR accident captured*
*on live network television. "The car rolled over and*
*over and he had his arm out the window. They didn't*
*have good safety equipment back then."*

Perhaps mindful of Howard's supplicants, Miller recalls "Leonard had the idea to start a union of drivers to look out for their benefits, just like all the major sports. I think Richard Petty was for it, too, but this guy Bill France [Founder and CEO of NASCAR] was opposed, and he was strong enough that he kept it down. He told the drivers it wasn't in their best interests and we got squashed, and to this day they don't have a union. But it was a lot of fun being involved with that, and I never would have been if it wasn't for Leonard."

★

Whenever Larry visited Chapel Hill in the off-season he'd stay with a professor friend, Gerald Unks—as did some of the other players—and for Timi it was the same deal as Greensboro: "We'd let the dogs out at night and then they'd come in. But one night Timi didn't come back again. I looked all over for her, but finally had to go back to Greensboro. And about three days later I got the call that she'd showed up again, and I got her back. So we dodged another bullet there."

Also crashing with Unks in those days was Dick Grubar, who was having an even tougher time going pro. The bad luck began in the 1969 ACC Tournament when, after scoring 23 points in a semifinal win, he injured his knee in the championship win over Duke, ending his UNC career as a spectator at the Final Four. Grubar was drafted anyway by the Indiana Pacers, had an operation, and fought through rehab—but when he rejoined the team in early January 1970, in only his second game back he tore the other side of his knee. Now, after rebuilding the knee again all spring in Chapel Hill, he was helping Larry out with the girls' session at the Charlotte camp and preparing to give the Pacers another shot.

It was during this summer that Larry met and began dating a schoolteacher in Hillsborough named Bonnie, who made a big impression on many of Larry's friends. Conveniently, Hillsborough was also home to the Occoneechee Speedway, first carved out as a colonial era horse race track and then adapted into one of the two original NASCAR dirt tracks before being abandoned in 1968. There, among whispering pines, Larry ran sprints on the rutted dirt oval for an hour in the middle of afternoons throughout the summer, building his wind for the Cougars' preseason.

One day, as Dick Grubar was driving from the Charlotte camp on his way back to Chapel Hill, some instinct told him not to pass through Greensboro without dialing Larry. "I said, 'What's going on, I'm just coming through,' and Larry said, 'No! You gotta come over—I got you a date, you'll love her!' And the next thing I know I'm meeting Bonnie's roommate, and she *was* great and we hung out for the rest of the year . . . and after five or six months we got married."

"He's probably still mad at me for that," cracks Miller of introducing Grubar to his first wife. "But she was a hottie. After they got married, they honeymooned at my house and I gave them my round bed."

\*

Larry kept his focus on basketball all summer by launching another basketball camp in early August—this one an overnight deal for boys in the Poconos—with the help of his Allentown buddy, Scott Beeten, then the recently named twenty-three-year-old head coach of East Stroudsburg High School. Beeten would be joined by coaches like Ken Rosemond (who had won Larry for UNC), Bobby Knight of West Point, and Lou Carnesecca who was taking over the ABA's New York Nets. "And one of the first speakers at camp—we gave him his first speaking engagement—was a fella named James T. Valvano," Beeten recalls.

"The camp was only 40 minutes from Allentown, not that far. When we started, we all did a little of everything, but Larry was such a big name that the camp would fill up early. So we hired someone to supervise the kids so we didn't have to be there all night, and we managed to get out and find some hot spots and have a pretty good time."

Beeten already knew that Larry's idea of summer conditioning was serious business. "When I was still in college and he was in the pros, we would go into his high school gym in the middle of summer with the doors locked and the windows shut, and we'd play one-on-one, full court, sometimes to 100 points. And Larry would play in that heat and humidity with a rubber sweat suit on. In those days we didn't know it was dangerous. We didn't have the scientific training and personal trainers they do now. And by the end of summer he'd be in good shape."

This summer there had been no beach bacchanals ballooning Larry's weight up to super-chunk, so he was already in good form. "While we were at camp, Larry would spend a lot of time working out and getting in shape. I remember one day he, Randy Denton and I decided we were going for a run in the mountains. They took off and I ran after them, falling behind . . . until

I realized, 'Hold on, the only thing I need in shape is my voice for yelling at other guys' . . . We'd also play counselor games at night, bringing buddies up from Allentown like Reidy. It was a way for all of us to get together to spend quality time during the day, and nights drinking beer."

By the time Larry broke camp to head for North Carolina in mid-August he was already a trim 200 pounds and, three weeks short of the Cougars' preseason, still struggling to understand what McKinney's problem with him was. (Recall that Miller, for all his off-court antics, was always considered eminently coachable and respectful.) Ultimately he addressed the situation the only way he knew how—with hard work. "I decided that second year I would do everything possible to do the right thing—and that started with being in good physical shape. I was known for my hard workouts, but this time I took it to a new level. In the heat of summer I worked out three times a day for weeks leading up to preseason. I sprinted, I did distances, I lifted, I exercised, I played—I was so disciplined. And by the start of the team camp, when I got my physical exam, the doc said 'I'm glad you told me you've been working out so hard, because had I not known that I would have thought you were dying and rushed you to the hospital, because your pulse is so low.' It was in the 40s, something like that, my heart was so relaxed."

Hearing of it later, Scott Beeten wasn't surprised. "The man could push himself so hard, and that mental toughness translated to the court. It's why he made so many plays, why he scored so many baskets in the clutch—because he had that mental toughness."

*

Arriving in Laurinburg where the Cougars camped, Larry found his room-mate was George Lehmann who had joined the team in the off-season. Recalls Lehmann of Bones McKinney's grueling schedule, "We were doing a long three sessions a day—7:00 AM . . . afternoon . . . and at night—and after the first session I'm looking around for Larry to go back to the room. And I look out on the track and Larry is out there running! Man, we just finished and he's out there running? But there's an adage in basketball—'When you're shooting two hours a day, someone else is shooting three hours a day'—and I knew this was a big year for us, so I started going to the track with him."

*Larry demonstrates he's mastered ABA defense by snagging the Celtics' Dave Cowans.*

Even Larry thought three sweltering practices a day for two weeks were way too much, but at least he was the one player ready for them: "That first evening we had a full-court scrimmage, and I just tore everybody up. I guess Bones wanted to see who was in shape and I just ran everybody to death—I stole the ball from everybody, must have had 50 points, I was light-years ahead of anyone else. As this went on, guys would sit out, but I never sat out. Every game I gave everything I had . . ."

*

Meanwhile, Dick Grubar had gone to Indianapolis in the best shape of his life . . . only to find his shot with the Pacers was abruptly over before it really began. Already ABA champs, Indiana had fortified itself that spring by drafting local hero Rick Mount of Purdue, and Grubar's services were no longer needed. "Coach Bobby Leonard was a great guy and said, 'I know you want to play and I want to be good to you. Where do you want to go? I think you could go to the Cougars and have a great chance to make that squad.' And the Cougars had finished last the year before, not even in the playoffs, so I thought that was an opportunity."

Cougar management jumped at the trade reuniting the Butch & Sundance of Carolina hoops, but by the time Grubar got down there the team had already broken camp and was playing exhibition games. In his first preseason appearance, Grubar played very well, scoring 14 points in less than a half . . . whereupon Bones McKinney decided he'd seen enough of that! Grubar never got another sniff of court time and, inevitably, was cut from the team.

"I don't think Bones and I saw eye to eye. He was a little bit different," Grubar reflects, trying to be diplomatic . . . before adding, "He was kind of an egomaniac. I have no respect for him at all. And that ruined my chance for a career, so I decided that's enough."

*

Even Miller, still on the roster and expending a summer's worth of effort, had a hard time pleasing the frustrating coach: "Every game I gave everything I had . . . And it still didn't work. Before the first game of the season, it was at Miami—I'll never forget this—Bones came up to me and said, 'Larry, I've never seen anyone deserve to start more than you—you worked so hard. But I can't . . . I gotta start this other guy.' And, like I said, I wasn't going to argue with him about anything he'd say at that point. I took that as though I expected it . . . and I still got in that game and scored 21 points [second highest on the team]."

"Larry was really bringing it," Lehmann confirms, "and I knew he thought he would play right away . . . but I knew he wouldn't because Bones McKinney was extremely favorable to Bob Verga at that time, who played at Duke and was his leading scorer. They were playing that old Duke bullshit where the ball always comes outside to the same guy to set up a play again for Verga. Verga was just running their system and Bones wasn't doing much coaching, just going along with it . . ."

Larry ended up playing sixth man, seeing 20–25 minutes a game, and was leading the team in scoring until . . . "Lo and behold, as the season went on, I got less and less time. It was like whatever I put into it, it didn't really matter. The guy just didn't want me to play. It was a losing situation, but I kept my head up and did what I was told and tried to get through it and hoped for the best . . ."

⋆

Larry did have certain consolations, like Bonnie who George Lehmann to this day calls "one of the most beautiful women I've ever seen in my life." And he still had the wine cellar and the wall-to-wall smoke glass mirror on the bedroom wall to enjoy the view. But the big event in the party house that fall of 1970 occurred one low-key night when hardly a creature was stirring.

"I'd met a girl downtown somewhere and we became friends, and one night she was out there studying. It wasn't a romantic thing at all—that's unusual for me, not to have an interest like that back then—it was just a quiet Sunday night. My roommate [center Rich Niemann] was asleep and I was listening to some low music, dozing off . . . and I heard a chain rattling. I finally woke enough to realize 'That's not right,' because the chain was to the cellar stairway—the door before you got to the bathroom. So I got up and went to the bathroom door, but there's no lights on, no one there . . . and then I realized the girl had fallen down the cellar stairs. I found her lying with a pool of blood around her head and called Emergency immediately—I was afraid she was dead. It turns out she had a fractured skull and almost died right there, at the base of those steep stairs.

"Naturally the police were asking questions—'Did we fight? Were there any drugs?'—they thought I might have something to do with it. I had a pretty good reputation for partying, and you could see how someone could go to prison for life. If she died, that could have changed my life because my roommate couldn't clear me, being asleep, and she was in a coma. They put her in critical ICU and she was pretty bad off for a while. I told her people, 'Whatever she needs I'm glad to help'—I tried to help her financially. But they wouldn't accept it because they thought I'd done something wrong and got some lawyers, and I started getting sick threats."

*

"Larry had the playboy image," George Lehmann acknowledges, "but it didn't affect him on the floor. Larry would be killing guys in practice but getting no game time—and it was weird. So I wasn't playing, and Larry wasn't playing that much. And meanwhile the game was changing. Players were getting bigger and faster, so Larry should have been in there because Larry could shoot the three, he was strong, he could go backdoor on God, and he could defend people and was extremely tough.

"Don't misunderstand, Verga was a good player—but he wasn't George Lehmann and he wasn't Larry Miller. We couldn't understand why Verga wasn't coming out when he was playing bad, and it was killing Larry . . . and me, too. It was a mystery to everybody." (Only decades later would Lehmann learn that their time on the bench had nothing to do with basketball—they were collateral damage from Bones once again doing something clandestine which he ought not to have done.)

*

By mid-December, *Charlotte Observer* columnist and five-time NC Sportswriter of the Year Bob Quincy was already throwing in the towel for Larry, writing that he was "a Tarzan figure in superb shape who aches for duty" . . . but little used, despite drawing the most lavish applause from fans who saw him as "a dynamic piece of property going to rust" on the bench.

And now, sometimes spending entire games on the bench, Larry's vaunted confidence began to crack for the first time. You could hear the resignation when he noted in one interview, "Someone must sit on the bench. I think I understand my destiny. Now it's up to the fans to begin understanding." Added sympathetic Quincy, "It's like Howard Hughes accepting poverty."

Bones McKinney, shedding crocodile tears, offered no explanation beyond, "It's a shame" . . . as if there were nothing the coach could do about it.

A funny thing happened, though, on Miller's way to the scrap heap: playing as sixth man he could still produce. In the first game of 1971 he hit 11 of 12 shots on his way to 27 points and headlines clamoring that he'd earned a starting spot. And now Bones was hastily making nice, conceding, "For the fourth straight game Miller has been out of sight. I guess I didn't have the faith in him that I should have had, and he's been picking up lots of splinters. Oh, we of little faith! Everybody makes mistakes sometimes, I guess."

The olive branch came too late. Apparently someone in management had noticed the team's 17-25 record and done the math: Miller on the bench—the team in the cellar. And suddenly it wasn't Larry who was finished—Bones was.

"They fired Bones that first week of January," Lehmann recalls, "and Jerry Steele became head coach. That's when Larry got more time, and I took over for Verga, and that became my best year in pro ball. Jerry Steele knew the whole time that the guys who should have been playing weren't." That year, in fact, George Lehmann became the first professional basketball player in history to make more than 40% of his 3-point attempts in a season.

Happy to bring Larry to the fore where he belonged, Cougar management even arranged a "Win a Date with Larry Miller" contest during halftime of a mid-January game, just two weeks after Bones' dismissal. "We were in limbo for a while," Larry remembers, "and the rest of the season was up and down, but I got along well with Jerry Steele and he liked me. I could have played for him, and was looking forward to the future . . ."

That spring, the future got even brighter when Larry's lawyer called. After six months, the coma victim had finally recovered her memory, realized what actually happened, and fully exonerated him. "Even though the cops and an ambulance had come, there hadn't been much mention of it in the papers, so it was never a PR problem," he recalls. "But I can tell you, if she had died it would have been something." What Larry couldn't know was that, about a year later, that house would claim two victims with Larry powerless to stop it.

*

Out from under Bones McKinney's thumb and the cloud of possible manslaughter charges, Larry knew he had a fresh start coming. His initial three-year contract had expired, but the strong second half of his season opposite Lehmann (averaging in the high teens) meant the Cougars renewal was certain. Meanwhile, his sap was rising with plans to stay in shape with his mountain camps and a pretty girlfriend, and all was on the uptick when—BANG—Larry got the shock of his life.

In the first week of June, Larry received an official letter saying he'd been reclassified medically fit by Selective Service and, on orders from the Allentown draft board, had to report to Charlotte for a draft induction physical. This was toward the end of the effort in Vietnam—even the White House knew the war had no future—but the first draft lottery pegged men with Larry's birthday at #81 out of 366 (accounting for leap year babies), making him certain to be drafted. And although Larry had already been disqualified three times by prior physicals (most recently the previous May), he saw a bad omen in this doctor's actual name: Richard Nixon, Jr.

"He's the one who approved me for the draft," recalls Larry, noting the effect this would have on the already short career span of any pro athlete. "If I was in the Army for two years, that would have taken away the prime of my career right there. So that really threw a wrench into my future. I didn't know if I'd ever play again." (Neither did the Cougars, equally caught by surprise, who put renewal of his contract on hold, effectively taking his living off the table.)

"I had no time to think about it, no time to plan. And I never considered the alternatives, never thought about being a Conscientious Objector or going to Canada. So I went into basic training in flux, because I had to think on my feet and adjust to play both ends: I had to do well if I was staying in, but I had to try to get out so I could play."

That summer of 1971 Larry dutifully reported to Fort Jackson in sweltering South Carolina. But he also hired Charlie Dameron's legal firm in Greensboro to find out why the Army had changed the rules on him. "It turns out there was a clause saying any civilian who, in pursuit of his civilian activities, so demonstrates that he can overcome a physical disqualification or handicap, that overrode the injury. If you had the will to overcome, you should be waived in. So if you did good, you were punished for it."

The lawyers set out to lobby the Department of the Army that Miller's induction was "arbitrary and capricious." But they would soon learn it was more than that—it was personal.

The first oddity was the discovery by *The Morning Call* that the incoming chairman of Allentown's Local Selective Service Board 89 was baffled, saying, "It's news to me. I don't know what it's all about." He noted the board had not yet conducted its June meeting, and he remembered no special mention of a case involving Miller at the board's prior meeting.

Further inquiries pointed to the executive secretary of Board 89, a woman named Mamie Bramwell. Miller's lawyers claimed that a physical exam report was "altered after the completion of the examination . . . to falsify findings of disqualification and substitute findings of acceptability" and that the case indicated "a personal dislike of the plaintiff (Miller) and his family" by Bramwell, leading to Larry being railroaded into the service. Recalls Larry, "When they finally got my file from the draft board, it was 120 pages thick with articles about my whole life. Nobody else got that kind of attention, so this lady basically had a hard-on for me." Ms. Bramwell refused to comment, but before long the State Selective Service office in Harrisburg directed the Philadelphia regional legal staff to launch an investigation.

Meanwhile, Larry was excelling at Fort Jackson, leading the mile run (of course), becoming a platoon leader (of course), and qualifying as a rifle marksman (of course). But it was a miserable time, with Larry noting the out-of-state kids were the worst of the worst on the rifle range, almost shooting other people. Because he was a platoon leader, though, Larry did have his own private barracks and an officer's batch right next to him where he could park his Jaguar.

"There was a Lieutenant I met from Winston-Salem; he kept me out of a lot of stuff, like the shots. They'd have us lined up like lab rats. They had these guns that shot all kinds of chemicals into you, I don't know what it was for—and he got me out of that stuff by pulling me out of line saying he had other duties he needed me for.

"I used to wear civilian clothes under my uniform, and take it off whenever he and I went out on the town, or when Leonard and Bonnie came down to see me and keep my spirits up. They really got me through that, because that was a different time. That summer I would have been working with Billy, doing camps all over the East Coast, so I missed out on a lot."

*

Scott Beeten picks up his end of the story: "Meanwhile, I'm wondering how we're running this summer basketball camp in the Poconos without the main attraction. Then Larry calls from basic training and tells me, 'Coach Smith is going to come up and spend as much time as you need him for during the week. And he's bringing another surprise.' So Coach made his own arrangements, and Billy Cunningham came to spend a few days with us as well. They both did that for Larry . . . and for me.

"Coach Smith was one of the greatest people I ever met. I became part of that 'family' because I was Larry's friend, and I couldn't begin to tell you all the things he did for me. One time, walking into Princeton for what used to be the Nike camp, my sons and I are looking for a place to sit and I hear Coach Smith—who traditionally would never sit with anybody—calling, 'Hey, Scott, come on up here—bring your sons!' And while the counselors are playing, he turns to my sons and says, 'Watch this, you're really going to enjoy it.' And some guy shuffles out on the court and starts playing—and it was Michael Jordan.

"Another time, when Carolina was going to play LaSalle at the Palestra and the place was filling up before the game, I look over and there's my sons

sitting with Coach Smith and he's telling them stories. As technical and ana-
lytical as the game has become, it's still a people business. As innovative as he
was as a coach, one of the reasons that Carolina is Carolina is because of what
Dean did as a person.

"When I was coaching at Penn there was an Ivy League rule that you
couldn't start practice until October 22—all the rest of the NCAA started
October 15—so instead of wasting the week I'd go down to watch three
or four days of practices at Carolina. Everybody sat upstairs, except Coach
Smith had me down on the floor. And later on, when the others had to leave,
I'd go into the coaches' room with Eddie [Fogler] and Roy, and then we went
out for dinner. And that was all because of Larry."

*

Back in South Carolina, Private Miller had been going to the doctor at every
twinge to have it on record. He was also giving his lawyers weekly updates on
conference calls to Greensboro every Friday, running up a $13,000 tab for the
summer—"so there went my spending money." Finally, at the end of August
he took another physical on the base, this time with a Colonel Broadus. "He
said I should not be there, because my knee did not qualify me for their standards [i.e., a knee collapse on jungle patrol would be more consequential than
in a gym]—and that I should be released." By now, though, Larry had learned
to be wary of the military bureaucracy.

"You had to get your paperwork from your company clerk, carry it to
the doctor, and then bring it back to the clerk. What I did was make copies of
everything—especially that order that I should be released—send them to my
attorneys, and *then* take the papers back to the clerk. Well, when my lawyers
called the Department of the Army to follow up, the DOA said 'We have his
file right here and we don't have anything saying he should be released.' So
my lawyers said, 'Oh, we have copies right here—shall we send them up to
you?'

"Needless to say, within a couple of days I received paperwork that I
was being honorably discharged out of the service. And after that, the clause

that overcoming a handicap as a civilian waives your deferment was revoked and got known as 'The Miller Clause.' So I was famous for a day. And of course the draft didn't last that much longer."

*

Leaving the Army after ninety-one days, Larry was so excited he took the first contract the Cougars offered him—a $10,000 bump up to $45,000, but for only one year. Understanding he needed to produce or hang up his sneakers, Larry went straight to Laurinburg and caught the last half of training camp that September. "I was in good shape," he recalls, "but totally different shape—mostly muscles instead of running. And they'd hired Tom Meschery as the new coach, who had that stereotype that I was a 'tweener,' so I had to do that thing all over again."

Meschery was a ten-year NBA vet, who'd played power forward along-side Wilt Chamberlain and led the league in fouls one year. (He was also a Russian with the soul of a poet, who later received an MFA from Iowa and published several volumes.) At this point, though, he was a beginner coach and in Lehmann's candid opinion, "Meschery was brain-dead."

(Larry has a more nuanced take on that: "He was the only coach I know who smoked pot with his players. I was at his house once after a game and he offered us some, but I just couldn't do it. I felt that was crossing a line. I might have a beer with a coach, but not a joint because that was still illegal.")

George Lehmann: "Now we come back to training camp at Laurinburg, and the new coach is 'Talk a lot, do nothing.' He's not playing Larry, I have a little run-in with him and he's not playing me. The team goes off on a losing streak, and we get blown out by Utah by like 55 points. Larry is in the game maybe a minute and I don't play at all . . ."

"George was a phenomenal shooter, plus a great passer," swears Miller. "He would've been one of the all-time greats if he kept his mouth shut. But he was hotheaded and said what was on his mind, mouthing off to the coach because he was a lot smarter than a lot of the coaches—and he had more experience than most of them."

Lehmann: "And now we're going to Memphis to play the former Buccaneers. At 8:00 AM the phone rings, and it's Carl Scheer the GM, saying 'George, the owner is here and we want to talk to you.' I figure, here I go again—I'm either getting cut or traded. I go down to the breakfast and Carl says to me, 'How can we straighten out what's going on?' I said, 'Easy—I'll straighten this thing out for you right now: You start me tonight, put Larry alongside me, put Eddie Manning [Danny Manning's dad] in the corner, and we'll beat the crap out of Memphis tonight.' The owner's looking at me like I'm some nut. But that night Larry goes off, I go off, Manning does his job—and we beat 'em. We return home to face Utah again—Larry starting, George starting, Manning starting—we beat them in our building. And that continued on . . ."

Miller started for the rest of the season and—gee, what a surprise—had his most productive pro year, hitting for more than 30 points a number of times and in one seven-game stretch averaging 25.3 points (roughly his old usual). Once, he was even selected by *The Sporting News* as Player of the Month for all of pro basketball, the NBA included. ("That's not a fluke, for a whole month.") To paraphrase Mark Twain, Bob Quincy's report of the death of Miller's career at the hands of Bones McKinney was apparently greatly exaggerated.

Lehmann knew they had something special, noting "At that time, Larry and I could dance with anybody in the league in the back court, because we could play off each other. Larry could run like a deer, could move without the ball, then catch and shoot. He could light it up in the right system, and we made the system right. The game was changing, because the ABA was all about running and shooting the three—we basically gave birth to the basketball that's being played today—although the guys today took it to a whole different level."

By the end of November, the Raleigh paper wrote, "It seems the Carolina Cougars might finally have discovered that big, irrepressible guard they've been searching for since the team's inception three years ago . . . and he has been sitting right there beside them all along, gnawing with frustration.

Larry Miller! He's the man, but not until recently did the magnitude of his talents become fully manifested to the Cougars coaches and management."

"It's the best stretch I've ever had," a vindicated Miller told the paper that winter. "Everything's falling into place right now."

So of course, this being the ABA, management found a way to screw it up.

*

George Lehmann: "When Jerry Steele told me they were signing Joe Caldwell [a two-time NBA All-Star], I said, 'You don't want to do that. Great player, best defensive player in the league, but he can't shoot and he can't rebound'— and it turned out to be the truth. But they signed Caldwell [for $200,000], and we didn't get along but I could play with him. He was the so-called 'star' from the NBA, and he didn't understand how I was playing and Larry was playing, always making snide remarks. We got into a fight in Utah [where George scored 36, Larry 25, and Caldwell only 10], and next thing I know they're shopping Caldwell—the Cougars didn't want to shop me—but nobody wanted to touch his big contract.

"We were in third place, and I was home for New Year's break [averaging 26 points in his previous five games], when I got the call from Meshery telling me they'd traded *me*. And that was devastating to me, because I knew that situation Larry and I had was never going to be as ideal again. We had half a season together. Larry was a star—liked to party, but no drugs were involved when I was there—really a neat guy, a quiet guy, never challenged authority. It was just a weird situation in both of our lives. Looking back, I should have straightened it out with Caldwell. But I had my hard head and didn't do what I needed to do."

Miller was also devastated at losing the best situation he'd ever had. "We were as good together as anybody in pro basketball—we could just give a look and know what was coming—a combination that could have dominated for years. And just like that it was gone. It stunned me when George got traded, because things were going so well and why would you mess with good chemistry?

"Joe Caldwell was a tremendous athlete, and in the flow of the game he'd do incredible things. But he couldn't dominate by himself, he couldn't create shots. And he was a strange personality. He had a local TV show there—I guess it was part of his contract—and one time he told me I was supposed to be on his show. I told him I was supposed to go to dinner at one of the coach's or general manager's house—and they made fish for me because they knew I didn't eat meat—but he said, 'Don't worry, I'll take care of it.' I said 'Okay, you explain to them.' So I went on his show that night . . . and later they called me up and said, 'Where were you? We had everything ready for you!' And right away, I said 'Oh, no . . . he didn't.' But Caldwell never told them—and he did that on purpose."

\*

Larry poured in 35 points in the first game of 1972 without Lehmann, but by the middle of March the magic had faded. His output was up and down, speckled with single-digit nights, and after eleven scoreless minutes in Denver he was benched for the rest of the game with a goose egg. Scott Beeten remembers going with Buff Schwenk and some other Catty guys to watch Larry play against the Nets the following night and imbibe with him after the game.

"Across from Nassau Coliseum was a bar called the Salty Dog that was owned by the Nets' center, Billy Paultz, who they used to call The Whopper. We were there until literally 4:00 in the morning and then took Larry back to his hotel." Larry remembers groggily watching a "Mr. Moto" movie on TV before heading off to catch the team's 7:00 AM flight back to Greensboro. There, he crashed at home for a few hours before heading to the Coliseum, where the franchise was honoring the king of stock car racing, Richard Petty. Suiting up, Larry had no clue that the best and worst nights of his professional life were upon him . . . within days of each other.

"During warmups I felt a little bit queasy, and I even said to someone that I wasn't feeling that good and maybe I shouldn't play—but I did."

And so he made history.

That night, Larry got hot, his teammates kept feeding him, and suddenly he had 38 points at halftime. He flew in the zone all night long and finished the game with 67—at that time the most points a pro basketball guard in either league had ever scored in a single game. And it could have been more, to the point that Larry began to feel embarrassed.

"In the fourth quarter I already had 60 points, and they threw me the ball and I threw it back to them because I already had enough points. Even Caldwell, he'd be there for a layup and turn and throw it out to me. So he could be that way, too. He could be good and then be a pain in the ass. I probably could have gone for another 18 or 20. I proved at every level I could score tons if people just fed me the ball, if I'd wanted to be Maravich and only a shooter. But I didn't want to be the only guy scoring. I wanted to play the complete game."

*Carolina Cougars GM Carl Scheer presents the game ball to Miller after he sets the ABA single game scoring record with 67 points on March 18, 1972—a record he now holds forever.*

After the game, Richard Petty found Larry and told him, "It started out being my night, but ended up being your night." He also stole the single-game scoring record from his idol Jerry West and now, with the league long extinct, it remains an ABA record that Larry will own forevermore.

\*

Three nights later, Larry woke up in the predawn darkness of his Greensboro bedroom hearing a crackling noise. "I ran down the hall, and when I saw the flames blazing it felt like pure evil in the house. I ran back to get Bonnie out the front door—she was sleeping, so if I hadn't woken up to that noise we wouldn't be alive now. Fortunately, I'd learned that it's better to have your bedroom door closed in case something happens in your house, and it turns out that's what saved our lives."

It didn't save the dogs, though. Larry smashed his bedroom window, cutting his hand as he climbed back in to rescue Timi and her pup who were sleeping under his big round bed. "But there was no movement at all . . . and then I couldn't breathe anymore. They said smoke came under the door and under the bed, so they were probably already dead by the time I woke up."

Larry then ran in just his underwear through the late winter chill, a quarter mile barefoot on gravel around the lake to the neighbors to sound the alarm. By the time firemen contained the blaze the house was practically destroyed. Meanwhile, Larry's left (shooting) hand was bleeding so badly it required eleven stitches, he had to have X-rays for smoke inhalation, and have his feet treated. And, yet, with Larry's team needing a win to make the playoffs, the insurance agent rounded up some clothes and he was flown to New York on a private plane, where a waiting limo whisked him to the game with the Nets . . . which the Cougars won with 15 points from stitched-up Larry.

"I wanted to play. That was better than sitting around thinking about it when you can't change things. The cause of the fire was unexplained, but they made the observation it may have been lightning, which I did hear earlier in the evening, starting in the den where the TV was plugged in. It was somewhere on the far end from the bedroom and was burning for hours before I knew about it.

"That house had a spooky history: First that girl fell down the cellar stairs and into a coma . . . then the fire killed Timi and her pup . . . and that same night my teammate Wendell Ladner had been over for dinner and sometime afterward he died young in a plane crash.

"The firemen asked what to do with the dogs, and we buried them on the property because that's what they loved. So after all the dangers she survived, Timi died the way she lived, right there under my bed with me the whole time. She was a beautiful dog . . . I think about her to this day."

*

The Cougars closed out the season with 5 wins in their final six games, Larry averaging 27.5 ppg over that span despite his gashed shooting hand, but they again fell short of the playoffs. Even so, Larry had good reason to feel he'd redeemed his place in the Carolina firmament. Playing more minutes per game than anyone else on the team that year, he'd clearly answered the call to produce by averaging more points than anyone (including Caldwell) other than the 6'11" center, and earned a featured role in the team's future. Now it was just a matter of negotiating the fruits of his labors with GM Carl Scheer, who was saying, "Larry's an all-star in our book, and we'll pay him as an all-star."

*

Buoyed by his prospects, Larry bought himself a condo in Greensboro, and some friends tried to soothe his soul by giving him an English sheep dog puppy named Poco. "But of course when I went on the road it wasn't like in the country where dogs could roam. Luckily the next door neighbors had young kids who fed and walked him for me—they loved the dog."

Meanwhile, if it was spring in the Carolinas, it was time for Larry to enjoy getting to know his fans . . . some better than others. One night, at the request of a young pen pal, Mr. Nice Guy showed up at a local high school prom and proceeded to play deejay, introduce songs, and judge a dance contest for the kids. All was going along fine until "some lady in charge" objected that Larry appeared to be halfway hammered. Larry politely pointed out that he was doing this on his own time out of the goodness of his heart, there was no pay involved, and he wasn't doing anything wrong. And then he concluded quite logically, "I'm sorry, but it's Saturday night—what did you expect?"

Most often, though, Larry preferred playing with the big girls. One of his favorite impromptu stunts occurred one day while driving the highway from Charlotte to Greensboro, as he came upon a carload of girls outside China Grove. The girls began waving and flirting with the guy drinking beer in the Jaguar, and soon began pleading for a couple of brews. "So I told them, 'Just drive steady on and keep your eyes on the road, and I'll do the rest.' So I pulled a couple of beers from the cooler, pulled in close beside them, passed them over going about 65 mph, and waved goodbye. That's what it was like back then—Boom—do it."

Another road trip might have turned out worse if not for his statewide reputation. This was during a period when Larry had made the acquaintance of a couple of well-known, well-endowed exotic dancers, one named Morgana (a comedic stripper who danced with a snake around her shoulders and was known as The Kissing Bandit for her affection for athletes) and another called Hot Tamale (real name none of your business).

"I'm not much on strip clubs, but Leonard took me to C'est Bon in Charlotte for kicks where he knew the owner, and that's how I met Hot Tamale. She told me she'd just dated David Janssen from "The Fugitive" the night before. I said, 'Wow, I'm really happy for you.' So we went out to the basketball camp grounds that night to fool around, and then I'm taking her back to Greensboro, and I'd had a few beers and was kind of weaving a little bit—and a cop stopped me. And when he asked why I was weaving, I just pointed to her and said, 'Well, she was . . . you know . . .' And the cop says, 'Oh, I'm sorry, Larry'—and he let me go! Would that happen these days?

"Later that summer, still with the Cougars, I used to get a couple of guys and we'd put the top down and drive around. And one time we stopped at a small place, went in and Richard Petty was in there filming something. And he sees me and says, 'I can't go *anywhere* without seeing you!' "

But that was about to change.

\*

That spring, as Larry prepared his usual summer camps, word had come that following an interleague court battle Billy Cunningham would be leaving the NBA to join the Carolina Cougars. Miller was psyched to play with Billy at last, and further happy to hear that Larry Brown was taking over his first pro head coaching job. "With Billy and Larry Brown coming in, that was exciting. I knew these guys, the style they'd be playing, and we could have had a good team and could have won." Everything was lining up perfectly. Except . . .

By early July, Larry was candidly telling his hometown *Morning Call* that a hassle was developing with the Cougars despite his outstanding season for them. Larry felt he'd earned an above-average salary (as Sheer had acknowledged), and asked for a bump from $45,000 to $60,000 a year. (The pro average was then around $50,000.) "I thought I deserved a raise because I had the best season of anybody on the team—it seemed normal." Scheer, however, claimed the team couldn't afford that and countered with no raise at all. The problem wasn't Larry's bid—it was the other guys capitalizing on the war between the leagues. It took $300,000 to lure Billy, a genuine star, from the NBA . . . a rookie center (who proved to be fool's gold) was getting $125,000 . . . and Caldwell was still dragging in $200,000. On a franchise struggling to break even, that top-heavy payroll left bupkis for everyone else—even though Larry's full asking price was easily the best value on the roster.

Scheer (the widely respected inventor of the slam dunk contest) didn't really want to lose Miller, so he took a gamble. He contacted the GM of the new expansion team in San Diego, which would have its pick of unsigned free agents, and talked about making a deal for Miller in which he bluffed that Larry was asking for an enormous salary (clearly not true). When San Diego turned down the trade, Scheer crossed his fingers he'd scared them off.

Then the Cougars turned up the pressure on Larry, knowing how much he wanted to stay. "I loved it there, and they told me if I didn't sign, they'd put me on the unprotected list. They thought I wouldn't be picked, and then they'd use that as a bargaining chip with me—thinking I'd sign for less when no one took me. Matter of fact, it was Larry Brown who called me up when he'd just signed to coach, to give me a heads-up about what they were doing if I didn't sign. And here I was just asking for a nominal raise."

In the end, Larry stood firm. The Cougars played their bluff, and that August San Diego pounced on the virtual all-star—he was second of the seventeen players they took—a steal for them at his full asking price.

Boom—Larry Miller was suddenly no longer a Cougar, and the Carolinas were in an uproar. Within a week the team received thousands of protest letters, an all-star game was picketed, and 700 season ticket orders to Cougar games were cancelled (costing them easily more than five times what Larry's raise would have).

According to *The Pocono Record*, "Some quick businessman came up with buttons which showed a smile on the top half, proclaiming 'Billy C is back,' and a tear on the bottom, saying 'but Larry's gone.' And now the Cougars have second thoughts. They want Miller back. But San Diego, realizing the prize plum it picked, wants two players, four draft choices, plus cash for the deal."

It didn't happen.

"So I went to the Conquistadors. And ironically the Cougars made the East finals the next year, but they lost there because they couldn't get any scoring out of the guard position. So there you go." Ultimately, the Caldwell deal that George Lehmann warned against had cost the Cougars both guards in one of the best backcourt pairings the ABA had ever seen.

*

"He was a special dude," reflects George Lehmann of his favorite running buddy. "Larry was the best player I ever played with, all around, on and off the court. Even in today's game, there are certain players on certain teams that are really good players, but would not be good players on other teams—only because of the system. And some players never get the chance to get to that level. Larry had all the things necessary to be extremely successful—the only problem Larry had was who was in charge of the team.

"Larry was in the middle of this game when it was going from a half-court, slow-it-down, throw-it-in, post-up to use the big guys game . . . to speed and explosiveness and the 3-pointer. Larry and guys who played in our era were in that switch-over—and Larry got caught in the switches. If he was coming out today, this game that they're playing now has 'Larry Miller' written all over it."

CHAPTER 10

# CRUNCH TIME

SAN DIEGO:

Despite reaping his richest contract yet, Larry didn't descend on San Diego to be the talk of the town, or try to be anyone's savior. He knew better than to put down roots buying real estate . . . or shipping his Jaguar in . . . or falling in love . . . only to have them ripped away again. After giving his all for Lehigh Valley pride, and then for love of the Carolinas, Larry parked his heart in the east and treated this startling next step as little more than an extended business trip.

He rented his Greensboro condo to Tar Heels-turned-Cougars Dennis Wuycik and Steve Previs, and gave the new dog to the neighbors. ("I didn't really want any more dogs after losing mine in the fire.") He put his furniture into Greensboro storage, where it remained for seven years, not getting it out until well after he'd finished playing. And instead of styling around the Golden State in a supercharged machine, "I think I just rented cars out there at the airport." Because by now Larry had learned that the "pro" game in the ABA was really played by executives calling the tune in a warped version of musical chairs that, for players, always ended in sudden death.

*

The San Diego Conquistadors—known by all as "the Qs"—were the first and only expansion team added to the ABA, hastily contrived to even the league at ten teams after Pittsburgh and Florida franchises folded. A local orthodontist-turned-investor convinced other owners to give him a go, which alienated the spurned manager of the 14,400-seat San Diego Sports Arena. That left the new team relegated to the owner's alma mater, at San Diego State's 3,200-seat Peterson Gym (described as "atop a remote mesa"). There were no refreshment stands, and also no turnstiles, which allowed the team's GM to invent attendance figures at will. What could go wrong? Larry, it seems, was fated to help launch new franchises with the best of intentions and a lack of most everything else.

The Q's had one remarkable asset, though, an LA Lakers assistant swiped from Bill Sharman and now making his debut as a pro head coach, named K.C. Jones. A proven winner, Jones had played college hoops with the great Bill Russell as a San Francisco Don, and then for many years together on classic Celtics teams, winning eight NBA titles. So, although this was not Miller's town and not Miller's team, in K.C. Jones and assistant Stan Albeck he did find someone worth playing for.

Larry appreciated the low-key style of a coach who didn't have to raise his voice to command attention, telling *Sports Illustrated*, "In the huddle during a time-out, K.C. will stand quiet a moment and then look at the guy or guys who have been messing up the most. He'll say something like, 'That guy too much for you?' And you say, 'Er, ah, nah, he's not.' Then he'll look you right in the face and say very clearly in that soft voice, 'Then why don't you *do* something about it?' "

As the Q's only white starter, Larry also noted, "Kase had instant respect when he got here, just because he had his reputation as a great player.

But I think he gets extra respect because he's a brother who made it. Most of the players in the pros are brothers now, and I don't think there's any more logical thing for a team to do than hire a good black coach."

*

True to form, Larry rented a place in Mission Beach right on the ocean, and to this day says he enjoyed San Diego as a beautiful city. But this was no Hollywood spree, replete with starlets and famous names. Sure, he took a trip or two down to nearby Mexico, "but that wasn't my cup of tea." And one night when Richard Howard and moonshine-runner-turned-NASCAR-legend Junior Johnson were out in Los Angeles, Larry flew up there to meet them for dinner. "Back then a flight to LA was five or ten bucks, every hour on the hour. So I did things like that."

Larry never got around to dating anyone, though, because he still considered himself involved with Bonnie . . . from afar. So perhaps Leonard Laye's view from back in North Carolina was right on the mark: "He and Bonnie had been going on for a good while—for Larry a real long time. And I think they talked on the phone most nights of the week, I'd say for six to eight months. But that's tough to keep a relationship going like that. He was playing in the Western Conference and they didn't come to play the Cougars, so it wasn't like they could see each other. And then it just gradually dissipated. And I hated it. I really liked Bonnie . . . and he did, too."

*

The Q's were given a break by the league, launching their brief history with a long home stand during which they won five of their first six games (easily downing the Cougars when Larry scored 23 points, nipping opponent Billy by 1). The rest of the season was not particularly memorable, but K.C. Jones was astute enough to encourage the league's single-game scoring leader to shoot and keep shooting all night long.

"K.C. gave me the green light to shoot 20 times a game—and I'd proven I could light it up at every level—but I wasn't selfish enough to light it up all the time. That wasn't my style, to hunt my shot, because in the course of a game it would come my way because of my activity. I wanted to play the team game and win. What management didn't understand is that when you steal a ball, or set a screen for somebody, or hit the open man—all those things that we learned from Dean—that would make other players better and win you games."

What Miller didn't understand until later, though, was that amateur owners loved the instant gratification of scoring so much that soon putting up numbers was the only way to stay in the game—and get a big contract. (Coaches, of course, knew the value of playmakers, but they were at the mercy of owners wanting to see their dollars on the court.) "But if you only get rewarded when you score, there's a conflict there, right? Every time you get the ball you're going to gun it, rather than pass it around for the better shot.

"You didn't have the strong general managers then because, with so few teams, there were not that many role models to learn from—just guys who came off the street and got that position—and you see some of the draft picks those people made. If you look back at that time, a lot of the draft choices could shoot . . . but that's all they could do. They didn't have any game at all. It was almost sad."

The Q's rookie owner was typical of the breed, a casual fan who had been a track star at San Diego State and, now in his late thirties, still had something to prove. "He was maybe 5'9", but he liked to try out players himself at halftime or after the games. It was just bizarre. After one game we had a seven-footer try out—an Englishman—and the owner decided to play this guy one-on-one, full court, to evaluate him. Which is dumb because you know a center can't run with a guard. But that's the story of the ABA . . ."

*

After that season, Larry delayed his return to North Carolina because the Cougars were still in the playoffs—and attention was the last thing he wanted while that was going on. "I still had bad feelings about them, and there would've been a lot of questions that it was better not to answer." So he waited a while, catching up with friends and preparing his basketball camps, before eventually coming to check on his investments.

Soon after getting out of college, Larry had bought a couple of Chapel Hill duplexes for rental income and a piece of commercial property on 15-501 (the main drag of Tobacco Road) right as one enters town that eventually became a Wendy's restaurant. Fortunately, these ventures made on his own were faring much better than the con man sports agent's pipe dreams.

"I'd also gotten involved in a women's clothing store in the west end of Greensboro, which I knew nothing about, but my friend Nick wanted to do it, so I'd put money into it. It was called Reflections, and the shop was really well done. We got our stuff from California so we were way ahead, fashion-wise, and we had young ladies running it doing fashion shows and whatever. We even hired a fashion buyer out in LA, and once in a while I'd fly up there, going to shows with her. But that whole thing was a mess because I was not involved beyond putting money in and being the front man. Like anything, it's about management. It was dumb—just like throwing money away—and it only lasted two or three years."

*

Following his usual mid-August camp in the Poconos with Scott Beeten and other roundball buddies, Larry returned to the West Coast looking forward to another productive year. But, once again, the ABA's wheel of misfortune turned . . .

"After that year in San Diego, I could have stayed with those guys still there. K.C. Jones and I used to go out and have drinks after a game. Sharman you could never go out with; he chastised me because he knew I drank. But at the start of the second season K.C. left to take an NBA job [later coaching the Celtics to NBA championships], and I believe Stan Albeck was the interim coach. I would have flourished under Stan, too, who had a good coaching career after that [thirty years and head coach of four NBA teams]. But, typical of my luck in the ABA, they didn't believe Stan was good enough, so they had to go out and spend a million dollars to get Wilt Chamberlain to come coach. Which was a joke."

In fairness, San Diego's management was paying Wilt $1.8 million over three years to be an intimidating player-coach—but when the NBA sued for their rights to him as a player, Wilt's height was good for nothing but blocking the view on the sideline. Where coaching was clearly not his strength.

"Wilt hardly ever showed up to practice," Larry recalls. "He had his white houseboy come down and throw the ball up and run practice or follow a script." Sometimes Wilt even skipped the games for book signings. (Ironically, whenever Wilt missed a game, Albeck would fill in as head coach—and he won them all.) "Hiring Wilt was the dumbest thing I ever heard of. But maybe they were counting on him filling the stands with all his conquests. That's when I gave up on them.

"I didn't fit into Wilt's plans. He wanted real small guards running up and down, and I don't know who was running the court better than I did . . . but obviously he didn't see it that way." As a result, Larry played in only seven games that fall, averaging a measly 9 minutes per game—in sports parlance, "he saw limited action"—before being abruptly traded to the Virginia Squires.

This was more than just dandy with Larry—and although he couldn't know it at the time, this deal would shape the rest of his life.

*

VIRGINIA BEACH:

Batted between coasts like a badminton birdie for the fourth time in five years, Larry was "very, very happy" to be back in ACC territory—still on that healthy Qs contract—four hours from Chapel Hill and an eight-hour drive from Pennsylvania. Similar to the Cougars' business model, Virginia's regional team played in several coastal cities like Norfolk, Hampton, and Newport News, all clustered around Chesapeake Bay. Featuring the natural beauty of endless bays and good-time beaches, and a large military population, the area was a tonic for Larry. He also respected Squires coach Al Bianchi, the former guard he'd met at Billy Cunningham's wedding and knew to be a really good guy. The respect was mutual as Bianchi told the press, "We were looking for a good, strong guard and Larry fits this. He's very aggressive and plays great defense."

Arriving in the Tidewater area, Larry's choice of lodgings was a no-brainer: In those days, all the teams and local players would stay at the Admiralty motel (ahem, "an Executive Inn Motor Hotel") conveniently located on Military Highway right between Norfolk and Virginia Beach—because in the ABA everyone was always just passing through. (And now, even the motel itself has passed away.) Also rooming at the Admiralty was "Chopper" Travaglini, a beloved figure who was perhaps the most famous trainer in pro basketball and who hosted a regular card game. "We were always playing cards in there," Larry recalls. "After games we'd play all night long—Julius Erving, George Gervin, Alex Hannum—you name it, they played. It was fun. So for Christmas I got him a nice card table."

Living out of motel rooms made for an itinerant love life as well, much to the regret of well-meaning friends like Leonard Laye. "One of the greatest ironies, when Larry wound up with the Virginia Squires, is that around that time Bonnie had landed a management job with the Los Angeles Convention Bureau. So they kind of crisscrossed the country. And I often wondered if he'd still been out west, what would've happened . . ."

*

The ABA was founded on a shrewd business plan based on the recent lesson of the football leagues: Like many business start-ups, the new league didn't need to defeat the NBA to succeed—just bedevil the established teams enough to push them into ridding themselves of the competition by absorbing the ABA's stronger markets and buying the weaker ones out—banking a profit for the owners. Consequently, even the money-losers were desperate to hang on long enough to share in that pot of gold at the end of the rainbow.

Unfortunately, one of the few ways a struggling team like the Squires could stem the financial rot was by trading away its most promising players, and so Julius Erving—already famous as "Dr. J"—was sent to the New York

Nets for cash before the season even began. Before long, Larry got a firsthand look at the shoestring operation in action.

"The way that league was running, you didn't know where the checks were coming from—or *if* they would come. I remember, over the Christmas holiday, our owner, Earl Foreman, flew down from Washington, and Chopper and I went out and met him at the airport, and he gave us the checks for the next pay period. For doing that for us, alone, he was a good man. But that's how it was run."

Before the season was over, on the night of the All-Star Game, it was announced that George "The Ice Man" Gervin—you only get a nickname if you're really good—was being sent to San Antonio for $225,000. Thus, it was foreordained that this team, sapped of its stars, would end with a seriously bad record, losing twice as many games as it won. The Squires did salvage a measure of pride, though, by snagging the final playoff spot, making it to the league semifinals where, ironically, they lost to the Nets and their own recent teammate, Dr. J.

Larry, himself, had an okay year, playing in seventy-three games with the sixth-most minutes, resulting in the sixth-best scoring average of 9.5 ppg—not terrible on a roster with lots of turnover, but hardly special. Far more important for Larry's future was a happenstance meeting while tooling down the highway to see a girl one Sunday afternoon.

\*

Larry was driving his white Chevy Monte Carlo on Route 44, the express toll road from Norfolk down to Virginia Beach, on his way to hang out with a woman he knew only casually, when he noticed a guy in the car next to him. The guy nodded and Larry nodded back . . . just two strangers passing on the road.

"And then—talk about kismet—I go visit this woman, and it turns out the guy lives in the apartment right across from her door. So she introduces me to Larry Weldon and we start chatting . . . and after a bit he says he's going down to The Shack to have a couple of beers. Do we want to come? But she had things to do for a while, so he told me 'You can wait here, or we can go down and have a beer.' And I said, 'Let's go have a beer!' [Does this sound familiar, Billy?] And we became best friends from there on."

Larry Weldon was in the real estate business, then working for a developer in the nearby Nag's Head area of North Carolina's Outer Banks. Larry Miller, already a small-time investor, had moved beyond youthful brainstorms of one day running a nightclub for kids and was looking into an eventual real estate career, himself. Clearly they had plenty to talk about. One wrinkle that caught Miller's attention was this: In Virginia you had to work five years toward qualifying for a real estate broker's license. In North Carolina, though, you could get your license and become a broker right away. And then, after only *one* year's experience there, you could get reciprocity to operate in Virginia—effectively saving yourself four years of apprenticeship. Before long, even before basketball season ended, as the Squires traveled around the country, Larry Miller's airplane reading began to be all about real estate.

*

That spring, the Squires signed a younger guard, and Coach Bianchi tried to do the right thing by Larry. "Al was kind of hinting to me that he didn't think the Squires were going to pick up my contract, and asking if I had any interest in becoming an assistant coach with him. We had a good relationship, and I think he would have wanted me back as a player because we got along well. I played the way he wanted me to, and I wasn't a problem. I think letting me go was management's decision. The Squires just didn't want to pick up my salary."

Larry had no desire to become a coach, though—essentially beginning a new career in the same unstable league he knew as a player—so he began that off-season by calling Billy Cunningham for advice. Billy put him in touch with his own agent, Irwin Weiner, and they began to explore Larry's options. Meanwhile, free of team obligations, Larry began preparing for life after basketball by commuting to the Greensboro Realty School for classes a couple of days a week.

In May, Larry flew to Catasauqua briefly to be the featured speaker at the same high school sports banquet he'd skipped as a player. There he spoke candidly to the kids about the arc of his unusual career: "I like the job, I love playing basketball . . . I have been a success at it and it has been rewarding . . . I really enjoy it and have no complaints. But I am now at a crossroads . . . Virginia is about to fold. The owners want to sell the team . . ." Then, acknowledging that his future was uncertain, he shared his interest in real estate and that he was currently studying for certification as a real estate broker.

(Larry's hunch that it was time to move on seemed prescient that summer, when word came that, despite having one of the ABA's most loyal fan bases, the Cougars were finished in the Carolinas. In the course of merger talks with the NBA, it became clear the regional concept was not wanted—in part due to the added travel expense of bopping between several cities—and with no town deemed large enough to support a franchise, Carolina would be spurned. Realizing the gold at the end of their rainbow was just a mirage, the team's owners sold out to investors who moved the whole operation to St. Louis.)

\*

"I thought I was a free agent," Miller recalls, "and packed my bags and went up to New York to see Irwin Weiner. We were looking for deals anywhere, and he got me a tryout with the Utah Stars. I think when the Squires found out about that, they decided to do something about it." In fact, because Larry's Conquistadors contract had been signed just before that season, Larry was still technically Squires property through the end of the summer. That August, in what had become an annual rite of ABA teams shuffling their trading cards, the AP announced that Larry Miller had been swapped to the Utah team by the Squires, astutely getting value for him just before their rights under his Q's contract expired. The Virginia GM explained that the team had decided "to go with youth and to give the team a new look." (In other words, the strapped franchise was rebuilding on the cheap.) Larry, at twenty-eight now, was no longer young, nor cheap, and he took the idea of bouncing across the country for the fifth time with equanimity.

"I really enjoyed my time with the Squires," he says to this day. "I liked Al Bianchi, we had a good time, and we made the playoffs. And I had a decent year." (This would be the last season Virginia made the playoffs, and history would record that the new look team the following year "simply imploded with a lack of talent," losing sixty-nine games to finish with the worst record in ABA history.)

Larry was not imploding, but even as he set aside real estate studies for Mountain Time, he was ready to move on from the game he loved. "At this time, I knew my time was running out in pro basketball . . . as was my enthusiasm for the game. I had enjoyed it and loved it, but the extraneous things that surrounded basketball and became part of it were just too much.

"Jerry West and I talked about it one night. It's all about situations. He said he was lucky to play for one team in thirteen years with the Lakers. I played for one coach at Catasauqua, one coach at North Carolina, and then nine different coaches with different philosophies on five different teams in just six pro seasons—so that ought to tell you something right there. It was all about selling yourself, every year, and I just got tired of it."

*

UTAH:

Traveling light now, with tempered expectations, Larry flew into Salt Lake City, picked up a rental car, and booked himself into a hotel, already figuring he would one day settle back in Virginia. The former LA Stars were unrecognizable here—new city, new owner, new coach, and not one of his former teammates still on the roster—so Larry was just looking for an opportunity to make a difference.

What he found was a chaotic situation on a team overloaded with seven guards, but he also noticed a raw rookie just coming out of high school named Moses Malone. At that time, the future instant Hall of Famer and three-time MVP of the NBA was 6'10" and talented, but still just a skinny kid weighing around 205—and, to Larry's eyes, he needed some guidance.

"I'm saying to myself, 'I could really help this kid' because he was very shy, he really couldn't talk, and was real hard around the edges. Mentoring him would have appealed to me if they were going in that direction—but I don't think they had *any* direction at the time. And they were coached by another NBA guy who didn't think I could play."

Larry barely had time to whet his whistle in Utah, but he did harvest a memory that outlasted the Stars. "That's when I discovered Miller Lite beer, because that was a test market for it. When I got back to the east I told people about Miller Lite and, sure enough, it became a big hit."

After appearing in only five of the season's first nine games (averaging 5 minutes per game), in the first week of November the ABA's all-time single-game scoring leader was cut for the first time in his life. The team's explanation was that someone had to go and Miller was "pretty banged up." Larry, of course, never saw it that way. "I was fortunate, playing in there underneath with the big guys so much, that in my entire pro career I only missed one game when I sprained an ankle. In Utah I never really got an opportunity, though. When the guy came in to let me go, I said 'I wish you'd given me a chance.' But it was really unorganized, and that was a waste of time. I was just passing through."

*

By now, Larry's game had passed through so much amateur management that it was feeling foreign to him. For the blue-collar kid who had shoveled snow off the town court, relentlessly built up his body, and trained himself for teamwork, the slapdash style of the ABA was an affront to the soul. Finding it ever harder to know why he should care, he had finally arrived at a clarity understood on any playground: These were just not guys he wanted to play with anymore.

"It all just added up," he reflects now. "It wasn't fun anymore. When it doesn't make sense it'll drive you crazy, and eventually, it drove me away. That's when I left the game. I didn't want to be part of it anymore.

"I never went back, and turned down several offers to play or coach over the years. Larry Brown, when he was coaching out in Denver, asked me to go out there as a player to spell David Thompson. But I told him, 'No, that's enough. I'm ready to move on.' Once I decided it was over, it was over."

*

Larry Miller's retirement from the game he had loved and lost was little noted in the press that fall, even after establishing the single-game scoring record for a pro guard—which in all the decades since has been surpassed only by Michael Jordan, David Thompson, Pete Maravich, and Kobe Bryant. Even less noticed is that the "tweener" thought to be too short to play forward and too slow to be a guard averaged more rebounds per minute across his pro career than All-Star guards Jerry West, Jordan, and Bryant.

The much traveled Larry Brown, now a multiple Coach of the Year with three decades of NBA experience, has said "There's no doubt in my mind Larry would have been successful in the NBA. He was a great athlete, an unbelievable jumper at 6'4" with great strength. He could guard big guys; he could guard small guys. When I look at the way the game is played today on the perimeter, he's a guy who would really fit in now . . . If he was coming out of college today everyone in the NBA would want him."

That fall, Peggy Miller wrote a final entry in the scrapbook she'd been keeping since her son's school days: "The end has come after 18 years of basketball, 14 years in the limelight. I'm very proud of a great kid, and a terrific basketball player. You have more character in your little finger than a lot of men have in their entire bodies. Good luck and Good Health for the rest of your life, and I hope it will be a long one. Love, Mom."

*

Sitting in a Salt Lake taxi to the airport, Larry Miller knew he'd made the right decision when years of discouragement lifted from his shoulders, giving way to a sensation that was more like wings: Absolute freedom from schedules, skeptics, and the expectations of others. Basketball had given him the role every boy of his era wanted to play—a hero for his hometown, his university, and thousands of fans he would never know. "I guess a lot of people dream of living a life like that," he would say later. "I was one of the lucky ones, in that my dreams came true." But after dreams come true . . . what comes next?

CHAPTER 11

# BEACHED

Already way out west, Larry bought a ticket to Los Angeles to flop with friends at Hermosa Beach and consider what he wanted to do. He was set to tackle real estate back east, but first had to be sure about giving up acting. And checking in with Vincent Chase, he discovered Universal's offer was still on the table. Meanwhile, lingering for a couple of weeks, he reacquainted himself with the sprawling life he had already ditched once before, wondering how he'd fare now in such a difficult place to live. He got a taste of it one night when even his mojo with women let him down.

"This is how stupid I am," he remembers ruefully. "I was going to stay with my buddy that night, and I met this girl next door who seemed to like me. But I already had a date he'd fixed me up with, somewhere up north, who turned out to be Clint Eastwood's secretary. She was a hottie and we really hit it off. We had dinner and then she invited me up for a nightcap, but I said, 'No, I had to get back to the beach.' She said, 'Oh, come on, please come up.'

Nowadays you could just text. But I left her in the lurch to drive back to the neighbor, trying to do the right thing—and she was already with someone else! How many times have I learned that lesson? I had two sure things, and ended up with nothing."

Perhaps that flirtation with too much temptation reminded Larry of what he already knew—that Hollywood dreams were a bait and switch, with every day dangling just enough promise to tease you through a thousand let-downs. Larry may have been new to acting but he wasn't a rookie at earning, and unlike other wannabes he knew all about the fool's gold of fame. This was a business in which 90% of actors were unemployed at any given time—more time parked on the bench than Larry had in the ABA—and the studio's modest $700 monthly guarantee (advanced against nothing but pipe dreams) meant he'd often be working at something else. There was also the matter of that studio contract telling him where to go and who to be for the next seven years. Larry had been owned before, but not for that long and that cheaply.

Eventually he remembered what the former Duke star and pro Jeff Mullins once told him—that when he was through playing basketball he didn't ever want to have to punch a time clock. Larry didn't either, having done that back in high school. He wanted to work for himself, to come and go on his own time, where no one could bench him ever again.

"I told Universal I'd get back to them . . . but I never did. How many people do you know who turned down Hollywood? I had a legitimate sev-en-year offer, so I could have gone there in a heartbeat. But I didn't feel it in my heart, so it wouldn't have been fair. I just didn't want it."

*

Larry flew coast-to-coast one last time that winter of 1975, landing in Virginia Beach to work and play hard in a new arena but, typically, still at the beach. There he shared an apartment with Larry Weldon, at first the only friend he had in town, but Weldon knew everyone so Miller by proxy did, too, right away. Still living off his basketball winnings and real estate income, the UNC All-Star was the perfect hire for Weldon's employer, Ocean Sands, selling vacation properties to Tar Heels across the border on the Outer Banks. And Ocean Sands was perfect for Miller, too, suddenly a rookie again with no real estate license but legally allowed to make sales there in a closed development.

"Back then the concept was way ahead of its time. They were right on the ocean, but set back behind the dune line maybe two or three hundred yards, so the lots were small but the open spaces were big." Miller even took the plunge, himself, buying a stretch of oceanfront in partnership with Billy Cunningham, the agent Irwin Weiner, and Billy's former UNC captain Jim Hudock. "We had a beautiful lot—an end one—I'm sure that's worth who knows what now." At the same time, Larry resumed commuting to Greensboro, finishing up those state-approved real estate classes, and before long the former honor student had scored 277 out of 280 on his exam—the highest score his instructors had ever seen.

Off duty, Larry made himself at home by learning the local landmarks, like a hill called Mount Trashmore (no kidding, the original city dump made into a large park), and stayed in shape by running along the beach and boardwalks. It was on the beach at 58th Street that he met a Marine one day named Theo Cantana who still remembers, "I saw this guy run by wearing a headband like I did, so we met and started running together. And then we all hung out on the beach playing volleyball, relaxing, and running through the park. Larry was a good runner." And since running naturally led to cooling off with a few beers—which naturally led to picking up girls together—before long Larry had himself a new gang, same as it ever was.

The only puzzlement for many of Miller's longtime friends was: Why was he *here*?

*

Dick Grubar, who had coached for a few years following his pro experience, had lost touch with Miller but thought returning to the Tar Heel state was a no-brainer. "When I decided to get out of coaching, the next thought I had was to go back to North Carolina, because everybody knows who you are and you can pick and choose whatever you want to do—which I was able to do.

And if I could do that, Larry *really* could have done that. That was the biggest surprise to me—that he never took advantage of what everybody thought of him. I always wondered about that."

One clue may lie in Theo Cantana's observation: "The biggest thing I remember is, when I met Larry he wanted nothing to do with basketball. He wouldn't go to the Y, didn't want to dribble or even touch a ball. He didn't want anybody to know that he was 'Larry Miller.' I think he was tired of being hounded and just wanted to be left alone like a normal joe-shit-the-rag-man. He was very humble and wouldn't trade on his name in real estate—and he should have—but he didn't. I don't know what happened there. I basically said, 'You're nuts!' Because he was an idol."

Miller has said that, once he retired, the ball was like a foreign object, and except for one alumni game against UCLA in the 80s he never picked up a ball again. "It was like I'd never been there."

Willfully rebuffing stardom was a sharp U-turn from dreaming up a restaurant chain with his name up in neon alongside Roy Rogers. But perhaps Bones McKinney had simply taught Larry too much about the odds against recreating old miracles. Scott Beeten, for one, finds his teenage pal's decision pretty sensible by Lehigh Valley standards. "We were taught to never be real impressed with ourselves. Larry's dad worked on the assembly line at Mack Truck and lived in the same little house for forty years. Growing up in an area like that you don't get too caught up in yourself."

Beeten is one of those who invited Larry to coach with him, only to be turned down, and reasons: "I think, as much love as he had for the game, as much as he put into it emotionally and physically, my guess is one thing that soured him on pro ball was how little control he had. He was always a pretty individualistic guy who took a lot of pride in doing things his way and having a lot of control over things start-to-finish. He didn't trade on his name because he wanted to trade on the fact that he was a really good real estate guy."

Miller, for whom the beach had always been a refuge from the oversight of parents and coaches, explains simply, "I liked the area and figured I could get along well. So that's when I started the second part of my life." And perhaps this demarcation was fundamental to taking charge of new expectations. Perhaps, like a snake shedding a skin that no longer fits, Larry had to slip out of his old "Larry Miller" life in order to inhabit the next one.

*

One of the first women Miller met while playing with the Squires had been a girlfriend named Patsy, and when he retired back to Virginia Beach they began dating again. "We had a lot of fun together and became good friends, but after a year or two she had an opportunity to become a stewardess with Eastern Airlines—starting with school in Florida. She asked my advice about what to do, saying she wouldn't go if I wanted her to stay. And I said, 'Well, of course I'll miss you, but you'll be sorry for the rest of your life if you don't do it. Besides, I'll be here for you when you get back.' So she went, and we dated a few more years until she was stationed so far away that we eventually lost touch.

"Then, something like thirty years later, she called me out of the blue and asked, 'Do you know why I'm calling?' And I said, 'Yeah, you want to thank me.' She said, 'How did you know?!' and I said, 'Some things you just know.' So she went on to thank me for encouraging her to go with the airlines, she'd had a wonderful life, saw the world, and she never would have done it if I hadn't pushed her. I guess it's because playing had taken me all over the world, but I just knew it was the right thing to do."

*

After a few years selling vacation homes over the state line—now a certified agent with that reciprocal license in Virginia—Larry stopped commuting to the Old North State and began working with Everett Tolson, bringing the 7-Eleven chain into the area. "That was my induction into the commercial side of real estate. At one time, Tolson had or managed over 200 properties and I was mainly looking into sites for 7-Elevens and other commercial deals."

Now in his early thirties, Miller enjoyed what, for him, was a balanced life: earning in real estate by day . . . maintaining good habits by hitting the gym three times a week and running seven-mile loops through Seashore Park . . . and, of course, maintaining bad habits after the sun went down. This was an era when Larry and Theo—joined by a third musketeer, Gene Schmidt, who owned the town's Zero submarine shops—would patrol the night looking for damsels in distress or, lacking damsels, creating distress of their own. This often involved localized versions of "Chicken" in which it wasn't speed that could kill you; it was jackass impulses lubricated by too many beers.

Like the night Gene was cruising down the boulevard and thought to prank Miller by suddenly flipping into the back seat with Theo, just to see what Larry in the shotgun seat would do. As the car rolled driverless toward a line of cars stopped at a red light, though, unperturbed Larry calmly wondered, "What are you doing? It's *your* car." Prompting Gene to hurtle back over the seat, headfirst, to hit the brakes.

Another night Gene was so cockeyed that, gliding down the street, he drove his old brown convertible right up onto the top of a parked transport truck. Because what's the point of not settling down with a wife and kids if you don't court disaster instead now and then?

\*

As the years rounded into the affluent '80s, Larry got a good price for his properties in Chapel Hill and, flush with this grubstake, figured it was time he became his own boss at last. The first Larry Miller & Associates office—"which was a fancy name for me"—was on Virginia Beach's oceanfront where he and Larry Weldon shared a secretary. "Starting then I did all kinds of stuff—I built some things, sold a lot of land—I was a free agent and could do whatever I wanted to do. Until 1985, it all went through there."

Around this time, running buddy Theo left the Marine Corps and went to work in food distribution and serviced a big restaurant owned by an experienced real estate investor named Tom Coghill. Coghill was a force who flew his own plane and already knew Dean Smith. "I was a Ram's Club member long before I knew Mills. Back when it was legal, I used to fly football recruits to Chapel Hill in my plane. I took Ken Willard from Richmond to Chapel Hill the first time when he was fifteen. [The UNC fullback went on to become a four-time Pro Bowler.] And Dean called me once asking if I could find a summer job for JR Reid, because he was from Virginia Beach, and I said sure. I still have the letter Dean wrote to thank me."

Coghill guided Miller to various projects, like working on his oldest boy's house and at one point putting up a basketball pole and backboard for him in Croatan Beach. More important, though, Coghill and his wife Nancy—both about fifteen years older—became like second parents to Miller, sharing their lives and advice in the following years. Tom still enjoys the memory of an evening the three of them shared a table at Monterrey's, when Larry tried to chat up a girl at the table behind them with little success. "So Larry asks my wife, 'Would you please tell this girl that I'm okay?' And Nancy says 'How about I write you a letter of recommendation,' and she wrote it out right there on a bar napkin . . . which Larry handed to the girl. Well, she thought that was hilarious and they wound up dating a few times." (Assist: Coghill.)

Larry fared pretty well flying solo at Monterrey's, too. "One tip I learned a long time ago: If it's a crowded room, you want to stand at the end of the bar by the Ladies Room. That way, if you want to meet a good-looking lady, they're coming right at you."

With his business growing, Larry could now flex real estate muscle, as he did during what has since been dubbed "The Bank Robbery Without a Gun." It began with an impulse over beers one night when Coghill's other son, Tommy Jr., mentioned a friend in western Virginia who had a beautiful '55 Thunderbird for sale—turquoise and cream (and no car ever did turquoise better), the 50$^{th}$ car off the block with all the paperwork to prove it. "Like everything else in those days, we just looked at each other and said, 'We got this. Let's go get it!'

"Next morning—this was a Saturday—I went up to a teller I'd never seen before and said 'I'd like fourteen and a half thousand in cash, please." She stared at me, and asked if I had a check or a withdrawal slip. No, I didn't, but I told her my name and said the banker [a Carolina grad] would approve this in a heartbeat. See, back then I'd just call them up every Friday and tell them to put money in the account to cover bills. Totally unorthodox, but they knew me. She looked confused, went off to talk to some people . . . And then she came back, stacked all the bills together on the counter, put them into a paper bag, and just handed it over. She didn't even make me sign any paper! And I walked out thinking. 'Nobody does it that way . . . I should be in jail for this.'

"Then I chartered a plane; that's what the extra $500 was for. We flew out that afternoon with Tommy Jr.—it had to be in the fall it was so pretty—and we got the car. I don't know why, we had no idea. The night before it just sounded like the thing to do. But I never really drove it that much, just put it in the driveway looking good. And, by the way, that bank's not in business anymore."

*

Meanwhile, despite his reluctance to cash in his legend for real estate deals, the man once dubbed "Instant Party" could still score memories for his pals. In the fall of 1981, when Clemson alumnus Theo was dying to watch his undefeated Tigers play football at UNC on their way to a national title—but couldn't get tickets at sold-out Kenan Stadium—Miller showed he still had the stroke to make an unlikely shot with the clock winding down:

"Next thing I know, Larry's telling me Dean Smith was giving us his own tickets. I said, 'What about Coach Smith?' and Larry said, 'Oh, he'll watch at home instead.' So we went into the basketball office and met Coach Smith—and Dean was *so* happy to see him! It was like Larry was his favorite adopted son. I was very impressed by that. I think we actually sat in Coach Smith's box."

The following March, watching Carolina's semifinal in the '82 Final Four over beers at Monterrey's, Miller again showed he was still a closer. "Someone said, 'If Carolina wins this, let's fly down to New Orleans tomorrow for the championship game.' That's how we did things back then. Carolina won, so—Boom—I called up Tommy." Coghill remembers that call asking if he wanted to go. "I said no, and when I hung up Nancy said, 'You're going to hate yourself for that.' So I called Larry back and said, 'We're going!' " Whereupon Larry called Leonard Laye who wangled them the Louisville band tickets, third row right behind the basket. *Swish!* Miller from downtown . . . Virginia Beach.

Down on the court before the Championship game, Dean Smith spotted his former star and asked why Larry hadn't called him for tickets. "But I told him 'Coach, you have enough to deal with!' " This game against Georgetown was etched in Tar Heel lore when a skinny freshman named Michael Jordan sank the winning jump shot with 17 seconds left—at last consummating Smith's quest for a national title after six Final Four frustrations—right under the eyes of the player who'd established Carolina's dominance fifteen years before. And now Larry no longer had to sit politely sweating out locker room interviews, but could head straight for Bourbon Street to celebrate like a normal fan . . . he thought. "But everyone was mobbing me. They recognized me and came up hugging me like *I'd* won the game. We couldn't get anywhere down the street, and my friends threatened they might have to put a bag over my head."

Instead, they ducked into a place called Lucky Pierre's, where all the guys threw a hundred bucks down on the bar—pretty good money back then—with orders to keep the drinks coming. "Then all of a sudden these hookers showed up, so that's how I ended up taking this Cajun girl back to my room. We spent the night together and she never left." Coghill's understanding is that someone from Carolina—he never knew who—paid that girl to make a move on Miller. "And we were easy in those days. Mills called my hotel room the next morning saying, 'Would you come here and help me? She won't leave!' It turned out she wanted to go back to Virginia Beach with him so badly she put $500 on the dresser—she wanted to pay *him!*" Miller concedes that after lingering a couple of days, he ultimately felt bad for the woman and took her out shopping and bought her some clothes. But then the party was over, and it was time to go.

\*

Eight months later, UNC's favorite wayward player picked up *Sports Illustrated* and came across an article by Frank Deford titled "Long Ago He Won the Big One: Dean Smith's Best Victory." The first three paragraphs set the drama of freshman Michael Jordan's game-winning shot . . . but then the article suddenly veered to the Big One, himself: "*Larry Miller was watching from the third-row seats he had obtained at the last minute . . . Miller was 'the key, the one player who turned it around for Dean' . . . Carolina was ascendant, in the Final Four by Miller's junior year. The rest was a glide.*"

Larry closed the magazine without finishing the article, thinking, 'Uh-oh, I know what he's alluding to now.' The previous year Deford had flown down to Virginia Beach to interview Miller shortly before publication of his football novel, "Everybody's All-American." Larry had picked him up at the airport in the sassy T-bird convertible and breezed over to Monterrey's where they chatted over dinner—and it was there that he shared the story of Smith recruiting him out of high school (although Deford was kind enough not to source Larry on the hole in Dean's shoe).

"I cringed when I saw that," says Miller, who knew right away that pulling focus from the winning team would land him in Smith's doghouse one more time. So when the phone rang and Larry heard his coach on the line, it was not a surprise. "Dean gave me some grief, as if the story were my fault. But, heck, I didn't write it!"

\*

The early '80s running craze caught Miller in mid-stride, already in shape but now upping his distance to twelve miles a day training for marathons. His first big test was in Virginia Beach . . . and he did it all wrong: "I didn't know you're not supposed to run the day before, so I put in eight miles on Friday instead of resting. Then that night I bought my first running shoes—I'd been using basketball shoes until then—didn't even break them in, and next day it turned out they were a half size too small and I lost three toenails during the race. Also, I didn't know to drink water while running—I'd never done that before—so at some point I couldn't swallow. When I hit that infamous wall for the last six miles, every step was agony, and I was so dehydrated I lost sixteen pounds. But I did finish the race in just over three hours, and I came in thirty-eighth out of something like a thousand runners."

After that, Larry ran another marathon in Virginia Beach and one in Richmond, all around three hours—"because you had to break three hours to get into the Boston Marathon—but thank God I didn't make it, so I didn't have to run that one." Instead, he ran some 10k races (about 6.2 miles), notching a great time of 37:37.

*

By now Larry had found his most memorable Virginia girlfriend, a beauty named Carol who was whip-smart, athletic enough for ocean racing in a catamaran, and very ambitious—especially for Larry. Recalls Theo, who knew the woman before Larry met her, "Carol was married at the time, but she liked him—they liked each other. She was a good person and a motivating factor, wanting to get him moving. She was like me, trying to get him into building and using his own name and go to North Carolina . . . though he never wanted to do that."

Instead, Larry built two houses at 81st Street in Virginia Beach's north end. These were the first of about ten residential houses he built abounding a natural paradise of hidden bays and unspoiled woodlands, less than a mile but a world away from the ticky-tack of the downtown tourist traps. He and Carol lived in one for a while, backing up to an impenetrable forest primeval and swamp across the parkway from Fort Story. (Cracks Larry, "That's where I bury women foolish enough to run away from their husbands.")

After those he did a four-piece on Chesapeake Bay, two more units close to where the famous early 20th century clairvoyant Edgar Cayce operated, and two bayfront condos on Meer Street. This last was on property Larry bought from an old eccentric, known for picking up discarded soda bottles off the street to swallow any last backwash he found—but who had lived there forever and so was a "land millionaire" selling off parcels for income. Larry's was a waterfront lot, but when he went to drive the first pilings for his structures, one tap sank the logs into the ground like straws into a milkshake. It turned out the old codger had artificially filled in a marshy border, so Larry now had to build a retaining wall to solidify his lot—and get longer pilings—but the condos he built still stand to this day.

"I really liked doing real estate because of the flexibility. It gave me the freedom not to do that nine-to-five stuff. There were some dry times—in between I bought some houses over in Portsmouth for rental income, and I had some 7-Eleven commissions—but when you hit it, you hit it big. At least I did." Says Nancy Coghill of Larry's swagger in the '80s boom years of Wall Street money, "In North Carolina, Larry could have been Governor if he wanted!"

The catch, of course, is that Miller didn't want that job—all title and the trappings of state-owned money, but pestered by the needs and blandishments of others. His was the nature of a warrior—to battle, to slay and to celebrate—and then, after sleeping it off, to move on and do it all over again. "It was freestyle living," he says of the sweet spot he found beyond the reach of others' expectations. "I was working for myself with no commitments, not tied down, so I could come and go as I pleased." The captain of nothing more than his own soul at last.

*

One winter, restless while his houses were being built, Larry shut down his office and lit out for adventure with Carol, trying something he'd never done before—skiing—and in typical Miller fashion he went all-in for almost four months. It all began with a weekend up in the Poconos . . .

"We went up to Camelback on Christmas weekend—probably the only place in the Northeast that had any snow, because they made snow—and there must have been 10,000 people from all over. Carol had skied Aspen and I was using her old skis, way shorter than I needed and the bindings weren't tight, and I got on the chairlift and asked her, 'What happens when we get to the top?' She just said, 'You'll find out.' So I slid off, and of course I knocked everybody over. Then I did one half of one run—never been on skis before, I was knocking little kids down, and it was so crowded other people were running into each other—and finally I decided I'm not going to take a shot at hurting myself or someone else here. I know what I'm doing now. So I picked up my skis and walked down with my skis over my shoulder, and people were booing me. But I said, 'Hey, I figured it out!' I taught myself in one run.

"After that we skied all across the country. We skied a week in Vermont, then North Carolina near Boone, then Gatlinburg, Tennessee. We skied across Colorado—Loveland Pass right outside Denver . . . four mountains in Aspen . . . three mountains in Steamboat Springs . . . Vail had three or four and I did all those . . . Beaver Creek . . . We went all the way across the state, and by the end I actually came down a Black Diamond [Expert] trail without falling. I had all the ski tickets stapled to the zipper of my jacket—thirty-two mountains, I believe, and it was all beautiful, are you kidding me? I wish I had saved those.

*Free as a bird, Larry flies down the slopes, self-taught, during a four-month, thirty-two mountain ski sabbatical from the workaday world.*

"Meanwhile I was building homes and I'd call my banker from out west and say, 'I need $27,000 from my construction account for a deal' and get it approved. I thought I was in heaven.

"Then on the way back, we were packed to the gills in Carol's 280ZX, and it was so cramped we couldn't stand each other. Somehow the window got broken, so driving was cold—that exacerbated the problem—and finally she threw me out of the car somewhere at a crossroads in Kansas with one dime in my pocket. Luckily I also had an American Express card, so somehow I managed. I got on a bus to Manhattan, Kansas and told the driver 'I have to pay you when I get there,' and he took my word for it. Got there, paid him, booked a flight back to Virginia Beach, and I was home that afternoon. The next morning she came back to the hotel in Kansas looking for me—she thought she was teaching me a lesson—but I was already gone. And it took her four days to get back. So basically that was it for us."

Once again, Larry's wingman—this time Theo—was sorry to see a good woman go: "I figured they were in love. I thought they'd get hooked up. She was trying to get him to do something really big instead of just messing around, but he didn't get channeled the way a lot of people wanted him to be channeled." But Larry wasn't biting on a life coach. "She could have been a nice thing, it was fun, but she thought she was so much smarter than everyone else, and after that I realized what she was like.

"But that trip was one of those things that normally you couldn't do in a lifetime. That's a bucket list for a bunch of people. And that's what I chose to do rather than sit in an office and become a huge name in real estate, like maybe I should have. I could have paid more attention to detail and given the business my all—with my focus now it would be over the top—but I was still young and rambunctious back then, and I guess my 'all' just wasn't there."

*

In the mid-1980s, now fully launched into his second life but still in close touch with the Carolina program, Miller finally returned to Chapel Hill—not for business, but for unfinished business: "I felt a pressure to get my college degree—my own pressure—because that's when Dean was doing so well and the graduation rate of the teams was so high, and I was one of the few people who hadn't graduated. I was only one course away, and the Athletic Department treated me like any athlete coming into school and got me a tutor."

Turning his back on Virginia Beach, Larry finally checked off that "Incomplete" and got his Bachelor of Science in Business Administration in 1985. "It didn't mean anything to me in the long term—maybe my parents liked having two college grads, but Dean never bugged me about it—but I felt bad because Dean had that graduation rate that was almost 100% and basically I wanted to do it for him."

This was no headline item, but hearing about it only decades later Billy Cunningham thought it was wonderful news. "During my era, Larry may be the only guy who didn't get a degree from Dean's first years—so I'm happy he did that. If you look at later players, like MJ and Worthy, the beauty is they all went back and got their degrees. And they didn't need it from a financial standpoint, but they'd promised Dean Smith. That impresses me more than anything."

Larry's effort came at a cost, though. Focused on life in Chapel Hill, he sublet his Virginia Beach apartment leaving personal items sealed off in a locked room. "But the guy stopped paying me, and then he broke into my room and stole everything. I lost good stuff that I'd asked my mother to send down to me—sports memorabilia, and my contract with Universal was there—and I had no recourse, because there was no way to prove what I had there."

*

After getting his degree, the graduate decided to give Raleigh a shot by opening another Larry Miller & Associates office on Paddock Drive. There, for the next five or six years, he operated all over the region doing big tracts in Raleigh, in fast-growing Cary (dryly said to be an acronym for "Containment Area for Retired Yankees"), and in Hillsborough where he sold the land on which a Holiday Inn Express now stands. "I would go anywhere. At that time you couldn't do dentures in Virginia, so I put a denture office right across the border down in Moycock, so Jim Hudock and a group of North Carolina doctors could set up a practice there where it was legal.

"That may have been another of my faults: I didn't concentrate on a certain area, I just went off on different things. With two licenses to cover two states, if I heard about something way far away, I'd go look at things down on the lakes in North Carolina. I could have focused on one area and stuck to the office, but I took a different route for my career: I was kind of a wanderer—I liked that part of it—but it is harder to manage that way."

*

Miller had come back to UNC just in time for a milestone in the storied basketball program, the January 1986 opening of the state-of-the-art Dean E. Smith Student Activities Center (aka, The Dean Dome). He'd gotten to know Duke's former National Player of the Year, Art Heyman, and twenty years after Larry starred in the first game played at Carmichael Auditorium, he now proudly took Heyman to the next arena's inaugural game in which #1 UNC fittingly beat #3 Duke. "Bob Costas was doing media day with Art, Coach K, and Jeff Mullins, and I just sat and listened. I like K. We're almost the same age and played around the same time."

That September, Larry was back for the Smith Center's official dedication ceremony, watching his 44 jersey take its rightful place in the rafters between numbers 22 and 33—only now with names attached as they never were when the guys played in humbler times—a murderer's row of Cunningham . . . Lewis . . . Miller . . . Scott . . . stretching on to fifty-one jerseys at this writing and counting . . . always counting.

It wasn't long before Miller's reappearance in the area was noticed by sportswriters like Elton Casey, who ran across him on a business trip that year. The good-natured article that followed reported Larry was "doing quite well" in commercial land sales and development, was pleased to share details of many of his former teammates also doing well, and quoted Larry saying, "There's a closeness with all Carolina players and coaches. I'm glad to be part of it." Asked what he would do differently if he could do it all over again, he wisecracked the obvious: "Be six inches taller."

The article politely noted, however, that despite still running four miles every day, Larry appeared to be "a tad heavier"—the first report that, without a season of strenuous games to work off the communion brews of brotherhood, the UNC Tarzan was falling out of shape.

*

Now passing forty, still unfettered by family life but no longer bigger, stronger, and younger than anyone else, Larry was also no longer quite as reckless—but disaster would not stop flirting with him. "When I was in Raleigh we had a house on Nag's Head, and three or four of us would chip in to fly down for the weekend all the time, maybe $50 each for the flight and the whisky tab. We had a pilot, Fast Eddie, a good guy. But then there was a crash in Raleigh—the plane was demolished—and we heard it was Fast Eddie. He'd had a heart attack while flying."

*Nine feet tall and five feet wide, this display jersey once hung in the
Smith Center rafters . . . until so many more All-Americans joined
Miller's generation the university had to downsize them to make room.
The original is seen here hanging in Miller's backyard.*

Mike Cooke remembers these trips, noting "Larry and a couple of guys owned a house on Nag's Head, and when they sold it my wife and I bought Larry's part out—and he would come back on weekends and hang out with us down there, so I got to know him reasonably well. Larry was always shy. What Larry didn't realize was that he exceeded any expectations. He was everybody's hero. All the women at Carolina were in love with him, and all the guys wanted to be him. Everybody liked him. And for some reason there was a shyness about him that couldn't handle that. It was strange. Most guys would get real cocky and arrogant, but this was the reverse thing and he kind of went the other way.

"Well, I know he was comfortable with women because they were all in love with him. And he was a blow-it-out partier. With a few shots he was an addictive person. He had no limits. He was either On or Off—in sports or whatever—either at zero or wide open at a hundred. I remember they had a UNC-UCLA alumni game set up in 1987 and Mills weighed about 260—out of shape from drinking and whatnot—and he said 'I'm going to play in this game and I'm going to be good.' All of a sudden he's running up and down the sand dunes, dragging tires on the beach, and he goes from 260 down to 225—incredible shape—and he went out there and had a great game."

The 1987 College Legends Classic, a benefit broadcast by ABC-TV, was a rematch of alumni from the '68 National Championship contestants, again played in Los Angeles but this time at UCLA's Pauley Pavilion. The Heels were coached by Smith and the Bruins by Coach Wooden and Bill Walton, but the headliners were current pros Michael Jordan and James Worthy. (Alcindor/Jabbar did not play in the game.) Larry played his minutes with his old teammates and it was all good fun and sportsmanship, of course . . . until the clock ticked down and the struggle intensified. And this time the Carolina team won, much to Miller's satisfaction: "I got in for, like, 3 minutes. Ran over a couple of guys. Took a couple of foul shots and made one. We had a blast!"

This was very likely the last time Larry Miller ever shot a basketball, and it was Larry in a nutshell: Setting his mind to a task, working his ass off to make it happen, capturing the nugget of joy from being in battle with his guys . . .

Mike Cooke: "And then he went back to his old ways. He was driven—he had great discipline to accomplish what he wanted to do—and then he'd slide. I just didn't understand it. He's a complex person."

*

As word of Larry's ways beyond Chapel Hill reached the ears of Dean Smith, the patiently persistent coach—still serving his players beyond graduation—reached out with a smattering of letters during the winter of 1988–89.

In November: "Dear Larry, I hear you have been in this area for a while and we have not had lunch together. Why not give me a call to touch base before the basketball season begins . . . I'm free any day next week for lunch! Could meet you at Governor's Inn . . ."

In December: A handwritten scrawl below Smith's annual Christmas greeting to lettermen: "Larry—My luncheon invitation is on! Let me know where to reach you . . . Think of you often—DES."

In January: "I'm sorry we missed on the luncheon engagement. I had no idea you had called . . . I can meet you at the Governor's Inn if you are coming from Raleigh, or we could go to the Chapel Hill Country Club" . . . followed by an offering of five specific dates over the next two weeks.

Finally Coach Smith called up Mike Cooke, asking him to find a phone number for Larry, leading to a somewhat peculiar reunion beyond the prying eyes of the press. "So Coach called Larry in Raleigh and said, 'I'd like to have lunch with you, and they made a plan to meet at a certain restaurant. Then Larry calls all of his buddies—Grubar and Bunting and Joe Brown—and says come have lunch with me and Coach Smith.'"

Still pleased with his prank to this day, Larry explains, "I figured Dean always does these nice things for us, so it would be nice for him to see all these guys—because they were all right there, and I was in touch with them. And everybody said, 'Sure, I'll do it.' So Dean was buying me lunch and all these guys kept popping up as though they had other business there—Donnie

Moe . . . and Greg was there . . . Joe . . . and Grubes came . . . Bill Bunting—we had about six guys, and Coach said 'This is incredible!' We really surprised him and it was amazing. He loved it!"

Grubar remembers initially thinking this was a great idea, because he hadn't seen Larry in quite a while, but now he wasn't so sure. "When we showed up, I don't think Coach was too excited about that. We didn't know Coach just wanted Larry, or what that would be about. Afterward I heard rumors Larry was drinking a lot, but that's as far as I ever knew. And I didn't know it that day, I just sensed Coach wasn't too happy . . . but he was good at hiding stuff."

Mike Cooke, the only one clear on the coach's agenda from the start, says "Dean was so mad. Because he'd planned a little one-on-one with Larry—'You're going in the wrong direction, son, you need to get your act together'—not a one-on-five. But that's the way Larry would do stuff. He absolutely knew what was coming, and he was never a fan of talking about himself."

To this day, however, Miller doesn't see it that way. He points to a nice letter from Smith that spring, congratulating him on successful surgery to fix that ever-troublesome knee and then telling his player, "I should have known you would surprise me with an 'accidental' meeting of your teammates while we were to have lunch. It really was enjoyable, and I appreciate you thinking of this . . . Warmest regards, as always . . ." Then, scrawled at the bottom in longhand: "If I can help you in <u>any</u> way, let me know."

Thus continued the eternal struggle between good advice and deaf ears.

*

That same year, Larry experienced a middle-aged miracle when he was drafted for love by a younger woman . . . *much* younger. "I first met Erin when she wasn't yet twenty and I was forty-three. I'd invited this girl I was interested in for lunch one day at one of Thad Eure's restaurants, and Erin was there. But it turned out my date wasn't interested . . . and then she pawned me off on Erin, who was. So of course I was flattered, since I was almost her parents' age.

They only lived two blocks away from me—her mother made desserts for Sebastians and her stepfather worked for IBM—and they approved of me. So we just started dating, and I used to hang out with them all the time. There was nothing clandestine, we were out in the open. She was just a beautiful mind—a really good person."

Miller's luck continued one late afternoon on the Raleigh beltline when he pulled up to a stop sign, was rammed by the inattentive driver behind him, and launched into another car in front, as a fourth car hit the guy in back. None of this was his fault—but it was a problem if the police discovered Larry's car registration had expired. Fortunately he recalled his afternoon as a Pagan and quickly convinced the others to pull over, trade information, and avoid the cops. "And we saved the police a lot of work, too, because the damage was no big deal."

Larry and Erin lived happily together in Raleigh for a while, but not ever after. Barely five years after his return to the home base of stardom, Larry's misgivings were borne out. "All they did down there was talk about sports all year long. 'What do you think about this? What about that?' Actually, it drove me crazy." And meanwhile, still operating with two real estate licenses, Larry had a life-altering project underway with a friend working out of Virginia Beach.

*

"This woman was in the advertising business—I knew her from just hanging around, nothing romantic—and she had this new concept for in-store advertising: You know those little TVs you see in grocery lines and gas pumps? We were really early on that. We were going to try one in all the 7-Elevens, and then you sell the advertising on there because that's what she was good at. In the beginning she bankrolled the whole idea herself, but she asked me to help her find investors."

Intrigued that this could be a national deal, knowing he was in life's second half now, the Carolina big gun sensed it was Miller Time again . . . Time to shoot the moon by pushing his hard-won reputation and freedom into the center of the table and go all-in for the win. Larry worked his North Carolina connections by setting up meetings with Franklin Street Partners, run by Bob Eubanks (twice Chairman of UNC's Board of Trustees) and Paul Rizzo (a former vice-chairman of IBM and dean of UNC's Business School). And, sure enough, they got an investor in from New York to listen to the Miller team's spiel and commit to backing the whole project.

Encouraged, Larry took time off from his real estate business to fly around the country with his partner talking to grocery chains, sitting down with their boards to show them the concept. He even did the voiceovers for sample advertising. It was like playing road games again—flying somewhere to make his score, be the closer, and then move on to the next one—with a big prize waiting at the end. "We were all over the place. Went out to Salt Lake to present it to one of the big chains out there, and skied there, too. And they were excited about the deals. I worked that project for over a year, doing it on the cuff, and still paying my bills in Raleigh, because I was going to get stock—a percentage of the new company. We were all set to package the whole deal, the guy was ready to go to contract . . .

"And right at the last minute, this lady just decided she didn't want to do it! There was another guy, an airline pilot, and her son was involved, too—they had it all set up—and she just pulled the string on it. Later I was having lunch with Dean and Bob Eubanks and they asked why she did that, and I said I had no idea what happened to her. It was out of my hands—she had control because she sponsored the thing—and I never did know the reason. And now you can see that concept actually being used. I still see those little TVs at gas stations."

Decades later Miller is able to be philosophical. "It's like anything—you take a shot, and sometimes it works and sometimes it doesn't. I thought it was a good gamble. But anyway, that was a whole year down the drain. It was a learning experience. I've had a lot of those."

★

Inexplicably benched again, Miller's bold gamble in the early '90s went bust at the worst possible time. His Raleigh office, idle for a year, had no projects in the pipeline, and with national interest rates soaring to 20% there were no bank loans to be had—and thus no sales—for builders or buyers anywhere. The industry virtually ground to a halt.

Late in 1991, Larry wrote a thoughtful letter to Coach Smith, thanking him and the UNC family for all the things they had done for him in the past year . . . "But more importantly, I sincerely appreciate your genuine concern for my welfare and happiness, as well as that of fellow UNC players." Smith responded by encouraging Larry to give him a call, assured him he had two season tickets coming, and added "Hope you are selling some real estate in this 'down' market!" The Christmas letter that followed wished Larry a great Christmas "despite looking for a new job." But reentering the tanking real estate market was proving to be no easy task, and Larry found himself "just looking for something to do for the moment—this and that, like putting mobile homes on lots—trying different things to stay busy."

In the summer of 1992, Coach Smith sent Larry another nudge: "Phil Ford gave me the enclosed tapes which I find to be helpful and also funny. I should substitute the word "food" for "alcohol" as I am getting fat! You could substitute any habit you have which you would like to break."

Wham—the hint was just dropped. But Larry didn't mind. "That was just Dean being Dean. He always cared about all of his guys. It didn't offend me in any way at all." The coach also appended his usual handwritten scrawl, this time adding, "Larry—Same girlfriend? I'm going to Kupchak's and Lebo's weddings this week—DES."

Yes, Larry was still seeing Erin during this difficult time, but barely. She was with him in New Orleans in March of 1993 when the Tar Heels won their next National Championship—this time when a Michigan player called a phantom time-out, drawing a technical foul to seal the outcome. But there would be no wedding bells for the May-December couple. "I took Erin up to Virginia Beach a couple times, and she loved it there. But then she got work in North Carolina, and after I closed the Raleigh office and relocated back to Virginia we never did live together up there. And she was such a young girl, with all kinds of future ahead of her—stuff that I had already done. So as much as I really cared for her, I knew she was like a beautiful butterfly I had to set free."

*

With Erin disappearing down a different path, Theo off to Clemson for a job in sports medicine, and Coghill and Larry Weldon doing their own things, for the first time in his life the boy who thrived in the heart of the action was suddenly a man without a plan. Sensibly, Miller cut back by closing the office, even while keeping both licenses and his business card. "But by that time I'd lost interest in real estate. I had no focus, didn't really know where I was going or what I wanted to do." So, with nothing very promising, Larry was lured by other ventures that, one after another, stabbed him with more harpoons in the back.

Tom Coghill remembers, "He got hooked up with somebody else who was going to put prepaid cards in stadiums. He spent a year with that guy— just another person trying to take advantage of his name—and then he found out the guy didn't have any money. So that wasted another year."

Life got even more bleak that August when Larry learned his father had succumbed to prostate cancer at age seventy-two. The Lehigh Valley stepped up, though. "They had the funeral at St. Lawrence where I went to school and my parents went to church. A lot of his buddies that he played with as a kid, from his ward down in Allentown, and guys he worked with at Mack Truck, they came and asked me could they be pall-bearers? And I said, 'Absolutely— I'm proud that you guys want to do it.' "

The one emotional tether that kept Miller's deflating spirits afloat was Coach Smith. As he told *Carolina Blue* in 1995, "I've never married, my father passed away, and my mother lives in Pennsylvania, so Coach Smith and the Carolina family is like my family . . . When I was in his office recently, he started pointing at team pictures on the wall, updating me on what some of them are doing now. He is proud of the young men he brought through college . . . and life, really."

So it was puzzling that, for all his devotion to Smith, Miller now began living removed from Chapel Hill to the point the coach's 1995 Christmas letter admonished, "Larry—Don't be such a stranger. Hope you are enjoying your life and finding it meaningful." The following Christmas, Dean scrawled, "Larry—Do hope all is well with you. Look forward to seeing you on January 18th when your group is honored."

Larry was nowhere to be seen at the 1997 reunion banquet, though, even as players passed a microphone around until it got to Jim Frye—Dean called out "Slink!"—and Frye theatrically droned "Heeeere . . . come the Tar Heels!" Frye, the first to feel Miller's absence, admits he was disappointed. "For the longest time, I was the only player from the Class of '68 who ever came back, and it always bothered me." It would be twenty more years before the classmates would cross paths again.

Nor was Miller one of the eighteen former players at Winston-Salem's Joel Coliseum two months later when Coach Smith broke Adolph Rupp's record to become the winningest major college basketball coach of all time with his 877th victory. Miller did stay in touch from arm's length, though, writing to congratulate his coach: "There are many proud individuals all over the world who are thanking God to be lucky enough for the opportunity to have been part of the basketball program, the university, and having known all the wonderful people associated with it."

That fall the sixty-six-year-old Coach Smith jolted the program by abruptly announcing his retirement, and again the former captain reached out from afar, this time faxing, "Wish everybody the best on this decision" . . . and following up the next day with a fax to "Coach Bill" [Guthridge], Dean's assistant and now successor: "What a wonderful choice for this challenge. There is no better man for the job. You have always been a favorite of all of us . . . We are 100% for you."

As Christmas approached, the student turned the tables on the master, offering concern as Larry wrote: "Hope all is going well with you in your new 'position' . . . Selfishly, I believe we all wanted you to continue, but after seeing you at the press conference it was apparent you were at ease with your decision . . . Let me know what your new schedule is like so we can stay in touch. Best wishes for health and happiness . . ."

Miller's outreach earned him a personal letter in April of 1998, with Smith writing, "I am finally beginning to acknowledge those letters that were so meaningful to me . . . You are the first letterman to whom I am writing. Larry, you surely stay under wraps, but when you are in Chapel Hill please let me know . . . I am at the office most every day . . ."

This correspondence led to Dean treating for a 1999 St. Patrick's Day lunch at Alumni Hall, where they were joined by Larry's trusted former Rough Rider teammate, Jim Van Horn (for whom Larry was now coordinating joint business ventures in Virginia and North Carolina). Afterward, Van Horn wrote a letter to Smith that illustrates the far-reaching ripple effect of Larry's instinct to look out for his guys so many years before:

"Dear Coach . . . I am embarrassed that it has taken me thirty-five years to properly thank you for the educational and basketball opportunity that you provided me at Elon in 1964. If it had not been for the one-on-one with Larry during high school, and your kindness to help a young player, college would not have been part of my life. I would have been destined to continue my summer job as a blacksmith's helper in a steel forge foundry.

"However, because of the involvement both of you had in my life, I was able to earn a degree in economics, work for a Fortune 500 company, coach Division I basketball, own a company for twenty years, and assist several needy causes with over $500 million dollars of fund raising. Sometimes all it takes is someone to believe in you, and open the door of opportunity . . ."

*

Although Miller was falling off his teammates' radar, he continued slipping into town to see Smith, as confirmed by his old friend Suzi (Wood) Mutascio, who spoke with Catasauqua Athletic Director Tom Moll while tracking down Miller not so long ago: "The A.D. loves UNC sports and says he went down there during the playoffs—I want to say around 2000—and he's in the Athletic office one day and who comes through the door but coach Dean Smith, still on his own so he was reasonably healthy. And Tom said that was kind of cool, seeing him . . . and not too many minutes later Larry walks in!

"So this Tom Moll doesn't know Larry personally, but he recognizes him, and he's watching from a distance and he can hear them connecting. And Coach says, 'Okay, Larry . . .' and rattles off Larry's home telephone number in Catasauqua—off the top of his head—from when he recruited him thirty-five years before! I get goosebumps even talking about this. But Larry shoots back, very quickly, 'Well, you're almost right, Coach, but the area code changed.' Later I told this to Larry and asked, 'Did that honestly occur?' And he said, 'It sure did. The man's mind was like a computer.' Isn't that something? I think Coach Smith was a really fine human. He was just amazing with his kids, kept a lot of them out of trouble and helped them out along the way."

Although they remained in touch by mail and by phone, this may have been the last time Larry Miller and Dean Smith ever saw each other in person.

*

On September 11, 2001, Larry was in a Whitehall, PA Giant grocery store, checking out the little TV in the aisle—the very concept he'd pitched a decade earlier—when he realized he was watching a World Trade Center tower with smoke billowing out of the top. He'd been coming back to check on his mom at least once a year, ever since Julius passed away, and like any mom she wanted her son to linger: "I'd come back and she'd always have a list of chores for me. I'd get on it, and then she'd say 'I didn't want you to do them all right away!' "

By this time another business venture in Raleigh had fallen through, and once again Larry was fed up with people he didn't want to play with anymore. "He got very discouraged," concedes Tom Coghill. "A lot of people used his name supposedly to make him money—and it never happened.

There's no question he was too trusting. He thought everybody was honest like they were back home."

So when a call came from his mother in the first days of 2002, asking him to come look after her while she recuperated from having her gall bladder removed, Larry didn't hesitate. With no plan beyond getting there, he threw a few things together and hopped on a bus heading north from Newport News. Looking back on the Virginia years, Larry gamely says, "Certainly I've had a few bumps—most of them from my own doing or lack thereof—but most of it was a lot of fun. I think I was actually done with Virginia Beach at the time, though. It was pretty much the end of the run after that."

His mom couldn't have known it when she called, but Larry Miller was going to a better place . . . and her summons probably saved her son's life.

CHAPTER 12

# GOOD SOIL

If you plan to spend any length of time in Catasauqua, there's one thing you need to know: They're going to give you a nickname. "When I was growing up, everyone in town had one," Miller advises. "There must be a thousand of them. A guy named Wabs Chromiak, a retired math teacher who must be eighty now, has a list of maybe six hundred nicknames."

The good local athletes going back to the 1930s are revered and remembered by monikers like Birdie, Schwepp, Ikky, Deej, Yootsie, Tickles, Boopty, Carrots, and Mike the bedbug. One big Polish guy who worked at the General Ribbon Mills was so well known as Joe Palooka (after the comic strip boxer) that a local bank let him open a savings account in that name.

"My nickname was Lem," Larry recalls. "Geetz Groeller made up that my middle name was Ernest just so it would fit."

Everyone knew who headliner Lem was, of course, but the practice was so ubiquitous that over the years many close friends no longer remembered each other's given names anymore, leading one local professor to remark, "I'd be willing to wager not 10% of the guys who know Birdie well know his real name." As a result, local obituaries now routinely include these nicknames so that old friends reading unfamiliar names in the paper will understand just who it is that has died.

*

Peggy Miller's elective surgery left her feeling unwell, and shortly after her son arrived home at Wood Street, she asked him to stay on. "Right then and there I thought, 'What the heck, I'm not doing anything important.' "

The town Larry found had changed, its character shifting along with the country, and not for the better to many of his old gang. "We've lost the old-time America here," says Don Canzano. "This used to be a great blue-collar community. Everybody had jobs. You could leave your front door open. And people were crazy about high school basketball. But after the late '60s it started going downhill, and part of it is the industry moving out. I firmly believe with the steel and coal leaving, it took our soul away. Now you can get shot in the daytime. And now the kids here don't have the stories that I grew up with."

Scott Beeten, living in Las Vegas now, confirms "Allentown used to be the jewel of the area. Then Bethlehem Steel got shrunk up and Mack Truck moved out of town, and there weren't any jobs . . . and it changed the whole town. For someone like me, it's hard to go back. At the same time, when downtown Allentown city went bad and people moved out, the smaller towns around there flourished."

Catasauqua is one of those, and Miller's old Knee-Hi baseball teammate, Tim Fisher, points out, "Many of the residents stayed in town, although now blue-collar jobs are in warehouses and landscaping which do not pay nearly as much as previous jobs. Development has changed the rural nature of the place. I'm not saying Catty is not a nice town, but this is the way it was when Larry came back to his hometown." Even the Boys Club has now become a store for ladies' cosmetics and beauty supplies.

But Catty did have advantages found nowhere else on earth: the old familiar sidewalks he'd walked on to school and old familiar faces right where they belonged, whom no one could trade away. McCarty's was their rendezvous spot, where Larry's confession-skipping pal John (since dubbed "Sam") tended bar and was now the one hearing confessions. Buff was no longer running the Esso (now Exxon) station but still around, so Larry—living on standby—could study retirement.

And there were new guys, formerly too young for Larry to know but now grown up, like Joe Barczy, whose family owned the Little Brown Jug, a huge sports fan always ready to take a jaunt to games . . . and Bobby Folland, whose parents Larry knew before, who quickly became a sidekick . . . and Dale Wint, who had written a comprehensive history of Catty and would always drive.

This was useful because Larry had arrived home without wheels for the first time in his life since he was sixteen years old. He doesn't even recall his last car, which may explain why he left it behind in Virginia Beach as he hurried north. "Matter of fact, I think I left four cars down there and North Carolina over the years. I still have four car titles somewhere. Once I got up here, I used my mom's and it was easy getting around." Clearly, time and circumstance had moderated the former hot wheels mechanic's taste for the snazzy ride.

And let us not overlook a former girlfriend or two who were more than glad to see Larry back. Blessedly, nobody wanted his autograph or grinning selfies taken, or saw any profit in knowing him beyond the new stories he'd brought home to tell.

*

On January 9, 2003 Magdalene Miller passed away at eighty, having never really recovered from the effects of her surgery. Larry's devout mother was laid to rest in St. Lawrence Cemetery next to Julius, leaving Larry and sister Lorraine with a decision to make about 116 Wood Street: "My sister asked if

I wanted the house, but I said no because at that point I had no idea where I was going to go."

Suddenly free of his mother's care, nothing was now keeping Larry in Pennsylvania . . . but nothing attracted him elsewhere, either. His blue-collar hunger and wanderlust had been satiated by fame and prosperity. The pleasures of beach life had washed away on a tide of ill fortune. And now, with good years ahead of him at age fifty-six, he still had plenty of time for . . . what, exactly?

Ultimately, Larry did what most boys are trained to do if they get lost in the woods: Don't stride off randomly, making it worse—remain still until you get your bearings. This was not such a bad idea, since after a year he felt comfortable right where he was. The siblings put the house on the market, and as soon as it sold Larry moved out . . . taking with him a treasure trove that had been waiting on him for years.

*

In the summer of 2003, the boy from the mountains, Roy Williams—once a Dean Smith assistant and now honored with six league and three national coach-of-the-year awards after guiding the Kansas Jayhawks to four Final Fours—returned to his alma mater to steady the wobbling North Carolina program. Among his first decisions was to invite all the lettermen back for a reunion—but the player who electrified Williams' high school coach, who sparked the chain of events leading to the coach's triumphant return, never showed up. Recalls Williams, "I personally called him and left a message. Never heard back."

Thus began the disappearance of Larry Miller, at least in the eyes of teammates and fans who gradually realized as the years went by that Elvis had left the building. Says elder statesman Mike Cooke of Miller's withdrawal in the late 1990s, "He kind of fell off the face of the earth. We couldn't get him to come back for anything. Billy was totally different. He was outgoing, comfortable with people. He hasn't changed since 1962. I correspond with him at least every other week. A bunch of us stay together and talk together . . . and Mills just wasn't that way."

"Such a complicated young man," says Cunningham of the path Miller chose. "And a nice guy—I want to emphasize that—there's not a mean or bad thing I could think of to say about him. What's very strange is he and Bobby, from the time they left, I never saw either of them at reunions of any type. And we're talking about two young men, I wish I had the success in college basketball that they had. And then to fall off the face of the earth in the manner he did? I understand turning your back on the game. I have guys that I played with that couldn't care less. But it's his relationships that he walked away from which I will never understand—because these people cared deeply about him as a dear friend. And for whatever reasons he became like a recluse to them."

Tom Gauntlett: "I'd heard he was in Virginia Beach but would not make himself available. That was disheartening to me. We all had to stop playing basketball, but we didn't stop talking to each other. I never understood that, because people at Carolina *loved* Larry. I know the players loved him and Bobby, and we always missed them when they didn't come back."

Dick Grubar in particular mourned Miller's absence. "The sadness I have in my life with Larry is that we really lost touch for maybe thirty years in total, never spent any time together, and I'm sad about that because we had some great times together. And it was more than just the college thing, it was the playing and the competition together—that's such a unique thing, you hate to lose that."

"I never lost touch with Dean," Larry points out, although this was off the radar of most folks. "But when I got to Pennsylvania it wasn't like I was only four hours away anymore and could head right down there."

*

That October, thirty-five years beyond his last game as a Tar Heel, Larry received another letter from Dean Smith . . . still coaching: "Dear Larry, I saw some of your teammates this weekend at Homecoming. Joe Brown and

Bill Bunting were laughing about your inviting them to 'our' lunch at the Governor's Inn! It always was good to be with you. You and Lorraine must be missing your mom still. You had great parents raising you through the years . . . Let us hear from you. I'm enclosing the 'Acceptance Booklet' which I read once a month. I sent these to all the players a few years back and you may have misplaced your copy. Thinking of you . . ."

*

Larry settled a few blocks from home, in a rental on Bridge Street right by the post office that was just temporary . . . he thought. "I still didn't know if I was going back to Virginia Beach or North Carolina or someplace else totally off the wall. It had a nice patio out back where we hung out on weekends during the summer, drinking beers. People would just pop in and pop out. Dale was the one who started calling them 'The Summer of Larry' parties, named for The Summer of George on 'Seinfeld.' Sometimes I'd hire a girl to serve us beers, when all she had to do was walk in the kitchen and get them. It was just a bunch of nonsense." In other words, Miller felt right at home. The apartment also had a bus stop right out front that would take him anywhere he needed to go, so he gave up driving and kept in condition by walking.

In the fall of 2004, Larry got around to sorting through the treasure trove of memorabilia he'd brought from the trophy case and boxes his mom had stored in the basement at Wood Street. There were over a thousand items from high school, college, and the ABA—jerseys, basketballs, ACC trophies and awards, recruiting letters, fan letters and photos—and he wanted to get rid of them.

One could hear him still shedding the skin of his earlier life in what by now was a consistent refrain to the press: He had all this stuff his mom packed away that didn't mean a thing to him. It didn't do any good being in boxes. He didn't like living in the past; it was just something he'd rather not do. And most memorably, as he told "20 Second Timeout," "I'm even out of the reunion business."

At first uncertain about how to put the past in its place, Larry learned that Dean Smith had given money to the university library and resolved to follow suit by auctioning his souvenirs on eBay, with proceeds to benefit Catasauqua's Public Library. (He also donated five volumes of scrapbooks from his mom's attic.) Not only was Miller not trying to live on his legend, he was giving it away.

One of the first he told of his decision was Coach Smith, who admired it in a letter that November: "As you know, we are grateful that you chose Chapel Hill and we will always recognize how important you were to our University's basketball program. They are planning a basketball museum in a new building that will be built right next to where we play. If you have one item that you might want to send, you could write it off your taxes and many people would be delighted to see something from you. We certainly will honor you in this museum and . . . coming from you it would be important."

The auction conducted on eBay throughout 2005 was gratifying for all concerned: "I figured raising $3,000 would be cool, and $10,000 would be great. A lot of it wasn't even UNC stuff—programs from football games, and of course the letters from all the coaches. But even my high school programs sold, and it ended up bringing in over $20,000—and all because my mother saved all that stuff."

*

Meanwhile, Roy Williams had almost instant success with the Tar Heels, winning his first National Championship in 2005. Not long afterward he received a surprising call of congratulations: "I'm guessing my second year back, I get a call from Larry. He said some great things—'I love what you're doing, I love our team, I'm just calling to say I still love the program, nothing against it, nothing against you, but I've got to move on with my life and not live in the past so much. I'm getting rid of personal items, but want you to know I'll always be a Tar Heel.' And that's the last conversation I had with him for years . . ."

*

The year Miller turned sixty, he took stock of his condition and didn't much like what he saw: "After I got to Bridge Street I took to drinking vodka too much, and I knew it was getting the best of me—I wasn't exercising anymore, probably wasn't eating a lot—so I decided to quit. I thought I could quit cold turkey, and I told this girl I was friends with 'It's gonna be very bad, I might act a little goofy' . . . because I know what happens when you come down off that. But I didn't know how bad those withdrawals are. You don't know what you're doing and you lose control. I said 'Don't you dare call anybody' . . . but I probably would have died if she didn't. I was unconscious in the hospital, I think for almost a week. Some people stopped by to see me and said they thought I was gone. Everybody thought I was dead . . . And then I just popped up."

The reckoning came hard, but when Miller finally left the hospital he actually stayed quit and didn't drink alcohol for quite some time. And here, so many decades after he'd been the panacea for Catty's misery in the winter after JFK's assassination, the old borough that loved its prodigal son now became *his* aspirin. "Bobby Nemeth came out of nowhere. He reached out to me and we'd go out to lunch. He's like an angel that was there." (Nemeth, who coached Northampton High School to four Lehigh Valley League titles— once Miller was gone—is now a Hall of Fame coach with the Konkrete Kids' court named after him, and pays Miller the ultimate local compliment: "He never forgot his roots. A lot of guys do.")

*

Dry for the first time in memory since high school, Miller flexed his old self-discipline to structure his life with healthy activities, like gardening with his new pal Dale Wint. "I used to do that all the time in other places. In Raleigh I lived in an apartment, but a buddy had a farm down in Harnett County on a lake. We used to go down there every afternoon, drink beers on the way down, and do our gardening in a big garden, almost an acre of land. He had a tractor and everything, and I was into that.

"So Dale and I made a garden just up the street, maybe a quarter acre, where we raised vegetables and gave a lot of them away to whoever wanted them. His parents had a casket company. That's how we built the casket for my funeral."

Wait, what?

Let's back up . . . One day, some months after Larry's brush with death-by-detox, he was shooting the breeze with Sam and Dale—probably at McCarty's, but Larry wasn't drinking now—and he was idly wondering if anybody would have come to his funeral. "And Dale said, 'Well, let's find out.' And Sam says, 'Yeah, go for it.' And that's all they had to say to me! Again, this is how we did things back then. Instead of thinking about repercussions like I do now, it was just 'Let's do it!' It wasn't my idea, but it made sense because I'm not going to see my funeral.

"So we built the coffin in my basement at Bridge Street, and because Dale's family was in the casket business he helped me design it. We bought some upholstery and Dale helped me upholster the inside of it, and I went to Bed, Bath & Beyond and got the handles to make it look right—but you had to hold it by the sides.

"We took the coffin over to St. Lawrence Cemetery—Sam was there and Dale was there—and right in front of my tombstone with no name on it they laid me to rest in the casket. Then we had a moment when everybody said their farewells. I had some friends who wouldn't come—they thought it was nuts—and Sam was getting nervous, because it was a Sunday and other people were arriving to visit their loved ones and he didn't want to be disrespectful. So we had to rush my funeral.

"Then we went right across the street to the Jednota Club for my wake. I hired a guy to be my stunt double, to wear a coat and tie and lie in my casket while I was partying. Then after a while everybody was getting in the casket; they all wanted their pictures taken. Maybe forty-five people showed up, it was a little disappointing—and it was free beer, too. Then we took the casket home and later it became a work hut in my compost area.

*The faux funeral of Larry Miller—not only resting in peace,*
*but in sunglasses—mourned by his buddies Dale Wint*
*(coffin consultant), Sam McCarty, and Wilbur Hill.*

"I always recycle everything. For my real burial I just want a cardboard box. I told the guy my druthers would be to just go out into the woods and be recycled naturally. I'm so in tune with nature I feel I already am a tree. And it turns out I'm not having a funeral, they're just going to throw me into a cardboard box—I don't have to have a suit or anything—and bury me right there across a little road from where my parents are buried. The plot is there, the stone is up although it doesn't have any name on it. I'm bought and paid for."

But, wait—that's not all.

"A year to the day later, we had the Resurrection. That's even more sacrilegious. We had me rise from the coffin because, remember, I was almost dead . . . and that was the reason for another party. And we had twice as many people for that one." So Larry the instigator—the kid who once brought the smokes, the beers, the points, the wins, the girls, the trophies, the parties and, yes, even now some new memories—was back.

*

In the spring of 2007, Miller was sobered by a real loss when he learned that his friend Jim Hudock had died. "He and Mills were really close," recalls Mike Cooke. "So when Hudock passed away, I was trying to find Larry and I called the Scranton or Allentown newspaper and asked for the sportswriter. I said 'Do you know Larry Miller and where I can get in touch with him?' And he said, 'Well, you need to call this Irish bar at 5 o'clock' [clearly McCarty's]. So I did, and the man said, 'Oh, he's right here.' But when I told Larry about the service, he didn't come. He said, 'Mike, I can't face it. I can't come back.' "

Miller had reasons that were sensible: "I wasn't driving anymore, so it wasn't like I could jump in a car and drive down like I did from Virginia Beach when Tommy Lloyd's daughter got killed. She'd just turned sixteen, was down at the beach, and she got hit head-on. That time I didn't even pack a bag—I just got in my car and went. But here I didn't know anybody going back and forth. And once I was back in Catty, I was tired of traveling—because my whole life had been that."

Nevertheless, when Miller didn't show, some teammates began to wonder if he'd given up on them. Clearly this retiring Larry disturbed old pals like Billy Cunningham—perhaps unaware of how close he'd remained with Coach Smith behind the scenes. "I think it was admirable going home to take care of his mother. Obviously, he was a very bright man, on his way with great potential making money in real estate. Then, all of a sudden . . . *Poof.* I never saw that coming in a million years. I would have thought his experience playing basketball at Carolina would have been a wonderful experience. But the last time I spoke with him, letting him know his dearest friend Jim Hudock died of cancer, it was cordial but . . . 'I'm moving on with my life and goodbye.' "

By this time a book by *The Charlotte Observer*'s Scott Fowler titled "North Carolina Tar Heels: Where Have You Gone" was terming Larry's absence "mysterious." On the UNC message boards, fans began to write: "Sorry he has never come back to the Hill . . . just a mystery" and "Has been a recluse most of his nonprofessional life." While not entirely accurate, these reports served to ferment the Miller legend into myth. For latecomers only learning of his exploits by word-of-mouth in the absence of videotape, Larry Miller became as imaginary as Paul Bunyan . . . and eventually the Tar Heel faithful simply lost track of him.

∗

Meanwhile, up in Pennsylvania, Larry didn't feel lost at all. If anything, for the first time in years, the newly-renovated Miller seemed to be finding his way since, back in the familiar mores of a blue-collar town, he fit right in. As a pro athlete, he'd essentially been a highly paid blue-collar worker, for all his celebrity now sharing the same aches and pains as his new buddy Mike Bonds, an iron worker in his fifties already feeling the effects of climbing around skeletal I-beam frames for decades. "We relate because Coop's a gardener who grows more and cans more than I do. And he raises chickens for their eggs—what's why I call him 'Coop.' He's amazing because he works full-time, has a cabin in the mountains, he's raising three kids, and does all that besides spending time with us drinking. I don't know how he does it." Forever allergic to management, Larry knew he wasn't a "suit," and recognized that the whole point of sharing beers in the first place had been the camaraderie that flowed. Almost six years after coming back to Catty to look after his mom, Larry finally realized he was home.

"Once I figured I've got a lot of good buddies still around, I'm really happy here, I started to look around. It's hard to tell how I came to that. I was looking at real estate, thinking about what I wanted to do—did I want to get into the business again—looking for something to renovate and flip, maybe. This went on for about a year. But then I saw this house where I am now and it just clicked with me: 'This has potential; I could live here and *stay*.' Boom—I said 'I'll take it' and wrote a check. I don't know how I came to it, but I came to it there. It was a magical thing . . . and then everything became clear.

"It was right at the cusp of the market [2007 sliding into 2008]. I think the market went bust right afterward. But I have no regrets about that; it turned out fantastic for me." The house demanded commitment—for the first time in years he wasn't just passing through—and it's here that Miller developed a self-reliant routine that has served him well ever since: Growing and canning his own food, walking everywhere he could to stay fit, regimenting his socializing with friends with far fewer parties worthy of titles—"I figured I could handle beer every other couple of days, and it worked out I could"—and reading voraciously at home.

The key to making the place his own was the vacant hardscrabble lot behind the house, where before long he started a garden. "I didn't know I was going to do that when I bought the house," he admits. But the commitment to tending this living thing every day was absorbing and, in return, it rewarded him more with each passing year.

*

## LARRY MILLER DEAD AT 64

The February 2009 headline was a shock to the Lehigh Valley and the ACC. Some wondered if Miller's famous "play hard" karma had finally caught up to him. It startled Larry, too . . . until he learned the media was mourning the loss of a car salesman who had taken his place as "basketball's Larry Miller" by buying ownership of the Utah Jazz. (This man's personal sport was fast-pitch softball.) Somehow it was fitting that the ABA, where the suits stole the show, and especially the Utah team which administered last rites to the All-American's love of the game, would finally rewrite the Big Cat from public memory. Once so famous that he was on the cover of *Parade Magazine*, later the plain vanilla name often forgotten on the best All-America team ever, "Larry Miller" was not even him anymore. Larry, it seemed, had once and for all shed his fame.

*

A year later, in February of 2010, UNC invited a lineup of gray-haired let-termen to a celebration of 100 Years of Basketball at the Smith Center, fea-turing an old-timers' Blue v. White game. The packed house loved it, and roared loudest when Dean Smith took the court with Coaches Williams and Guthridge to hug his players and wave to the crowd before ambling off. As usual now, Larry Miller wasn't there.

Five months later, the coach's family released a public letter acknowl-edging that Dean Smith was suffering from a "progressive neurocognitive disorder." The man legendarily famous for instantly recalling hundreds of birthdays, children's names, and phone numbers—even plays on videotape he hadn't seen for thirty years—now had trouble remembering the names of some of his players. (But, they added, "he could not forget what his relation-ships with those players meant to him").

*

In 2012, the most notable event in Catasauqua was what *didn't* happen. Don Canzano points out, "Allentown goes back to 1762, and the 200th anniver-sary celebration in 1962 was a big deal for everyone here. But when we got to 2012 nothing ever happened for the 250th. Nobody even thought about it, because it's not a community anymore. It's all impersonal."

Not so in one corner of the borough, though, a Brigadoon of the old ways where a select group of Rip Van Winkles still gathers to celebrate any-thing, even . . . "Do you remember when the world was going to end?" says Miller, recalling the infamous Mayan Doomsday prophecy. "That's when we had the End of Days party at the Jed." Another impromptu gathering that year was held at Miller's garage, which by now was known as The Lizard Lounge. "My friend Lester was doing a pub crawl with some friends, and I said 'Why don't you stop by here?' I still had liquor to get rid of and a crate bar from Home Depot, and he came with thirty people. There was no charge for anything, but I put out a tip jar and they left $145. Didn't have to. And we honored Sam—that was strictly something I came up with on my own."

The Tar Heels will celebrate the 100th year of
Carolina Basketball throughout the 2009-10 season.

*Gone but not forgotten: When the Tar Heel program celebrated*
*100 Years of Carolina basketball, the marquee cover boy was,*
*of course, Michael Jordan . . . and featured right next to him,*
*Larry Miller, shooting his lefty jump shot.*

Sam had been at Larry's induction into the Catasauqua Hall of Fame, and piped up that he should be in the Hall of Fame, too . . . leading one of Miller's coaches to smile and retort, "For what—tiddlywinks?" That's all it took to inspire Miller to recycle a 100-year-old window he found in the basement of his house, channeling Julius's woodworking skills to make it a picture frame with a nice dedication. Larry wasn't sure whether Sam would like it or not—he had Tim Fisher present it to him—but the plaque is on the wall in McCarty's today:

## CATASAUQUA HALL OF FAME

*As a first-ever inductee, we are honored to enshrine John "Sam" McCarty
to this hallowed hall, not only for his prodigious prowess and abilities
in Tiddlywinks, but for the many things he has done for all of us over the years.
And most importantly, for being our friend.*

*

Around this time, Larry received the worst piece of mail he ever got from Dean Smith. "I sent him a card with a note over one of the holidays, and I got the note back with a reply he'd written on it—and it really didn't make any sense. I'd heard he had some dementia, but that's when I really found out." For Miller this was another death, severing his strongest tether to Carolina.

*

## MINUTES OF THE CATASAUQUA BOROUGH COUNCIL,
## SEPTEMBER 3, 2013

ORDINANCE 1293: Mr. Regits made a motion, seconded by Mr. McKittrick, to approve an ordinance establishing an additional one-way street on School Street from Howertown Road to Pineapple Street traveling east. Mr. Regits said that Larry Miller had planted flowers at the corner of School and Pineapple Streets.

A roll call vote was taken with six in favor, none opposed and one absent. The motion was passed.

\*

Coach Dean Smith passed away at home, surrounded by his family on the evening of February 7, 2015. Two weeks later, Tar Heels old and new gathered at the Smith Center to remember him, and Leonard Laye was there: "I know a lot of the former players came. I ran into several guys from the team, like Donnie Moe, and we started talking—'How about Mills, is he here? Anybody heard anything from him lately?' And Donnie said, 'I don't know anything, but wait a minute.' He went halfway around the floor and found Grubar, and he and Joe Brown came over. Nobody had had any contact with him."

By now, Grubar had heard that Miller sold all his awards to get them out of the house, and had a hard time understanding that. "We all try to move forward. But he was a big part of what we all accomplished—the biggest part—and we'd like to share that, but he wasn't willing to come and that was disappointing."

Charles Scott was troubled, too: "Especially when you get to be our age, you should be proud of what you accomplished in life—and don't let anybody take it from you. That's why I'm upset that Larry has not allowed people to come and tell him how much he meant to them. Sometimes that's all you have in life to live with. He has not allowed himself to enjoy what people wanted to give him for that, and I think it would make him happy to realize how happy he made other people. He should enjoy what he accomplished—and he accomplished a *lot!*"

But Linda Woods, Coach Smith's administrative assistant since 1977 and still called "Mama Woods" by some players, had mothered too many wayward boys to pass judgment. She still prefers to talk fondly of a road game in Virginia some twenty years after Miller graduated—it might have been at Richmond or Old Dominion—when Smith sent two tickets to his former star. On game day Larry appeared suddenly, dressed out in his old game uniform with sneakers, calling "I'm ready, Coach—put me in!" It was just to give his old coach a laugh and it worked. Recalls Woods, "We just fell out . . . He was the *sweetest* thing."

A month after the memorial service, every former letterman coached by Smith across thirty-six years received a letter from the Trustee of his estate. Inside was a check for $200 and the message: "Enjoy a dinner out compliments of Coach Dean Smith." Mike Cooke certainly wasn't going to argue: "I was quoted in a book about Coach Smith a couple times, and all of a sudden I get this letter from him thanking me for being part of the book—with a $100 bill in it. And I said, 'Coach, I don't want this, it was an honor to be part of it.' And he said, 'If you don't take the hundred dollars and take your wife out to dinner, you will insult me.' And after forty years, I said 'Yes, sir!' I'm not going to say no to him. So when we all got the $200 check after he passed away, people asked if I was going to save it, and I said 'No, I'm going to take a picture of it and spend it, because if I don't, Coach Smith will be upset—and I have proof!"

Billy Cunningham, who hadn't kept many souvenirs, was different: "The only thing I have is the check for $200—mine is hanging over my desk. I wonder what Larry did with his check."

In fact, Miller considered selling it on eBay and donating the proceeds to the library. But, realizing some would be unhappy about that, he followed his coach's instructions—this time for the last time—and took his sidekick Bobby Folland out to dinner at Red Lobster. He spent the check, he sold the trophies, and he couldn't face saying goodbye. But Larry Miller still has a collection of every handwritten note Dean Smith ever wrote to him.

*

In 1963 the *Evening Chronicle* had gushed that Larry Miller was "currently establishing a career record that promises to stand for generations."

So far, so true: More than five decades after his last high school game, Miller is still the all-time leading scorer in District 11 boys basketball history—a record that Don Canzano predicts will never be broken: "When my dad was almost on his deathbed, the whole sports situation came up with the good old days, and I remember him saying that our area can't ever produce a Larry Miller again, because the work ethic and the blue-collar mentality is gone. Larry's era was the last time Catty played big-time high school basketball. And then we all started sliding in the '70s, and it got worse with each passing decade. I can drive you inside a two-mile radius now to playgrounds where there aren't even basketball courts anymore. And once they were filled with kids. You played all day."

In Chapel Hill, too, the record stands tall: Among three-year players—those not permitted to play as freshmen and, later, those who jumped early to the pros—Miller remains #3 in all-time career scoring, just behind #2 Scott and leader Lenny Rosenbluth, and now eternally ahead of Jordan, Worthy, Jameson . . . pick any name you like. Meanwhile, remarkably, the program he kick-started with Coach Smith has appeared in over one-third of all Final Fours in the last fifty years.

*

Larry Miller is playing his endgame carefully now, playing like a man with 4 fouls who still has some scoring to do. His 800-plus FICO score—how does that compare with yours, pal?—shows his famous self-discipline is winning the old war with mischief and overindulgence, obviously well in charge of himself. He no longer tempts fate behind the wheel of a car—after all the near-misses he retired undefeated—and he's probably best described these days as "present," engaged in what's going on close by in the here and now: "The things I care about are the earth and bringing the good out of people."

He'll plan a five-day project creating a structure for his plants, but get into such a zone that he finishes in two days. He'll help a buddy move his fridge, or swap some of his ceviche for a dozen of Coop's eggs, but he won't follow sports scores, because that happens somewhere else. "About three years ago, I quit watching any sports—live games or broadcast—I just thought 'Why do I need this?' So I extricated it from my system, and it's not part of my life anymore. Same with driving. Those two things are so ingrained in society, and you really don't have to do them. That freed up my mind, and then I went through a stretch where I read a book a day . . . sometimes two or three."

Miller prefers doing his daily neighborhood rounds on foot—everything he needs is within a mile or two—because how better to come across a chance conversation or a small lucky Buddha someone dropped in the street. He always declines rides, even walking through brutal 55-mph March winds to finish his mission, although he's been known to stumble into McCarty's frozen like a popsicle and wryly concede that was stupid: "I was being vain today because it's Spring and I'm supposed to be the flower guy."

Some days Larry walks with a slight limp, still feeling the knee he wrenched in high school. "If I went to a doctor now, he'd tell me I need a knee replacement—but as long as I can get around, I'm not going for artificial body parts." He and doctors seldom have a meeting of the minds, most recently when a doctor became alarmed by his slow heartbeat.

"I just went in for a checkup, and ended up in the ER for about three hours because she thought my heart was stopping—but I wasn't sick or anything. I told her I've always been that way, how the Cougars doc said if he didn't know how I'd been working out, he'd think I was dying . . . forty years ago. My heartbeat has always been low and slow and especially now I'm older, not carrying as much weight. She said, 'I don't give a damn if you die—I'm worried about my reputation.' "

When he finishes his errands, Larry will angle over to one of several long established eateries to rendezvous for lunch according to a strict rotation observed by those in the know. Some days he'll go to Palace Pizza, where Don prefers to meet him because there's no smoking there. Fish might appear, too, reminding us that he was the batter on deck when Larry won that long-ago Knee-Hi baseball game—and amiably needling that Larry did so whiff by mistake on that dropped third strike and *not* on purpose.

Other days find Larry at Metro's (pronounced "meat-ro's . . . definitely *not* as in "metro-sexual"), where you can still enjoy $1 beers and a good plate of spaghetti for $2.50. There, he might run into Faye (Fink) Roman, who was a sixteen-year-old high school junior listening to that '63 playoff game on her bedroom radio when Larry's pass slipped through a teammate's hands, costing Catty its best ever shot at a state title: "I just bawled, everyone was so upset. But to this day Larry will not blame his teammate. He says he should have taken it in himself." (To this day, Miller will also pretend he's forgotten who the unfortunate butterfingers was . . . but query Faye and she'll explode with laughter: "Are you kidding?? Larry knows where that guy lives *today!*")

On certain afternoons every week, the guys will gather at their unofficial clubhouse, McCarty's, established when the Crane Iron Works was young, and if Sam puts down a small cup in front of you as a marker, someone has just bought you a beer. Here the men trade stories, some launching old brags about Triple-Lindy dives in the park's WPA pool that will never be equaled now that today's protective culture has made it shallower and removed all the diving boards. That loud voice is probably Bobby Folland, pulling for Notre Dame when his operational genius isn't troubleshooting for Amazon, but if he lowers his voice in Larry's ear they're probably scheming something, like a raid on some seafood worthy of Larry's ceviche.

Occasionally, one particular tippler will topple backward off his stool, land on the floor, and not move . . . drawing no reaction from Coop, discussing how other high schools used to be afraid of Catty, or from Sam who advises, "Just leave him." When asked what gives, Sam explains the first time that happened he called an ambulance that whisked the guy away. Next time the man returned, he groused that had cost him 200 bucks. Eventually the fellow had one too many and crashed to the floor again . . . this time moaning, "No ambulance! No ambulance!" The event has now become so routine that no one reacts anymore, just stepping around the body until he revives. But they have honored the guy's performance by rewarding him with a nickname—"Thumper."

McCarty's is not an evening hangout, and around 4:30—when blue-collar folks who start work at 8:00 AM are going home—Larry will lightly slap his palm on the bar and head for the door. They know better than to offer him a ride, of course, but the walls of McCarty's ricochet with hails of farewell because here, where a man's wealth is measured in the stories he has, Larry Miller who once climbed the glass mountain and returned to tell about it, is one of the richest men in town.

\*

Walk into Miller's garden in midsummer and you'll see a reflection of the man's character: The order, the labeling, the neatness. It's meticulous. This is where he works himself hard, building a healthy sanctuary with the same dedication he once applied to building basketball skills, shaping his life around the seasons now the way he used to obey a basketball schedule. After eight years—about as long as it took to become an All-American—he's turned the dead ground into a private refuge of towering arborvitae, knockout roses, peppers, and tomatoes so sweet they're treasured by his friends. There's already a picture book of it.

When the day's work is done, this is where he reads and meditates—sometimes approaching enlightenment, sometimes cleansing anger at himself, and sometimes just musing on that UFO he once saw about to collide with a plane before it disappeared. ("I spend a lot of time looking up.") Larry even creates pop art out here, like the glass lids for pots that he strung from a tree, making a flying saucer mobile to entertain the young kid from next door.

"I'm as happy as you can get," he'll tell you. "I'm relatively healthy. My mind is straight. And gardening became spiritual when I got up here. I used to do it on other people's land, but when I got my own place growing and living with the plants really became part of the deal. I spend a lot of time outside, because this is where I'm finding my roots . . . where it all comes together."

This is also where women will drop in with coffee and compliment him on what his spiritual renaissance has wrought. Larry looks around at the living Eden he's created and will now tend for the rest of his life. Then he shrugs and passes the compliment to the town that long ago and again has always nurtured him:

"Just good soil."

\*

The Miller kid is past seventy now, here in plain sight if you know where to look. He's not on a bench wearing a suit, or laughing it up on ESPN. Today

he's ambling through North Catasauqua Park on a sweet summer morning, shooting the breeze with a new friend who's hunted him down . . . until they pause by the basketball court where once, long ago, he made himself a name to remember.

The park is empty now, except for one lone kid at the basketball hoop. He's playing "Around the World," sinking basket after basket until he clanks a shot off the metal rim, and the ball skips over to Larry like it's eager to play.

Larry fields it as gently as an egg.

"Take the shot," his companion prods.

But Larry's already made all the shots—has shot his way so far around the world that he's come full circle back to where, once upon a time, everyone knew what to value and cheer for and who deserved to be respected. Instead, he rolls the ball back, still making the pass to the kid with a better shot. It's his game now.

The kid scoops it up without thanks or a glance at the old man limping away, heading past the mansions of men long forgotten . . . heading all the way back to a time before his father put a ball into his hands, where every day is Saturday and the boys still gather to see what new stories today will bring.

Meanwhile, out in Las Vegas, Scott Beeten is golfing and mentions his home town, causing another man's head to snap up and stare at him: "Larry Miller?" Yeah—*that* Catasauqua.

And down in Charlotte, a junior high school French teacher keeps a picture of Miller in her classroom where, year after year, she'll admit to students she dated him in college . . . but the rest is none of their business.

And on the Carolina message board, where fans reminisce in cyberspace, one old boy recalls a time when gods walked among us—and hitchhiked, too—causing him to yell at his parents to "Stop! That's Larry Miller!" . . . and again feels the pride of sharing the back seat of his family car with the most famous boy in Pennsylvania, hitching home from his draft physical, who graciously thanked him for the ride.

All across America, a constellation of happy moments traces the shape of Larry Miller's lifetime, uncounted thousands gratefully hitching their memories to days and nights he shared with them, some riding shotgun and others sharing the back seat, each in his or her own special way.

Thanks, Larry . . . Thanks for the ride.

# THE AFTER-PARTY

During the writing of this book Larry Miller emerged from hibernation, tentatively at first and then with a gathering appetite for friendships he'd left behind. Our earliest discussions were taped in Allentown over a few beers. Later, he agreed to dig out the old phone numbers of his pals, only to find that some of these connections are now lost forever. Those we did track down, however, were often surprised and delighted to learn their old teammate was back in the game.

Most of these men are retired, of course, and almost all enjoyed recollections of Miller, even those who have long been absent from Chapel Hill themselves, like Bob Lewis who returned to Washington, D.C. to work for the National Theater and Tom Gauntlett who ran a printing business in Pennsylvania. Even the irascible George Lehman, who shuns talking about his own career, willingly spoke for an hour about his favorite running buddy in the old ABA.

Eventually, Larry began giving us personal guided tours of the old days, bringing us to his first high school reunion in decades. Organized by his old Wood Street neighbor Nancy (Konye) Cunningham (who had a career in publishing), the event drew teammates like Jim Van Horn and other class-mates like Linda Thomas (the Valentine queen to Larry's king of hearts in a 1964 photo), who shared some useful old clippings.

Soon afterward, we drove down Maryland's Eastern Shore and across Chesapeake Bay to Virginia Beach—Miller's first road trip beyond the Lehigh Valley in many years—to the sound of Gregg Allman's "(The Road Is) My Only True Friend." There, over dinner with a side order of stories, he reunited with Nancy and Tom Coghill who, well into his eighties now, has earned the nickname "Double-Overtime." The following day, we rendezvoused with Theo Cantana at The Raven ("our daytime bar") before leaving Larry to spend the night with the Coghills, last seen trying to lure him to visit them in Florida.

The big event in the winter of 2018 was a weekend Tar Heel reunion hosted by Coach Roy Williams honoring the Classes of 1967–68–69—the "three-peat" teams that established North Carolina as perennial champi-ons—and this time, at last, Miller showed up. At halftime of the Saturday game twenty lettermen filed onto center court and stepped forward to warm applause as their names were announced. When #44's name was called the volume swelled, the surging welcome seeming to catch Larry by surprise. And then, as all players must, they filed out of the spotlight once again.

That evening, Larry hosted an oyster shucking around a fire by a pri-vate pool in nearby Hillsborough for about forty players and wives, mingling and taking selfies together. Linda Woods was there, with a gifted photo book of Larry's garden, and Charles Scott brought his wife and kids, and now it was Grubar and his wife urging Larry to visit them down in Florida. (The only defection from Team Miller on this night was the writer Jill McCorkle grinning to Dickie, "I'm a Grubar Girl now!") Before the evening was over, Joe Brown had Larry promising to make this rare trip south an annual visit.

*

*Nancy and Larry at the oyster shucking party they hosted after Coach Williams' three-peat reunion for the teams of 1967–68–69.*

By summertime, Larry's reflections on Catasauqua, UNC, and life in the ABA were stacking up in a thick ream of paper. Experienced interviewers will tell you that subjects often don't fully appreciate their own stories. (It was only during our third discussion of meeting Dean Smith in a high school gym that Larry dropped the choice tidbit that he was wearing a Duke sweatshirt at the time.) He remembers his favorite anecdotes well, but isn't always clear about the sequence of long-ago events—the progression of choices and accidents that shape the arc of a life—and nearing the end of our work together he seemed almost surprised to see how his story made sense.

And now Larry was feeling his old mojo again, especially when offered a bucket list acting role in an independent film called "Giants Being Lonely" (titled from a Carl Sandburg poem). Directed by the North Carolina artist

Grear Patterson and produced by Olmo Schnabel, it was shot partially on a Catasauqua baseball diamond—where Larry teaches his movie "son" how to throw a curve ball—and later in North Carolina. (It would go on to premiere at the prestigious Venice Film Festival.)

With filming completed, the suddenly busy retiree then joined other Tar Heel legends in Springfield, Massachusetts for Charles Scott's induction into the Naismith Basketball Hall of Fame, spending happy hours shooting the breeze with Coach Roy, Phil Ford, Jim Delany and Eddie Fogler . . . back in the family again.

*At Charles Scott's Naismith Hall of Fame induction*
*in Springfield, MA September 7, 2018: Roy Williams, Larry Miller,*
*Charles Scott, Jim Delany, Eddie Fogler.*

Most recently, Miller was called off the bench to make more history when Charles Scott phoned him to say a well-heeled Tar Heel alumnus wants to establish a private charitable foundation by and for former Tar Heel players—with a founding board of icons Lenny Rosenbluth, Phil Ford, Scott and Miller. Their weekend summit at UNC's Business School included a long dinner swapping inside stories from three decades of locker room lore so good that Miller wishes it had been recorded for posterity.

The next day he witnessed another Tar Heel win over Duke, echoing those contests in which his teams established what ESPN has since called the third greatest rivalry in all of North American sports. He had courtside seats, of course, but his knee makes sitting uncomfortable, so on this day he gave the precious tickets to the daughter of his Catasauqua pal Joe as a wedding present. Instead, the man without whom there might never have been a Dean E. Smith Center preferred to stand and watch from the concourse, a ghost legend content to be unrecognized now by the multitudes swirling past him. When last seen that weekend, he was boarding a plane back to Allentown. A few hours later, though, the telephone rang and it was Larry reporting a happy landing.

"Hey! You won't believe this, but half the people on that plane were Tar Heel fans just down for the game. The kid next to me spent the whole flight telling me everything he knew about Carolina basketball, and how great it was to be a Tar Heel."

Did Larry tell the kid who he was actually sitting next to?

"Nah," said Larry, savoring the moment. "He was having such a good time, I just listened . . ."

# SOLILOQUY

*When I leave my precious garden and become part of this earth,*

*I hope that in my life I left not a footprint, but did something of worth.*

*Blessed with great parents, family, and friends, along with strong values
and excellent health,*

*What better way to measure one's riches and ultimate wealth.*

*When things did go wrong with my life and well-being*

*Most of the blame for the situations and issues came from me not seeing.*

*If I hurt or wronged you, that was not my intent.*

*At times I was perhaps careless, insensitive nor content.*

*But as I matured, gained some knowledge, and looked to the light,*

*I realized that in my actions I could make things right.*

*So in passing words to those who have shared some moments of glee*

*I hope those memories reflect the true joy they brought to me.*

*I don't know where the journey goes from here, but in my eyes*

*My life, being here, I always thought I was in Paradise.*

*Be kind and sharing with all creatures of worth*

*And be especially gentle and caring with your home, the earth.*

—Larry Miller

# FOULS

This book contains errors, largely because it is based on the memories of older men. For example, one player remembered the first time he and Larry Miller met Roy Williams at Coach Smith's basketball camp when Roy was still just a teenager. Coach Williams, however, says he never attended such a camp. Another source tipped me that undergraduate Jeff MacNelly—later the Pulitzer Prize winning editorial cartoonist who created the comic strip "Shoe"—had drawn a cartoon for *The Daily Tar Heel* of Miller hoisting a State player off the ground. On locating the cartoon, exactly as described, however, I found it was not by MacNelly after all. I have caught enough instances of benign misinformation to suspect these pages must contain more. These are not willful falsehoods, but simply the patina that memories acquire from being handled too fondly over time. Any corrections will be welcomed by the author.

## ACKNOWLEDGMENTS

This book is a team effort, a meeting place for memories across many years, and I am grateful for the generosity and good will of the following contributors:

**Teammates:** Joe Brown, Mike Cooke, Billy Cunningham, Jim Delany, Eddie Fogler, Jim Frye, Tom Gauntlett, Dick Grubar, Bob Lewis, Charles Scott, George Lehmann

**In the Lehigh Valley:** Scott Beeten, Mike Bonds, Don Canzano, Wabs Chromiak, Nancy Cunningham, Tim Fisher, Bobby Folland, Sam McCarty, Bob Nemeth, Bob Riedy, Faye Roman, Linda (Thomas) Colgan, Austin Vitali, the Catasauqua Public Library and *The Morning Call*

**In North Carolina:** Jon Barett, Art Chansky, Kaye Chase, Monty Diamond, Ron Green Jr., Erin Hardy, Jim Heavner, Larry Keith, Steve Kirschner, Leonard Laye, Suzi Mutascio, Aaron Picart, Katharine Walton, Roy Williams, Linda Woods

**In Virginia Beach:** Theo Cantana, Tom and Nancy Coghill

**And my generous hosts:** The Curlee family at Arcadian I, Morgan Moylan at Oh Danny Bay, and Anne Eldridge and Cap Kane at Setters Run Farm

# ABOUT THE AUTHOR

Stephen Demorest is a six-time Emmy Award winner and recipient of the Writers Guild of America Award as head writer of the CBS daytime dramas *Guiding Light* and *As the World Turns*. He has also written for *All My Children, General Hospital, Another World,* and *One Life to Live,* as well as writing a script for *Law & Order.*

He was managing editor of the iconic rock magazine, *Circus,* where he interviewed and profiled scores of major rock stars, reviewed the first Talking Heads and Ramones albums for *Rolling Stone,* flew with Led Zeppelin, and landed the first adult at-home interview with nineteen-year-old Michael Jackson. His work has appeared in *The New York Times, New York Daily News, Saturday Review, Travel & Leisure,* Andy Warhol's *Interview* and other publications. He is a Tar Heel by marriage, and this is his first sports book.